Windows 95
The Cram Sheet

This Cram Sheet contains the distilled, key facts about Windows 95. Review this information last thing before you enter the test room, paying special attention to those areas where you feel you need the most review. You can transfer any of these facts from your head onto a blank sheet of paper before beginning the exam.

PLANNING AND INSTALLATION

1. SETUP.EXE command-line switches:
    - **/ID** Skip check for hard drive space
    - **/IM** Skip memory check
    - **/IQ** Skip cross-link drive check (used with /IS)
    - **/IS** Skip ScanDisk
    - **/T:<path>** Location to place temporary files, directory must already exist
    Additional DOS prompt setup switches:
    - **/IL** Install the drivers for a Logitec series C mouse
    - **<batch>** Name of batch file to use for setup details
    Additional Windows 3.x setup switches:
    - **/IN** Skip launching of the network module
2. For automated install use NETSETUP. EXE and/or BATCH.EXE to create MSBATCH.INF

ARCHITECTURE AND MEMORY

3. The Virtual Memory Manager manages 4 GB of memory address space. Memory comprises physical RAM and a disk swap file. Memory is paged in 4 KB segments. Address space is used:

    - **0 through 1 MB** (DOS, some Win16 apps). If no DOS VM, this area is reserved for Real Mode drivers.
    - **1 through 4 MB** Generally not used (used by Win16 apps for backward compatibility).
    - **4 MB through 2 GB** Used by Win32 and Win16 apps.
    - **2 through 3 GB** Used by DLLs and other shared components.
    - **3 through 4 GB** Exclusive use by Ring 0 components, i.e., virtual device drivers.
4. Know these Registry keys:
    - **HKEY_LOCAL_MACHINE** Contains hardware information and settings.
    - **HKEY_CURRENT_CONFIG** Contains settings for current hardware devices. This key is rebuilt or recreated each time Windows 95 boots.
    - **HKEY_DYN_DATA** Contains details about dynamic hardware devices, such as Plug and Play devices, PCMCIA cards, and removable media. This key is created dynamically each time the machine is booted.
    - **HKEY_CLASSES_ROOT** Contains data about OLE services and file associations.

Each DOS app has its own address space but does not use a message queue.

21. Windows translates 16-bit calls to 32-bit calls, and vice versa, known as "thunking." Sixteen-bit code is non-reentrant; when a thread uses non-reentrant code, the Win16Mutex flag is set.

22. Known DOS apps are initially launched with settings found in APPS.INF; otherwise the DEFAULT.PIF is used.

MOBILE SERVICES

23. The Dialing Properties dialog box controls how TAPI uses a modem to place calls: long-distance dialing, calling card use, prefix numbers, and tone/pulse dialing.

24. DUN can use POTS, ISDN, and X.25 networks.

25. Dial-Up Server, an add-on component from Microsoft Plus!, can accept a single inbound connection from Windows 95, WFW, LAN Manager, Windows NT, or any PPP client.

MICROSOFT EXCHANGE

26. Workgroup postoffices are created and administered with Microsoft Mail Postoffice applet.

27. The Mail and Fax applet is used to add, remove, and configure information services for the Exchange client.

28. A message profile is a collection of information services and their configurations that dictate what the Exchange client can do.

PLUG AND PLAY

29. A Plug and Play system must consist of: A Plug and Play operating system, a Plug and Play BIOS, and Plug and Play devices.

TROUBLESHOOTING

30. Detection log files:
    - **SETUPLOG.TXT** Logs installation, notes last action performed prior to a system halt.

- **DETCRASH.LOG** Logs hardware detection during setup. Binary file, readable only by setup to determine which module was running when the system halted.
- **DETLOG.TXT** Equivalent of DETCRASH.LOG written in a readable format.
- **NETLOG.TXT** Logs detected network component information.
- **IOS.LOG** Logs error messages from the SCSI drivers.
- **PPPLOG.TXT** Logs PPP and dialup activity.
- **BOOTLOG.TXT** This log file is recorded during the first boot sequence and written to later with Logged boot. It records all devices and drivers loaded by the system.

31. For Startup menu, press F8 when "Starting Windows 95" is displayed upon bootup.

32. The command line options for WIN.COM are:

```
win [/d:[f] [m] [n] [s] [v] [x]]
```

The **/d:** switch is used to initiate one of the following troubleshooting boot parameters:

- **f** Turns off 32-bit disk access; equivalent to 32BitDiskAccess=FALSE in SYSTEM.INI.
- **m** Launches Windows 95 in Safe Mode.
- **n** Launches Windows 95 in Safe Mode with Networking.
- **s** Instructs Windows 95 to not use ROM address space between F000:0000 and 1 MB for a breakpoint; equivalent to SystemROMBreak-Point=FALSE in SYSTEM.INI.
- **v** Forces the ROM routine to handle interrupts from the hard disk controller; equivalent to VirtualHDIRQ= FALSE in SYSTEM.INI.
- **x** Excludes all expansion card memory addresses from Windows 95's scan to find unused space; equivalent to EMMExclude=A000-FFFF in SYSTEM.INI.

Certification Insider™ Press

- **HKEY_USERS** Contains user preferences.
- **HKEY_CURRENT_USER** Contains the current user's preferences.

CUSTOMIZING AND CONFIGURING WINDOWS 95

5. Important Control Panel applets:
   - **Add New Hardware** Use to install new drivers for hardware. Hardware can be detected automatically, selected manually from a list, or installed using third-party drivers.
   - **Add/Remove Programs** Use to add or remove software components of Windows 95, remove 32-bit applications, and create a Startup disk.
   - **Display** Alter the background, enable screen savers, set Energy Star-compliant monitor activities, set the color and font scheme, set screen color depth and resolution.
   - **Mail and Fax** Use to add, remove, and modify information services.
   - **Microsoft Mail Postoffice** Use to create and administer postoffices.
   - **Multimedia** Use to set audio, video, MIDI, and CD functions.
   - **PC Card (PCMCIA)** Use to manage removable PCMCIA cards and drivers.
   - **System** Use to view installed devices, manage hardware profiles, and set system performance.

EDITING USER AND SYSTEM PROFILES

6. Profiles are stored in \WINDOWS\ PROFILES\<username> directories, where <username> is the name of the user. Each user's profile directory contains:
   - **\Desktop** A directory containing the desktop layout; e.g., shortcut locations.
   - **\Recent** A directory containing shortcuts to the last used documents.
   - **\Start Menu** A directory containing the Start menu structure.
   - **USER.DAT** This is a copy of the Registry key HKEY_CURRENT_USER.
   - **USER.DA0** A backup of USER.DAT.
7. System policies are created through the use of two file types:

- **.ADM files** These are template files that are modified and transformed into actual policy files.
- **.POL files** These are the actual policy files themselves.

8. Windows 95 applies policies in the following manner:
   1. System is checked for a user-specific profile; if found, it is applied.
   2. If a user-specific profile is not found, the default user policy is applied.
   3. If a user-specific profile is present, no group policies are applied.
   4. All group polices (for which the user is a member) are located and applied from lowest to highest priority.
   5. System is checked for a computer-specific profile; if found, it is applied.
   6. If a computer-specific profile is not found, the default computer policy is applied.
   7. If no network or server can be located or if no policy can be located, Windows 95 will use the settings currently found in the Registry.

NETWORKING AND INTEROPERABILITY

9. Windows 95 supports both NDIS (3.x and 2) and ODI network adapter drivers. A single instance of an NDIS 3.x driver can support up to eight adapters, whereas a separate NDIS 2.0 driver must be loaded for each adapter.

10. UNC is a method of addressing or locating resources on a network. A UNC name is constructed in the following manner:

    \\servername\sharename\path

11. Windows 95 can participate in either a workgroup or a domain but not in both simultaneously. A workgroup is a network of computers in which no single computer has any greater control or advantage over any other computer. A domain is a network of computers in which one or more computers maintain a security scheme and information services (known as servers) used by the other computers (known as clients).

12. Windows 95 has native support for several protocols, including: **TCP/IP**, **IPX/SPX**, **NetBEUI**, **DLC**, and **NetBIOS**.

- **TCP/IP** This protocol is the most widely used protocol in the world, mainly because it is used on the Internet. TCP/IP is robust, reliable, and based on open standards. This protocol should be installed for Internet access. It can be used on small networks but because of its overhead and system requirements, is more often reserved for larger networks. TCP/IP supports routing.
- **IPX/SPX** This protocol is a Novell IPX/SPX-compatible protocol, usually called NWLink. On an NT network, NWLink is good for small- and medium-sized networks, especially those requiring access to NetWare servers. NWLink supports routing.
- **NetBEUI** This protocol is a limited protocol that cannot be routed. It is small and fast but cannot be used on medium or large networks because it is limited to 254 nodes.
- **DLC** This is a protocol used in conjunction with TCP/IP, NWLink, or NetBEUI to access mainframes or network-attached printers.
- **NetBIOS** This is not an actual protocol but more like a communications interface between protocols and applications. Most of Microsoft's networking mechanisms use NetBIOS as a basis for communication.

13. Primary Network Logon should be set to the appropriate logon type:

- **Windows logon** To log into only the local machine.
- **Client for Microsoft Networks** To log into a Microsoft domain or workgroup.
- **Client for NetWare Networks** To log into a NetWare domain.

14. On the Identification tab of the Network applet you will find **Workgroup**= workgroup or the domain name.

15. On the Access Control tab of the Network applet you will find:

- **Share-level access control** Each share assigned a password. Specific users cannot be blocked.
- **User-level access control** User authentication from an existing network (Windows NT or NetWare). Individuals or groups can be granted or denied access.

16. Tools for remote administration:

- **Net Watcher** Manages shared resources and the users accessing those resources. ADMIN$, mapped to the Windows directory; IPC$, an interprocess communication channel.
- **System Monitor** Monitors the remote client. Requires Network Monitor Agent service on the client.
- **File System Administer** Manages resources on the remote client. Requires Remote Registry service on the client.

MANAGING DISK RESOURCES AND UTILITIES

17. Vital statistics for the VFAT file system:

Maximum volume size	4 GB
Maximum file size	4 GB
Maximum files in root directory	512
Maximum files in nonroot directory	No limit

MANAGING PRINTERS

18. The Spool Settings dialog box controls the spooling activities of the printer, including the following:

- The logical printer can be set to use the spooler or to send print jobs directly to the physical printer.
- If you use the spooler, you can choose whether to begin printing immediately or wait until the entire print job is spooled.
- The spooled data format can be changed between EMF and raw.
- Bi-directional support can be enabled or disabled.

RUNNING APPLICATIONS

19. The System VM hosts the kernel, Win16, and Win32 apps. A DOS VM hosts a single DOS app.

20. All Win16 apps share a single address space and message queue. Each Win32 app has its own address space and message queue.

Are You Certifiable?

That's the question that's probably on your mind. The answer is: You bet! But if you've tried and failed or you've been frustrated by the complexity of the MCSE program and the maze of study materials available, you've come to the right place. We've created our new publishing and training program, *Certification Insider Press* (www.certificationinsider.com), to help you accomplish one important goal: to ace an MCSE exam without having to spend the rest of your life studying for it.

The book you have in your hands is part of our *Exam Cram* series. Each book is especially designed not only to help you study for an exam but also to help you understand what the exam is all about. Inside these covers you'll find hundreds of test-taking tips, insights, and strategies that simply cannot be found anyplace else. In creating our guides, we've assembled the very best team of certified trainers, MCSE professionals, and networking course developers.

Our commitment is to ensure that the *Exam Cram* guides offer proven training and active-learning techniques not found in other study guides. We provide unique study tips and techniques, memory joggers, custom quizzes, insights about trick questions, a sample test, and much more. In a nutshell, each *Exam Cram* guide is closely organized like the exam it is tied to.

To help us continue to provide the very best certification study materials, we'd like to hear from you. Write or email us (craminfo@coriolis.com) and let us know how our *Exam Cram* guides have helped you study, or tell us about new features you'd like us to add. If you send us a story about how an *Exam Cram* guide has helped you ace an exam and we use it in one of our guides, we'll send you an official *Exam Cram* shirt for your efforts.

Good luck with your certification exam, and thanks for allowing us to help you achieve your goals.

Keith Weiskamp
Publisher, Certification Insider Press

Windows 95

Exam #70-064

Microsoft
Certified
Systems
Engineer

MCSE Windows 95 Exam Cram

The Coriolis Group, Inc.
An International Thomson Publishing Company
14455 N. Hayden Road, Suite 220
Scottsdale, Arizona 85260

602/483-0192
FAX 602/483-0193
http://www.coriolis.com

ISBN   1-57610-287-4

Printed in the United States of America
10 9 8 7 6 5 4 3 2 1

Publisher
Keith Weiskamp

Acquisitions
Shari Jo Hehr

Project Editor
Mariann Hansen
Barsolo

**Production
Coordinator**
Kim Eoff

Cover Design
Anthony Stock

Layout Design
April Nielsen

**Marketing
Specialist**
Cynthia Caldwell

an International Thomson Publishing company

Albany, NY • Belmont, CA • Bonn • Boston • Cincinnati • Detroit • Johannesburg • London • Madrid
Melbourne • Mexico City • New York • Paris • Singapore • Tokyo • Toronto • Washington

About The Authors

Ed Tittel

Ed Tittel is the president of LANWrights, Inc., and the originator of the *Exam Cram* series. With recent experience as a freelance writer, consultant, and classroom instructor, Ed has covered topics that range from network operating systems to Web software development tools and techniques. Ed is a member of the NetWorld + Interop Program Committee and also of the Interop faculty, where he teaches about Windows NT security and performance related topics.

Ed has contributed to over 50 computer books, including *HTML 4.0 For Dummies* (with Stephen N. James, 1998) and *Windows NT Networking for Dummies* (with Mary Madden and Dave Smith, 1996). Ed's most recent work has included contributions to the majority of *Exam Cram* titles and to *Exam Prep* titles on *Networking Essentials* and *Windows NT Workstation* (1998).

When he's not working, Ed is an avid cook who makes his own chicken stock. He is also a dedicated—if not quite professional—pool player. You can reach Ed by email at etittel@lanw.com or on the Web at www.lanw.com/staff/etbio.htm.

James Michael Stewart

James Michael Stewart is a full-time writer focusing on Windows NT and Internet topics. Most recently, he has worked on several titles in the *Exam Cram* series, including *NT Server 4*, *NT Workstation 4*, *NT Server 4 in the Enterprise*, *IIS 4.0*, and *Proxy Server 2.0*. Additionally, he has co-written the *Hip Pocket Guide to HTML 4* (1998) and the *Intranet Bible* (1997). Michael has written articles for numerous print and online publications, including CNet, *InfoWorld*, *Windows NT Magazine*, *Computer Currents*, and *Datamation*. He is also a regular speaker at Networld+Interop, and has taught at WNTIS and NT SANS.

Michael has been developing Windows NT 4 MCSE-level courseware and training materials for several years. He has been an MCSE since 1997, with a focus on Windows NT 4.0. He is currently pursuing MCSE+Internet certification, with his sights set on MCT.

Michael is also the founder of IMPACT Online, a Web design and computer maintenance company based in Austin, TX. IMPACT Online is both Michael's outlet for site design experimenting and distributor resource to sustain the LANWrights' arsenal of computing hardware.

Michael graduated in 1992 from the University of Texas at Austin with a bachelor's degree in philosophy. Despite his degree, his computer knowledge is self-acquired, based on almost 14 years of hands-on experience. He has been active on the Internet for quite some time, where most people know him by his "nom de wire" McIntyre. He spends his spare time reading, two-stepping, and remodeling his condo.

You can reach Michael by email at michael@lanw.com, or through his Web pages at www.lanw.com/jmsbio.htm or /www.impactonline.com/.

Acknowledgments

Ed Tittel

With six months of unbelievable sales under our belts, our thanks to the Coriolis team must escalate to similar heights of hyperbole and overstatement. We've all worked very hard, but Coriolis has created a genuine market phenomenon. So, I'll begin with a profound hats off to Keith Weiskamp, the enterprising publisher; Shari Jo Hehr, the acquisitions editor who made it all happen; the dynamic duo of Sandra Lassiter and Paula Kmetz, who oversaw all the down and dirty details; Ann Waggoner Aken, the series editor; and finally, Mariann Barsolo our champion project editor. Thanks also to Kim Eoff, the production coordinator; Cynthia Caldwell, the marketing specialist; and to the whole sales team. Special thanks and farewell to Josh Mills, who's moved on to pursue his dreams of higher education. And of course we remain eternally grateful to Anthony Stock for the cover design, and April Nielsen for the outstanding work on interior design.

But the real credit for this book goes to my right-hand man, James Michael Stewart. He worked miracles to finish this revision to reflect the passing of test 70-063 and the introduction of its replacement 70-064 in a remarkably short period of time. But we couldn't have delivered this new version without the efforts of our general manager David (DJ) Johnson and also Mary Burmeister, for whom this book represents her first solo editing effort.

Thanks to everyone at LANWrights for being such a great bunch of people and for sticking things out while we pulled all this material together. I'd also like to thank the gremlins at Microsoft—especially the training and certification team who put the MCSE tests together and keep them up-to-date—for giving us the opportunity to continue on our great adventure.

James Michael Stewart

Thanks to my boss and co-author, Ed Tittel, for including me in this book series. Thanks to all my co-workers, whose efforts in the trenches have enabled this series to come to fruition. To my parents, Dave and Sue, the soon-to-be goat farm is looking better than ever. To Sharon and Tommy, congratulations on the conception, good luck on the delivery. To Mark, if there really is alien

Acknowledgments

intelligence in the universe, with my luck it will be you. To HERbert, at one year and growing you are the best feline suitemate I could have. And finally, as always, to Elvis—I wanted to get Suede bucket seats, a leather bed liner, and gem-stone topped tassels for my new truck, but it seems that Dodge isn't into the Elvis motif.

Table Of Contents

Introduction

Welcome to the *Windows 95 Exam Cram*. This book aims to help you get ready to take—and pass—the Microsoft certification test numbered Exam 70-064, titled "Implementing and Supporting Microsoft Windows 95" (a revision of Exam 70-063). This introduction explains Microsoft's certification programs in general and talks about how the *Exam Cram* series can help you prepare for Microsoft's certification exams.

Exam Cram books help you understand and appreciate the subjects and materials you need to pass Microsoft certification exams. *Exam Cram* books are aimed strictly at test preparation and review. They do not teach you everything you need to know about a topic. Instead, we (the authors) examine the areas that you're most likely to encounter. Our aim is to bring together as much information as possible about Microsoft certification exams.

Nevertheless, to prepare yourself completely for any Microsoft test, we recommend that you begin your studies with some classroom training or that you pick up and read one of the many study guides available from Microsoft and third-party vendors, including the *Exam Prep* books by Certification Insider Press. We also strongly recommend that you install, configure, and interact with the software or environment that you'll be tested on, because nothing beats hands-on experience and familiarity when it comes to understanding the questions you're likely to encounter on a certification test. Book learning is essential, but hands-on experience is the best teacher of all.

The Microsoft Certified Professional (MCP) Program

The MCP Program currently includes five separate tracks, each of which boasts its own special acronym (as a would-be certified professional, you need to have a high tolerance for alphabet soup of all kinds): MCP, MCSD, MCT, MCSE, MCSE+I.

MCP (Microsoft Certified Professional)

This is the least prestigious of all the certification tracks from Microsoft. Attaining MCP status requires an individual to pass at least one core operating system exam. Passing any of the major Microsoft operating system exams—including those for Windows 95, Windows NT Workstation, or Windows NT Server—qualifies an individual for MCP credentials. Individuals can demonstrate proficiency with additional Microsoft products by passing additional certification exams.

MCSD (Microsoft Certified Solution Developer)

This track is aimed primarily at developers. This credential indicates that those who hold it are able to design and implement custom business solutions around particular Microsoft development tools, technologies, and operating systems. To obtain an MCSD, an individual must demonstrate the ability to analyze and interpret user requirements; select and integrate products, platforms, tools, and technologies; design and implement code and customize applications; and perform necessary software tests and quality assurance operations.

To become an MCSD, an individual must pass a total of four exams: two core exams plus two elective exams. The two core exams are the Microsoft Windows Operating Systems And Services Architecture I and II (WOSSA I and WOSSA II, numbered 70-150 and 70-151). Elective exams cover specific Microsoft applications and languages, including Visual Basic, C++, the Microsoft Foundation Classes, Access, SQL Server, Excel, and more.

MCT (Microsoft Certified Trainer)

Microsoft Certified Trainers are individuals who are considered competent to deliver elements of the official Microsoft training curriculum, based on technical knowledge and instructional ability. It is necessary for an individual seeking MCT credentials (which are granted on a course-by-course basis) to pass the related certification exam for a course and successfully complete the official Microsoft training in the subject area, as well as to demonstrate teaching ability.

This latter criterion may be satisfied by proving that one has already attained training certification from Novell, Banyan, Lotus, the Santa Cruz Operation, or Cisco, or by taking a Microsoft-sanctioned workshop on instruction. Microsoft makes it clear that MCTs are an important cog in the Microsoft training channels. Instructors must be MCTs to teach in any of Microsoft's official training channels, including its affiliated Authorized Technical

Education Centers (ATECs), Authorized Academic Training Programs (AATPs), and the Microsoft Online Institute (MOLI).

MCSE (Microsoft Certified Systems Engineer)

Anyone who possesses a current MCSE is warranted to possess a high level of expertise with Windows NT (either version 3.51 or 4) and other Microsoft operating systems and products. This credential is designed to prepare individuals to plan, implement, maintain, and support information systems and networks built around Microsoft Windows NT and its BackOffice family of products.

To obtain an MCSE, an individual must pass four core operating system exams plus two elective exams. The operating system exams require individuals to demonstrate competence with desktop and server operating systems and with networking components.

At least two Windows NT-related exams must be passed to obtain an MCSE: Implementing and Supporting Windows NT Server (version 3.51 or 4) and Implementing and Supporting Windows NT Server in the Enterprise (version 3.51 or 4). These tests are intended to indicate an individual's knowledge of Windows NT in smaller, simpler networks and in larger, more complex, and heterogeneous networks, respectively.

Two more tests must be passed: networking and desktop operating system related. At present, the networking requirement can be satisfied only by passing the Networking Essentials test. The desktop operating system test can be satisfied by passing a Windows 3.1, Windows for Workgroups 3.11, Windows NT Workstation (the version must match whichever core curriculum is pursued), or Windows 95 test.

The two remaining exams are elective exams. The elective exams can be in any number of subject or product areas, primarily BackOffice components. These include tests on SQL Server, SNA Server, Exchange, Systems Management Server, and the like. But it is also possible to test out on electives by taking advanced networking topics like Internetworking with Microsoft TCP/IP (here again, the version of Windows NT involved must match the version for the core requirements taken).

Whatever the mix of tests, individuals must pass six tests to meet the MCSE requirements. It's not uncommon for the entire process to take a year or so, and many individuals find that they must take a test more than once to pass. Our primary goal with the *Exam Cram* series is to make it possible, given proper study and preparation, to pass all of the MCSE tests on the first try.

MCSE+I (Microsoft Certified Systems Engineer Plus Internet)

This is the newest of the Microsoft certifications. MCSE+I is designed to certify MCSE level experts in the topical fields commonly associated with the Internet. This level of certification requires the completion of seven core exams and two electives. The core exams are Networking Essentials, TCP/IP, a client (Windows 95, Windows 98, or Windows NT Workstation), Windows NT Server, Windows NT Server in the Enterprise, Internet Information Server, and Internet Explorer Administration Kit. There are five tests that can be used as the two required electives—System Administration with SQL Server, Implementing Database Design with SQL Server, Exchange Server, Proxy Server, and SNA Server. Needless to say, this certification level is significantly more work to achieve than the standard MCSE.

A related certification is that of MCP+I (Microsoft Certified Professional plus Internet). This midlevel MCSE certification is attained by completing three core exams: Windows NT Server, TCP/IP, and Internet Information Server.

Finally, certification is an ongoing activity. Once a Microsoft product becomes obsolete, MCSEs (and other MCPs) typically have a 12- to 18-month time frame in which they can become re-certified on current product versions. (If individuals do not get re-certified within the specified time period, their certification is no longer valid.) Because technology keeps changing and new products continually supplant old ones, this should come as no surprise.

The best place to keep tabs on the MCP Program and its various certifications is on the Microsoft Web site. The current root URL for the MCP program is Certification Online at www.microsoft.com/mcp/. Microsoft's Web site changes frequently, so if this URL doesn't work, try using the Search tool on Microsoft's site with either MCP or the quoted phrase "Microsoft Certified Professional Program" as the search string. This will help you find the latest and most accurate information about the company's certification programs. There is also a special CD-ROM that contains a copy of the Microsoft Education and Certification Roadmap, which covers much of the same information as the Web site and is updated quarterly. To get your copy of the CD-ROM, call Microsoft at 800-636-7544, Monday through Friday, 6:30 A.M. through 7:30 P.M. Pacific Time.

Taking A Certification Exam

Alas, testing is not free. You'll be charged $100 for each test you take, whether you pass or fail. In the United States and Canada, tests are administered by Sylvan Prometric. Sylvan Prometric can be reached at 800-755-3926 or 800-755-EXAM, any time from 7:00 A.M. to 6:00 P.M., Central Time, Monday through Friday. If you can't get through on this number, try 612-896-7000 or 612-820-5707.

To schedule an exam, call at least one day in advance. To cancel or reschedule an exam, you must call at least 12 hours before the scheduled test time (or you may be charged). When calling Sylvan Prometric, please have the following information ready for the telesales representative who handles your call:

➤ Your name, organization, and mailing address.

➤ Your Microsoft Test ID. (For most U.S. citizens, this is your Social Security number. Citizens of other nations can use their taxpayer IDs or make other arrangements with the order taker.)

➤ The name and number of the exam you wish to take. (For this book, the exam number is 70-064 and the exam name is "Implementing and Supporting Microsoft Windows 95.")

➤ A method of payment must be arranged. (The most convenient approach is to supply a valid credit card number with sufficient available credit. Otherwise, payments by check, money order, or purchase order must be received before a test can be scheduled. If the latter methods are required, ask your order taker for more details.)

When you show up to take a test, try to arrive at least 15 minutes before the scheduled time slot. You must bring and supply two forms of identification, one of which must be a photo ID.

All exams are completely closed-book. In fact, you will not be permitted to take anything with you into the testing area, but you will be furnished with a blank sheet of paper and a pen. We suggest that you immediately write down the most critical information about the test you're taking on the sheet of paper. *Exam Cram* books provide a brief reference—The Cram Sheet, located inside the front cover—that lists the essential information from the book in distilled form. You will have some time to compose yourself, to record this information, and even to take a sample orientation exam before you must begin the real thing. We suggest you take the orientation test before taking your first exam; they're all more or less identical in layout, behavior, and controls, so you probably won't need to do this more than once.

When you complete a Microsoft certification exam, the software will tell you whether you've passed or failed. All tests are scored on a basis of 1,000 points, and results are broken into several topical areas. Even if you fail, we suggest you ask for—and keep—the detailed report that the test administrator prints for you. You can use the report to help you prepare for another go-round, if needed. If you need to retake an exam, you'll have to call Sylvan Prometric, schedule a new test date, and pay another $100 to take the test again.

Tracking MCP Status

As soon as you pass any Microsoft operating system exam, you'll attain MCP status. Microsoft also generates transcripts that indicate the exams you have passed and your corresponding test scores. You can order a transcript by email at any time by sending an email addressed to mcp@msprograms.com. You can also obtain a copy of your transcript by using the transcript tool on the secure private MCP Web area. This is accessed by clicking the "For MCPs Only" link on the MCP page. You'll need to provide your unique MCP number and password to gain entry. Details about what your password is will be included in your MCP welcome that Microsoft will send you two to six weeks after you complete your first operating system exam.

Once you pass the necessary set of six exams, you'll be certified as an MCSE. Official certification normally takes anywhere from four to six weeks, so don't expect to get your credentials overnight. When the package arrives, it will include a Welcome Kit that contains a number of elements, including:

➤ An MCSE certificate, suitable for framing, along with an MCSE Professional Program membership card and lapel pin.

➤ A license to use the MCP logo, thereby allowing you to use the logo in advertisements, promotions, documents, on letterhead, business cards, and so on. An MCP logo sheet, which includes camera-ready artwork, comes with the license. (Note: Before using any of the artwork, individuals must sign and return a licensing agreement that indicates they'll abide by its terms and conditions.)

➤ A one-year subscription to TechNet, a collection of CDs that includes software, documentation, service packs, databases, and more technical information than you can possibly ever read. In our minds, this is the best and most tangible benefit of attaining MCSE status.

➤ A subscription to *Microsoft Certified Professional* magazine, which provides ongoing data about testing and certification activities, requirements, and changes to the program.

➤ A free Priority Comprehensive 10-pack with Microsoft Product Support, and a 25 percent discount on additional Priority Comprehensive 10-packs. This lets you place up to 10 free calls to Microsoft's technical support operation at a higher-than-normal priority level.

➤ A one-year subscription to the Microsoft Beta Evaluation program. This subscription will get you all beta products from Microsoft for the next year. (This does not include developer products. You must join the MSDN program or become an MCSD to qualify for developer beta products.)

Many people believe that the benefits of MCSE certification go well beyond the perks that Microsoft provides to newly anointed members of this elite group. We're starting to see more job listings that request or require applicants to have an MCSE, and many individuals who complete the program can qualify for increases in pay or responsibility. As an official recognition of hard work and broad knowledge, MCSE certification is a badge of honor in many IT organizations.

How To Prepare For An Exam

At a minimum, preparing for the Windows 95 test requires that you obtain and study the following materials:

➤ *Supporting Microsoft Windows 95*. Microsoft Press, 1995. ISBN 1-55615-931-5. This boxed set should be purchased only if you have not already spent time using Windows 95, since it covers much introductory material and costs a whopping $199.95 (list price).

➤ The exam prep materials, practice tests, and self-assessment exams on the Microsoft Training And Certification Download page (www.microsoft.com/mcp/). Find the materials, download them, and use them!

➤ This *Exam Cram* book! It's the first and last thing you should read before taking the exam.

In addition, you'll probably find any or all of the following materials useful in your quest for Windows 95 expertise:

➤ **Classroom training** ATECs, AATPs, MOLI, and unlicensed third-party training companies (such as Wave Technologies, American Research Group, Learning Tree, Data-Tech, and others) all offer classroom training on Windows 95. These companies aim to help prepare network administrators to understand Windows 95 concepts and pass the MCSE tests. While such training runs upward of $350 per day in class, most of the individuals lucky enough to partake (including your humble authors, who've even taught such courses) find them to be quite worthwhile.

➤ **Other publications** You'll find direct references to other publications and resources in this book, but there's no shortage of materials available about Windows 95. To help you sift through some of the publications out there, we end each chapter with a "Need To Know More?" section that provides pointers to more complete and exhaustive resources covering the chapter's information. This should give you an idea of where we suggest you should look for further discussion.

➤ **The TechNet CD** TechNet is a monthly CD subscription available from Microsoft. TechNet includes all the Windows NT BackOffice Resource Kits and their product documentation. In addition, TechNet provides the contents of the Microsoft Knowledge Base and many kinds of software, white papers, training materials, as well as other good stuff. TechNet also contains all service packs, interim release patches, and supplemental driver software released since the last major version for most Microsoft programs and all Microsoft operating systems. A one-year subscription costs $299—worth every penny, if only for the download time it saves.

Microsoft periodically offers a free trial issue of TechNet as part of a special promotion. Keep your eyes on the TechNet CD Web site (www.microsoft.com/technet/) for these promotions. As of April 1998, a free issue of TechNet was available by registering on the IT Home Web site (www.microsoft.com/ithome/).

The above set of required and recommended materials represents a nonpareil collection of sources and resources for Windows 95 topics and software. In the section that follows, we explain how this book works and give you some good reasons why this book should also be in your required and recommended materials list.

About This Book

Each topical *Exam Cram* chapter follows a regular structure, along with graphical cues about especially important or useful material. Here's the structure of a typical chapter:

➤ **Opening hotlists** Each chapter begins with a list of the terms, tools, and techniques that you must learn and understand before you can be fully conversant with that chapter's subject matter. We follow the hotlists with one or two introductory paragraphs to set the stage for the rest of the chapter.

➤ **Topical coverage** After the opening hotlists, each chapter covers a series of at least four topics related to the chapter's subject. Throughout this section, we highlight material most likely to appear on a test using a special Study Alert layout, like this:

This is what a Study Alert looks like. Normally, a Study Alert stresses concepts, terms, software, or activities that you should understand thoroughly. For that reason, we think any information found offset in Study Alert format is worthy of unusual attentiveness on your part. Indeed, most of the facts appearing on The Cram Sheet appear as Study Alerts within the text.

➤ **Tables** Occasionally, you'll see tables called "Vital Statistics." The contents of Vital Statistics tables are worthy of an extra once-over. These tables contain informational tidbits that might well show up in a test question.

Even if material isn't flagged as a Study Alert or included in a Vital Statistics table, all the contents of this book are associated, at least tangentially, to something test-related. This book is lean to focus on quick test preparation; you'll find that what appears in the meat of each chapter is critical knowledge.

➤ **Tips** We have also provided tips that will help build a better foundation of Windows 95 knowledge. Although the information may not be on the exam, it is highly relevant and will help you become a better test taker.

This is how tips are formatted. Keep your eyes open for these, and you'll become a Windows 95 expert in no time.

➤ **Exam Prep Questions** Although we talk about test questions and topics throughout each chapter, this section presents a series of mock test questions and explanations of both correct and incorrect answers. We also try to point out especially tricky questions by using a special icon, like this:

Ordinarily, this icon flags the presence of an especially devious question, if not an outright trick question. Trick questions are calculated to "trap"

you if you don't read them carefully and more than once, at that. Although they're not ubiquitous, such questions make regular appearances in the Microsoft exams. That's why we say exam questions are as much about reading comprehension as they are about knowing Windows 95 material inside out and backward.

➤ **Details And Resources** Every chapter ends with a section titled "Need To Know More?" That section provides direct pointers to Microsoft and third-party resources that offer further details on the chapter's subject. In addition, this section tries to rate the quality and thoroughness of the topic's coverage by each resource. If you find a resource you like in this collection, use it, but don't feel compelled to use all the resources. On the other hand, we recommend only resources we use on a regular basis, so none of our recommendations will be a waste of your time or money.

The bulk of the book follows this chapter structure slavishly, but there are a few other elements that we'd like to point out: the answer key to the sample test that appears in Chapter 18 and a reasonably exhaustive glossary of Windows 95-specific and general Microsoft terminology. Finally, look for The Cram Sheet, which appears inside the front cover of this *Exam Cram* book. It is a valuable tool that represents a condensed and compiled collection of facts, figures, and tips that we think you should memorize before taking the test. Because you can dump this information out of your head and onto a piece of paper before answering any exam questions, you can master this information by brute force—you need to remember it only long enough to write it down when you walk into the test room. You might even want to look at it in the car or in the lobby of the testing center just before you walk in to take the test.

How To Use This Book

If you're prepping for a first-time test, we've structured the topics in this book to build on one another. Therefore, some topics in later chapters make more sense after you've read earlier chapters. That's why we suggest you read this book from front to back for your initial test preparation. If you need to brush up on a topic or you have to bone up for a second try, use the index or table of contents to go straight to the topics and questions that you need to study. Beyond the tests, we think you'll find this book useful as a tightly focused reference to some of the most important aspects of this operating system.

Given all the book's elements and its specialized focus, we've tried to create a tool that you can use to prepare for—and pass—Microsoft Certification Exam 70-064, "Implementing and Supporting Microsoft Windows 95." Please share your feedback on the book with us, especially if you have ideas about how we can improve it for future test takers. We'll consider everything you say care-fully, and we'll respond to all suggestions. You can reach us via email at examcram@lanw.com. Please remember to include the title of the book in your message; otherwise, we'll be forced to guess which book you're making a sug-gestion about. Its also a good idea to list the page number which relates to your questions or comments. And we don't like to guess—we want to KNOW!

You should also visit our *Exam Cram* Web site at www.lanw.com/examcram/.

Thanks, and enjoy the book!

Microsoft
Certification
Exams

Terms you'll need to understand:

√   Radio button

√   Checkbox

√   Exhibit

√   Multiple-choice question formats

√   Careful reading

√   Process of elimination

Techniques you'll need to master:

√   Preparing to take a certification exam

√   Practicing—to make perfect

√   Making the best use of the testing software

√   Budgeting your time

√   Saving the hardest questions until last

√   Guessing (as a last resort)

Exam taking is not something that most people anticipate eagerly, no matter how well-prepared they are. In most cases, familiarity helps ameliorate test anxiety. In plain English, this means you probably won't be as nervous when you take your fourth or fifth Microsoft certification exam as you will be when you take your first one.

Whether it's your first exam or your tenth, understanding the details of exam taking (how much time to spend on questions, the setting you'll be in, and so on) and the exam software will help you concentrate on the material rather than on the environment. Likewise, mastering a few basic exam-taking skills should help you recognize—and perhaps even outfox—some of the tricks and gotchas you're bound to find in some of the exam questions.

This chapter explains the exam environment and software, and describes some proven exam-taking strategies that you should be able to use to your advantage. This information has been compiled from the 30-plus Microsoft certification exams that the authors have taken themselves. The authors have also drawn on the advice of friends and colleagues, some of whom have taken more than 30 tests each.

The Exam Situation

When you arrive at the Sylvan Prometric Testing Center where you scheduled your exam, you'll need to sign in with an exam coordinator. He or she will ask you to produce two forms of identification, one of which must be a photo ID. Once you've signed in and your time slot arrives, you'll be asked to deposit any books, bags, or other items you brought with you, and you'll be escorted into a closed room. Typically, that room will be furnished with anywhere from one to half a dozen computers, and each workstation will be separated from the others by dividers designed to keep you from seeing what's happening on someone else's computer.

You'll be furnished with a pen or pencil and a blank sheet of paper or, in some cases, an erasable plastic sheet and an erasable felt-tip pen. You're allowed to write down any information you want on both sides of this sheet. You should memorize as much of the material that appears on The Cram Sheet (inside the front cover of this book) as you can and then write that information down on the blank sheet as soon as you are seated in front of the computer. You can refer to that piece of paper any time you like during the test, but you'll have to surrender the sheet when you leave the room.

Most test rooms feature a wall with a large picture window. This permits the exam coordinator to monitor the room, to prevent exam takers from talking to one another, and to observe anything out of the ordinary that might go on.

The exam coordinator will have preloaded the Microsoft certification exam you've signed up for—for this book, that's Exam 70-064—and you'll be permitted to start as soon as you're seated in front of the computer.

All Microsoft certification exams allow a certain maximum amount of time to complete your work (this time is indicated on the exam by an onscreen counter/clock so you can check the time remaining whenever you like). Exam 70-064 consists of 49 questions. You're permitted to take up to 90 minutes to complete the exam.

All Microsoft certification exams are computer-generated and use a multiple-choice format. Although this may sound quite simple, the questions are constructed not only to check your mastery of basic facts and figures about Windows 95; they also require you to evaluate one or more sets of circumstances or requirements. Often, you'll be asked to give more than one answer to a question; likewise, you may be asked to select the best or most effective solution to a problem from a range of choices, all of which are technically correct. Taking the exam is quite an adventure, and it involves real thinking, but this book will show you what to expect and how to deal with the problems, puzzles, and predicaments you're likely to find on the exam.

Exam Layout And Design

The following shows a typical exam question. This multiple-choice question requires that you select a single correct answer.

Question 1

What is the name of the Windows 95 utility that enables you to recover deleted files?

○ a. Undelete

○ b. Trash

○ c. Recycle Bin

○ d. Undo

The Recycle Bin is the deleted-file-recovery utility of Windows 95. Therefore, answer c is correct. Undelete is the process used to recover deleted files, not the specific utility. Therefore, answer a is incorrect. The Trash is a utility found on Macintosh computers. Therefore, answer b is incorrect. Undo is a command used in many applications to repeal the last change made to a document. Therefore, answer d is incorrect.

This sample question corresponds closely to the type you'll see on the Microsoft certification exams. To select the correct answer, position the cursor over the radio button next to answer c and click the mouse. The only difference on the exam is that questions are not followed by the answer key.

Let's examine a question that requires choosing multiple answers. This type of question provides checkboxes rather than radio buttons for marking all appropriate selections.

Question 2

> Which of the following are true for VFAT? [Check all correct answers]
>
> ❑ a. Allows file names up to 255 characters long
>
> ❑ b. Maximum volume size of 4 GB
>
> ❑ c. Limited to 8.3 file names
>
> ❑ d. Supports file-level security
>
> ❑ e. Maximum of 512 root directory entries

VFAT supports 255-character file names, has a maximum volume size of 4 GB, and has a maximum of 512 root directory entries. Therefore, answers a, b, and e are correct. FAT, not VFAT, is limited to 8.3. Therefore, answer c is incorrect. VFAT does not support file-level security. Therefore, answer d is incorrect.

This type of question requires more than one answer. As far as the authors can tell (Microsoft won't comment), such questions are scored as wrong unless you choose all of the required selections. In other words, a partially correct answer does not result in partial credit when the test is scored. For Question 2, you'd have to check the boxes next to items a, b, and e to obtain credit for a correct answer.

Although these two basic types of questions can appear in many forms, they constitute the foundation on which all of the Microsoft certification exam questions rest. More complex questions may include so-called exhibits, which are usually screen shots of a Windows 95 utility. For some of these questions, you'll be asked to make a selection by clicking a checkbox or radio button on the screenshot itself; for others, you'll be expected to use the information displayed therein to guide your answer to the question. Familiarity with the underlying utility is the key to the correct answer(s).

Other questions involving exhibits may use charts or network diagrams to help document a workplace scenario that you'll be asked to troubleshoot or configure.

Careful attention to such exhibits is the key to success. Be prepared to toggle frequently between the picture and the question as you work.

Using Microsoft's Exam Software Effectively

A well-known principle when taking exams is to first read over the entire exam from start to finish while answering only those questions that you feel absolutely sure of. On subsequent passes, you can dive deeper into more complex questions, knowing how many such questions you have to deal with.

Fortunately, Microsoft exam software makes this approach easy to implement. At the top-left of each question is a checkbox that permits you to mark that question for a later visit. (Marking questions makes review easier, but you can return to any question if you are willing to click the Forward and Back buttons repeatedly.) As you read each question, if you answer only those you're sure of and mark for review those that you're not sure of, you can keep working through a decreasing list of questions as you answer the trickier ones in order.

There's at least one potential benefit to reading the exam over completely before answering the trickier questions: Sometimes, you find information in later questions that sheds more light on earlier ones. Other times, information you read in later questions may jog your memory about Windows 95 facts, figures, or behavior that will also help with earlier questions. Either way, you'll come out ahead if you defer those questions about which you're not absolutely sure.

Keep working on the questions until you are absolutely sure of all your answers or until you know you'll run out of time. If questions are still unanswered, you'll want to zip through them and guess. Not answering a question guarantees you won't receive credit for it, and a guess has at least a chance of being correct. This strategy works only because Microsoft doesn't penalize for incorrect answers (i.e., it treats an incorrect answer and no answer as equally wrong).

At the very end of your exam period, you're better off guessing than leaving questions unanswered.

Exam-Taking Basics

The most important advice about taking any Microsoft exam is this: Read each question carefully. Some questions are deliberately ambiguous, some use double negatives, and others use terminology in incredibly precise ways. The authors have taken numerous exams—both practice and live—and in nearly every one, have missed at least one question because they didn't read it closely or carefully enough.

Here are some suggestions on how to deal with the tendency to jump to an answer too quickly:

➤ Make sure you read every word in the question. If you find yourself jumping ahead impatiently, go back and start over.

➤ As you read, try to restate the question in your own terms. If you can do this, you should be able to pick the correct answer(s) much more easily.

➤ When returning to a question after your initial read-through, read every word again—otherwise, your mind can fall quickly into a rut. Sometimes, revisiting a question after turning your attention elsewhere lets you see something you missed, but the strong tendency is to see what you've seen before. Try to avoid that tendency at all costs.

➤ If you return to a question more than twice, try to articulate to yourself what you don't understand about the question, why the answers don't appear to make sense, or what appears to be missing. If you chew on the subject for a while, your subconscious may provide the details that are lacking, or you may notice a "trick" that will point to the right answer.

Above all, try to deal with each question by thinking through what you know about the Windows 95 utilities, characteristics, behaviors, facts, and figures involved. By reviewing what you know (and what you've written down on your information sheet), you will often recall or understand things sufficiently to determine the answer to the question.

Question-Handling Strategies

Based on the exams the authors have taken, some interesting trends have become apparent. For those questions that take only a single answer, usually two or three of the answers will be obviously incorrect, and two of the answers will be plausible—of course, only one can be correct. Unless the answer leaps out at you (if it does, reread the question to look for a trick; sometimes, those are the ones you're most likely to get wrong), begin the process of answering by eliminating those answers that are most obviously wrong.

Things to look for in obviously wrong answers include spurious menu choices or utility names, nonexistent software options, and terminology you've never seen. If you've done your homework for an exam, no valid information should be completely new to you. In that case, unfamiliar or bizarre terminology probably indicates a totally bogus answer. As long as you're sure what's right, it's easy to eliminate what's wrong.

Numerous questions assume that the default behavior of a particular utility is in effect. If you know the defaults and understand what they mean, this knowledge will help you cut through many Gordian knots.

As you work your way through the exam, another counter that Microsoft thankfully provides will come in handy—the number of questions completed and questions outstanding. Budget your time by making sure that you've completed one-quarter of the questions one-quarter of the way through the exam period (or 13 questions in the first 22 minutes) and three-quarters of them three-quarters of the way through (37 questions in the first 66 minutes).

If you're not finished when 85 minutes have elapsed, use the last 5 minutes to guess your way through the remaining questions. Remember, guessing is potentially more valuable than not answering because blank answers are always wrong, but a guess may turn out to be right. If you don't have a clue about any of the remaining questions, pick answers at random or choose all a's, b's, and so on. The important thing is to submit an exam for scoring that has an answer for every question.

Mastering The Inner Game

In the final analysis, knowledge breeds confidence, and confidence breeds success. If you study the materials in this book carefully and review all of the exam prep questions at the end of each chapter, you should become aware of those areas where additional learning and study are required.

Next, follow up by reading some or all of the materials recommended in the "Need To Know More?" section at the end of each chapter. The idea is to become familiar enough with the concepts and situations that you find in the sample questions so that you can reason your way through similar situations on a real exam. If you know the material, you have every right to be confident that you can pass the exam.

Once you've worked your way through the book, take the practice exam in Chapter 18. This will provide a reality check and help you identify areas you need to study further. Make sure you follow up and review materials related to the questions you miss before scheduling a real exam. Only when you've covered all the ground and feel comfortable with the whole scope of the practice exam should you take a real one.

If you take the practice exam and don't score at least 75 percent correct, you'll want to practice further. At a minimum, download the Personal Exam Prep (PEP) exams and the self-assessment exams from the Microsoft Certification and Training Web site's download page (its location appears in the next section). If you're more ambitious, or better funded, you might want to purchase a practice exam from one of the third-party vendors that offers them.

Armed with the information in this book and with the determination to augment your knowledge, you should be able to pass the certification exam. You need to work at it, however, or you'll spend the exam fee more than once before you finally do pass. If you prepare seriously, the execution should go flawlessly. Good luck!

Need To Know More?

By far, the best source of information about Microsoft certification exams is Microsoft itself. Because its products and technologies—and the exams that go with them—change frequently, the best place to go for exam-related information is online.

If you haven't already visited the Microsoft Certified Professional Web pages, do so right now. The Microsoft Certified Professional Web page resides at www.microsoft.com/mcp/ (see Figure 1.1).

> *Note: This page may not be there by the time you read this, or it may have been replaced by something new and different because things change regularly on the Microsoft site. Should this happen, please read the sidebar titled "Coping With Change On The Web."*

Through the menu options offered in the left-hand column of the Microsoft Certified Professional Web page, you can access information about individual tests, certification levels, training materials, and more.

Coping With Change On The Web

Sooner or later, all of the information we've shared with you about the Microsoft Certified Professional Web page, and all of the other Web-based resources we mention throughout the rest of this book, will go stale or be replaced by newer information. In some cases, the URLs you find here might lead you to their replacements; in other cases, the URLs will go nowhere, leaving you with the dreaded "404 File not found" error message.

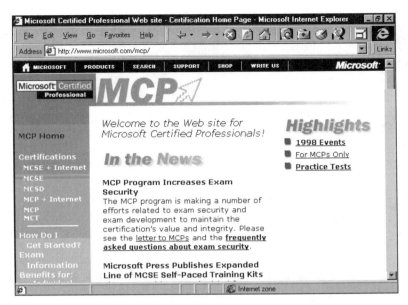

Figure 1.1   The Microsoft Certified Professional home page.

When that happens, please don't give up! There's always a way to find what you want on the Web—if you're willing to invest some time and energy. To begin with, most large or complex Web sites—and Microsoft's qualifies on both counts—offer a search engine. Looking back at Figure 1.1, you'll see that a Search button appears along the top edge of the page. As long as you can get to the site itself (and we're pretty sure that it will stay at www.microsoft.com for a long while yet), you can use this tool to help you find what you need.

The more particular or focused you can make a search request, the more likely it is that the results will include information you can use. For instance, you can search the string "training and certification" to produce a lot of data about the subject in general, but if you're looking for the Preparation Guide for Exam 70-064, "Implementing and Supporting Microsoft Windows 95," you'll be more likely to get there quickly if you use a search string such as this:

```
Exam 70-064 AND preparation guide
```

Likewise, if you want to find the Training and Certification downloads, try a search string such as this one:

```
training and certification AND download page
```

Finally, don't be afraid to use general search tools such as www.search.com, www.altavista.digital.com, or www.excite.com to search for related information. Even though Microsoft offers the best information about its certification exams online, there are plenty of third-party sources of information, training, and assistance in this area that do not have to follow a party line like Microsoft does. The bottom line is: If you can't find something where the book says it lives, start looking around. If worse comes to worst, you can always email us! We just might have a clue.

Need More Practice?

LANWrights, Inc., the company behind this book, also offers practice tests for sale. You can order practice exam diskettes via snail mail. Because we wrote them ourselves, we don't feel comfortable telling you how great they are—but they surely are a good deal! Currently available tests include NT Server 4.0, NT Server 4.0 in the Enterprise, NT Workstation 4.0, Networking Essentials, TCP/IP, Proxy Server 2.0, IIS 4.0, and Windows 95. Please send a check or money order to the following address: LANWrights, Inc., P.O. Box 26261, Austin, TX 78755-0261.

Each diskette includes two complete practice tests. Either Netscape Navigator 3 (or higher) or Microsoft Internet Explorer 3 (or higher) is required to use the Java-based testing system on the diskettes. Single exam diskettes are $25 each. Multiple diskettes can be purchased at a discount, as follows:

➤ Two exams for $45

➤ Three exams for $65

➤ Four exams for $85

➤ Five exams for $100

➤ Six exams for $115

➤ Seven exams for $125

➤ All eight exams for $130

Prices include U.S. shipping and required taxes. (Mexico and Canada add $5; all other countries outside North America add $10 for additional shipping charges.) Please be sure to include your name, shipping address, contact phone number, and the number and titles for those practice exams you wish to order.

Overview
And Installation
Of Windows 95

Terms you'll need to understand:

√   General Protection Faults (GPFs)

√   SETUP

√   Plug and Play

√   MSBATCH.INF

√   Automated installation

√   Dual boot configuration

√   BOOTSECT.DOS

Techniques you'll need to master:

√   Knowing whether to upgrade or perform a clean installation

√   Installing and configuring Windows 95

√   Troubleshooting failed Windows 95 installations

√   Uninstalling Windows 95

Windows 95 is the premier desktop operating system from Microsoft. Windows 95 is a significant improvement over Windows 3.1 in many respects, including memory usage, reliability, and network/Internet support. In this chapter, we introduce you to Windows 95.

Overview Of Windows 95

Windows 95 was designed with specific operating goals in mind. These goals were selected to provide the home and office user with the widest range of use and the most reliable environment possible on a personal computer. These goals are:

➤ **Compatibility** Windows 95 supports most existing hardware (i.e., at the time of its deployment in 1995) and all Windows 3.x applications.

➤ **Speed** Windows 95 is designed to support existing applications as fast as Windows 3.x and to outperform 3.x with new software and hardware. The 32-bit Protected Mode storage cache is one feature that improves Windows 95's performance.

➤ **Reliability** Compared to Windows 3.x, Windows 95 is better equipped to recover from General Protection Faults (GPFs) and hung applications.

➤ **Ease of use** Windows 95 is easier to use, supports Plug and Play technology, and simplifies configuration changes.

➤ **Networking** Unlike Windows 3.x, Windows 95 has native network capabilities, 32-bit Protected Mode drivers and protocols, and faster, more reliable network access to both LAN connections and the Internet.

Details of the Windows 95 architecture are discussed in Chapter 3.

Windows 95 Compared With NT Workstation

Windows 95 was such a revolutionary and successful operating system that Windows NT Workstation 4, the high-end operating system, adopted its look and feel, its ease of configuration, and several of its native utilities. Thus, distinguishing between Windows 95 and Windows NT can be difficult. Windows 95 was designed for compatibility, whereas NT Workstation was designed for security.

These two operating systems have the following features in common:

➤ Ability to run both 16-bit and 32-bit applications

➤ Preemptive multitasking

> ➤ Multithreaded operation

> ➤ File and printer sharing

> ➤ Web server hosting

> ➤ User profiles

> ➤ System policies enforcement

> ➤ Use of the Registry instead of INI files

> ➤ Can be clients for Microsoft or NetWare networks

> ➤ Intel CPUs

However, Windows 95 and Windows NT are different in more significant ways (see Table 2.1).

The details listed in Table 2.1 are important for one reason: They help determine which situations are better suited for Windows 95 and which are better suited for Windows NT. Such situations include security, compatibility, and legacy application/driver support.

Installation Overview

From the user's point of view, installing Windows 95 is smooth and simple, but the many complicated tasks accomplished behind the scenes are what enable such a pleasant experience. You'll need to understand the following information about the installation process.

Table 2.1   Differences between Windows 95 and Windows NT.

Item	Windows 95	Windows NT
16-bit drivers	Yes	No
Plug and Play	Yes	No
DOS applications	Yes	Most
Direct hardware access	Yes	No
16-bit applications in separate memory space	No	Yes
Multiple CPUs	No	Yes
C2 level security	No	Yes
Secured logon	No	Yes
Alpha, PPC, MIPS CPUs	No	Yes

Installation starts with the Real Mode SETUP, which, though very brief, performs five important activities:

➤ **File system** ScanDisk checks the integrity of the storage device.

➤ **Windows 3.x** SETUP checks the system for a previous version of Windows. If a previous version is found, the user is prompted whether to use this version to host the installation. If the user answers no, or if Windows 3.x is not found, SETUP loads its own minimal version of Windows to host the installation.

➤ **System composite** SETUP inspects the system to verify that it can support Windows 95 by looking at the CPU, storage space, and memory, and by determining which version of DOS is present.

➤ **Memory** SETUP checks for an extended memory manager, such as HIMEM.SYS. If one is not found, SETUP loads one. Setup will also load SMARTDRV, a disk-caching utility, if such a utility is not present.

➤ **TSRs** SETUP will attempt to unload any Terminate and Stay Resident (TSR) programs that may conflict with the installation. Setup gathers this information from the CONFIG.SYS and AUTOEXEC.BAT files and ignores TSRs it doesn't recognize.

Once these Real Mode activities are complete, the computer is switched to Protected Mode, and the Windows installation interface is loaded. In this mode, hardware is detected, files are copied, and boot records are modified. The details of this mode are discussed in "The Installation Process," later in this chapter.

Installation Vs. Upgrade

The Windows 95 distribution media are available in two media formats (floppies and CD-ROM) and two installation formats (full installation and upgrade). Both installation formats require the hard drive to be partitioned and formatted with the FAT or VFAT file system (file systems are covered in detail in Chapter 7). Either installation method can be used to install Windows 95 on a system with just DOS, but the upgrade version requires the first floppy from Windows 3.x to verify that you are legitimately upgrading.

Two issues are involved regarding full installation or upgrading. The first is the media type. The full installation format does not require any previous version of Windows to perform the installation, but the upgrade format requires Windows 3.x to be present on the system or for you to have the setup floppies for that version on hand. However, either installation format can be used to perform a "full clean install." The second issue is the actual upgrade of an existing version of Windows 3.x. Both the full and the upgrade formats can be used to upgrade Windows 3.x. The upgrade is performed by instructing the SETUP utility to use the same installation directory as the existing Windows version. The existing settings and configuration are then transferred into Windows 95. If an alternate or different installation directory is defined, none of the configuration of the existing Windows version is transferred to Windows 95.

Nearly all of the data stored in Windows 3.x is transferable to Windows 95, but only if you upgrade using the same installation directory. This means that if Windows 3.x is installed into the C:\WINDOWS directory, you must install/upgrade Windows 95 into the same C:\WINDOWS directory to retain the existing configurations. If you install/upgrade Windows 95 into a different directory, the existing configuration (such as user preferences and program groups) will not transfer into Windows 95.

The SETUP process for the full and upgrade installations is exactly the same, other than selecting the installation directory of the existing Windows version.

 If you failed to install Windows 95 into the same directory as an existing Windows 3.x installation, you can still transfer your program groups into Windows 95 by using the GRPCONV utility (Start|Run|GRPCONV).

Shared Installations Of Windows 95

Windows 95 can be used in a network in which the client machines either do not have hard drives or have only limited hard drive space. In such situations, you can use a shared Windows 95 network installation. A shared installation is one in which most of the system files for Windows 95 are stored on a network drive, and clients load Windows 95 from this network drive each time they boot. The clients have either a boot floppy or a network bootstrap routing on their small hard drives that establishes a network connection and initiates the transfer of the necessary files from the network drive to the client's memory. Windows 95 operates as it does normally, except instead of looking to a local drive for system components and drivers, it looks to a network drive. However, because Windows 95 is not local, it does slow the performance of the OS considerably.

The basic steps of performing a shared installation are as follows:

1. From a Windows 95 client on a Banyan Vines 5.52, Microsoft Windows NT Server, or Novell NetWare 3.x or 4.x network, launch the NetSetup

tool from the ADMIN\NETTOOLS\NETSETUP directory of the Windows 95 distribution CD.

Note: The NetSetup tool is present only on the original release CD of Windows 95; it does not appear on the Windows 95 with Plus or the OSR2 release. You must download the file from the Windows 95 Web area: www.microsoft.com/windows95/.

2. Define the following: a network path in which the Windows 95 files will be stored; how installation can occur—local hard disk, shared copy, or user choice; default setup scripts; and the CD key number. Then, allow the tool to copy the distribution files.

3. Use the NetSetup tool to create machine directories on a network server to host the user and machine-specific files, such as WIN.INI, SYSTEM.INI, SYSTEM.DAT, USER.DAT, user profile, and print spool.

4. Use the NetSetup tool to create a setup script to use in launching the shared installation of Windows 95.

Some additional items to remember about shared installations:

➤ **MS-DOS mode is disabled** When the system shuts down to switch to MS-DOS mode, access to the network is lost; thus, MS-DOS mode cannot be activated.

➤ **Network adapter hot-docking is disabled** Because network access is required, removal of network interface cards (NICs) is not possible.

➤ **Users cannot log off, then log on as different users** A reboot must be performed with a different boot strap routing to access a different machine directory for an alternate user.

➤ **Safe Mode startups still load all configuration files** Because network access is required, these files must be loaded.

Automated And Network Installation

In addition to the standard installation options, Windows 95 offers several other unique setup routines and operational methods. These include server-based and batch installations.

The server-based option installs Windows 95 onto a server in a shared folder. This folder can be used by clients to run or to locally install Windows 95. This type of shared installation requires very little drive space but demands significant network bandwidth, and performance is poor.

The batch option uses a script to provide the installation details without requiring user input. A batch installation can use the distribution files from a CD-ROM or from a server-based installation. The installation script must conform exactly to the required syntax, so Microsoft provides a utility that writes the script for you. The NETSETUP.EXE utility (found on the Windows 95 installation CD in the \ADMIN\NETTOOLS\NETSETUP\ directory) and the BATCH.EXE utility (found in the Windows 95 Resource Kit) can be used to create the MSBATCH.INF files to automate the installation.

The following is a sample MSBATCH.INF file:

```
[Setup]
Express=0         ; allows user input
InstallType=1     ; Typical Setup
EBD=1             ; create startup disk
InstallDir=C:\WINDOWS
Verify=0
PenWinWarning=1
ProductID=999999999


[NameAndOrg]
Name="User One"
Org="Your Company Name"
Display=1          ; User Information dialog box is displayed


[OptionalComponents]
"Accessories"=1
"Communications"=1
"Disk Tools"=1
"Multimedia"=1
"Screen Savers"=0
"Disk Compression Tools"=1
"Paint"=1
"HyperTerminal"=1
"Defrag"=1
"Blank Screen"=1
"Scrolling Marquee"=1
"Calculator"=1
"Object Packager"=1
"Backup"=0
"Phone Dialer"=1
```

```
"Clipboard Viewer"=0
"Microsoft Fax"=0
"Microsoft Fax Services"=0
"Microsoft Fax Viewer"=0
"Accessibility Options"=0
"The Microsoft Network"=0
"Audio Compression"=0
"Video Compression"=1
"Sound Recorder"=0
"Volume Control"=0
"Media Player"=1
"Microsoft Exchange"=0
"Microsoft Mail Services"=0
"Briefcase"=0
"Document Templates"=1
"WordPad"=1
"Dial-Up Networking"=0
"Direct Cable Connection"=0
"Mouse Pointers"=0
"Windows 95 Tour"=0
"Online User's Guide"=0
"Desktop Wallpaper"=0
"System Monitor"=0
"Net Watcher"=0
"Character Map"=0
"Curves and Colors"=0
"Mystify Your Mind"=0
"Flying Through Space"=0
"Games"=0
"Quick View"=0
"Sample Sounds"=0
"Musica Sound Scheme"=0
"Jungle Sound Scheme"=0
"Robotz Sound Scheme"=0
"Utopia Sound Scheme"=0
"CD Player"=0

[System]
"Display"="Tseng Lans ET4000"
"Keyboard"="Standard 101/102-Key or Microsoft Natural Keyboard"
"Machine"="MS_CHICAGO"
"Monitor"="NEC MultiSync 2A"
"Mouse"="Standard Serial Mouse"
"Power"="No APM"
"Locale"="L0409"
"UI Choice"="Win95UI"
"Multilanguage"="English"
```

```
[InstallLocationsMRU]
MRU1=C:\WINDOWS
MRU2=C:\User
MRU3=\\win_svr\source files\home_dir

[Network]
Display=0                ; Network Options do not appear in Setup
ComputerName=W95_1
Workgroup=test_group
Description="This is a lab test computer"
Clients=vredir,nwredir
Security=Domain
PassThroughAgent=Test_domain
WorkstationSetup=0       ; not a shared installation of Windows 95
HDBoot=1

[VREDIR]
ValidatedLogon=1
LogonDomain=test_domain
```

In addition, the INFINST.EXE tool from the Windows 95 Resource Kit can be used to add more details to the MSBATCH.INF file to install other applications, such as Microsoft Office, at the same time. Therefore, several common applications can be automatically installed.

You can use the NETSETUP utility to place the Windows 95 distribution files on a network share or you can perform this transfer manually. Simply create a network share with a share name of eight characters or less. Then, copy the entire contents of the Windows 95 distribution CD into this share. Grant read access to all users.

System Requirements

Microsoft has outlined the minimum and recommended requirements for computers hosting the Windows 95 operating system (see Table 2.2). It is important to follow these recommendations.

In addition, a pointing device, such as a mouse, simplifies interface interaction. A modem is required for dial-up access, and a network interface card (NIC) is required for LAN access.

As already mentioned, Windows 95 installation requires the computer's hard drive to be partitioned and formatted with the FAT or VFAT file system. Although DOS 6.2x is preferred and recommended, the following alternatives are supported:

Table 2.2 Requirements and recommendations for Windows 95.

Item	Requirements	Recommendations
Processor	386 DX	486 DX66 or better
RAM	4 MB RAM	16 MB RAM
Floppy drives	3.5" floppy	3.5" floppy
CD-ROM drives	CD-ROM drive	CD-ROM drive
Disk space	55 MB free disk space	55 MB plus twice the amount of RAM or more
Video	VGA	SVGA

➤ DOS 3.2 or later

➤ DR DOS

➤ Novell DOS

➤ IBM PC-DOS

➤ OS/2 with dual boot to DOS

The Installation Process

Installation is started by executing the SETUP.EXE file from either a DOS prompt or from the Windows 3.x File|Run command. Depending on the environment in which SETUP is launched, different command-line parameters can be used.

The following is a list of DOS prompt SETUP switches:

➤ **/ID** Skip check for hard drive space

➤ **/IL** Install the drivers for a Logitech series C mouse

➤ **/IM** Skip memory check

➤ **/IQ** Skip cross-link drive check (used with /IS)

➤ **/IS** Skip ScanDisk

➤ **/T:<path>** Location to place temporary files; directory must already exist

➤ **<batch>** Name of batch file to use for SETUP details

➤ **/?** Help

The following is a list of Windows 3.x SETUP switches:

➤ **/ID** Skip check for hard drive space

➤ **/IM** Skip memory check

➤ **/IN** Skip launching of the network module

➤ **/IQ** Skip cross-link drive check (used with /IS)

➤ **/IS** Skip ScanDisk

➤ **/T:<path>** Location to place temporary files; directory must already exist

➤ **/?** Help

Once SETUP is launched, individual steps of the installation process occur in the order shown in Table 2.3.

The first five steps of the Real Mode portion of SETUP were described earlier in this chapter; their completion is often nearly instantaneous. Once Windows is launched (Step 6), the Protected Mode portion of SETUP is started (Step 7).

Hardware Detection (Step 8)

The hardware detection phase is a multipart activity that identifies the computer's components. The first step polls the components to determine whether any Plug and Play devices are present. The second step, a safe detection method, searches the CONFIG.SYS, AUTOEXEC.BAT, and INI files for device drivers. The third step, an invasive method, systematically sends signals to various memory locations and IRQ channels. This final method can cause some systems to crash or lock up, in which case restarting the computer by turning off the power allows SETUP to start over and try again.

Table 2.3 The order and modes of the setup process.	
Real Mode	**Protected Mode**
1. ScanDisk	7. Protected Mode started
2. Look for existing Windows	8. Hardware detection
3. System composite check	9. User detail selection
4. XMS check	10. Files copied
5. TSR management	11. Boot record modification
6. Windows started	12. Restart
	13. First run of Windows 95

You can troubleshoot a crashed system by looking at the log files DETLOG.TXT and SETUPLOG.TXT. The SETUP utility can bypass any invasive steps that caused the previous crash and move on to the next address or channel. It does this by using DETCRASH.LOG, which records system crashes. It is possible that SETUP will lock up a machine several times, requiring you to cycle the system's power to continue the SETUP process. SETUPLOG.TXT contains a detailed, ordered list of everything that occurs during SETUP, including crashes. DETLOG.TXT lists the configuration parameters of all located and identified hardware.

User Detail Selection (Step 9)

The SETUP Wizard offers four types of installation:

➤ **Typical** This is the default SETUP type and is recommended for most desktop computers. This selection has the least number of user prompts.

➤ **Portable** This SETUP type is optimized for notebook installation (e.g., Briefcase), direct cable connection, and power management tools.

➤ **Compact** This SETUP type uses the least amount of hard drive space and installs only required files.

➤ **Custom** This SETUP type allows you to specify which components to install. This option will bring up additional windows within which to make component selections. This is the only option that offers Mail and Fax.

The remaining user input prompts include:

➤ Destination directory

➤ Name and organization

➤ Agreement with the license

➤ CD key

➤ Prompt to create a Windows 95 startup disk (see the next section for more details)

Completion (Steps 10 Through 13)

The final steps of installation include copying all of the appropriate distribution files to their "permanent" locations on the system, modifying the boot record, and restarting the computer into Windows 95 for the first time.

Once the distribution files are copied, you can create a Windows 95 startup disk (a useful tool for troubleshooting boot problems). The Windows 95 certification exam assumes that you will create the startup disk during installation, even though, in practice, you should wait until the configuration of other applications, utilities, and drivers is complete. The following files are copied to the Windows 95 startup disk:

➤ **ATTRIB.EXE** File attribute utility

➤ **CHKDSK.EXE** Lightweight disk-scanning utility

➤ **COMMAND.COM** Command interpreter

➤ **DEBUG.EXE** System-level debugging utility

➤ **DRVSPACE.BIN** DriveSpace compression driver

➤ **EBD.SYS** Windows 95 startup disk flag/identifier

➤ **EDIT.COM** Text editor

➤ **FDISK.EXE** Disk partition utility

➤ **FORMAT.COM** Disk format utility

➤ **IO.SYS** System boot file

➤ **MSDOS.SYS** Boot setting information

➤ **REGEDIT.EXE** Registry editor

➤ **SCANDISK.EXE** Disk status and repair utility

➤ **SCANDISK.INI** ScanDisk configuration file

➤ **SYS.COM** System transfer utility

➤ **UNINSTAL.EXE** Windows 95 uninstall utility

The modifications to the boot record include:

➤ Renaming COMMAND.COM, CONFIG.SYS, and AUTOEXEC.BAT to COMMAND.DOS, CONFIG.DOS, and AUTOEXEC.DOS, respectively

➤ Copying new IO.SYS and MSDOS.SYS files over the existing ones

➤ Modifying the boot record and track to point to the correct IO.SYS

Windows 95 by itself does not need the CONFIG.SYS and AUTOEXEC.BAT files, which often are created or used by other utilities or device drivers.

The following final configurations occur after Windows 95 is launched for the first time (the final step of the installation):

➤ Initial logon occurs, and a password file is created.

➤ All Plug and Play devices are initialized.

➤ Start menu items and the Control Panel are created, the Help system is built, and default DOS application parameters are defined.

➤ Time zone settings are defined.

➤ If Microsoft Exchange was installed, the Installation Wizard is displayed to configure the services of Microsoft Network, Mail, or Fax. A modem, if required by these services, is installed.

➤ A printer can be installed.

➤ The computer is restarted to complete the installation process.

At this point, installation of Windows 95 is complete.

Dual Booting

Windows 95 can exist with other operating systems on a single computer if a dual boot is set up properly. Dual booting DOS 5.0 or later (5.0 is the earliest version to allow dual booting) and Windows 3.x requires only two steps:

1. Install Windows 95 in a directory other than that of Windows 3.x.

2. Modify the MSDOS.SYS file so BootMulti has a value of 1 instead of 0 (see Chapter 4 for details on MSDOS.SYS editing).

Once these two steps are complete, press F4 (to boot to a previous operating system) or F8 (to get a menu) when "Starting Windows 95" appears after the CMOS specification.

Setting up a dual boot with Windows NT is easiest when Windows 95 is installed before NT. The Windows NT installation routing automatically configures the system to be a dual boot system, unless you direct the installation to use the same main directory as Windows 95. Fortunately, this is not an easy mistake to make. Windows NT offers a full installation or an upgrade installation. The full installation method uses a default installation directory of \WINNT, which you'll have to change to \WINDOWS (or \WIN95, etc.) to overwrite an existing installation of Windows 95. The upgrade installation places NT into the same main directory as Windows 95. Only the upgrade installation of Windows NT will retain Windows 95 settings. Performing a full installation into the same main directory as Windows 95 overwrites only the existing files.

The Windows NT boot menu displays the boot selections for NT (NT and NT VGA) plus a third for the previous OS. This is listed as MS-DOS. To change this to read Windows 95, you'll need to edit NT's BOOT.INI file.

However, if NT already exists on the system, the following steps must be completed:

1. Boot to DOS.

2. Remove read-only status from BOOTSECT.DOS and BOOT.INI (attrib -r <filename>).

3. Copy BOOTSECT.DOS to BOOTSECT.BCK.

4. Install Windows 95 into a directory other than that of Windows NT.

5. Rename BOOTSECT.DOS to BOOTSECT.W40.

6. Rename BOOTSECT.BCK to BOOTSECT.DOS.

7. Edit BOOT.INI to reflect the following:

   ➤ <ARC NAME>\WINNT="Windows NT"

   ➤ <ARC NAME>\BOOTSECT.DOS="MS DOS 6.22"/Win95dos

   ➤ <ARC NAME>\BOOTSECT.W40="Windows 95"/Win95

8. Reboot.

Windows 95 can be dual booted with OS/2, but OS/2 must already exist on the system. If it does not, any HPFS (High Performance File System) volumes will be inaccessible to DOS and Windows 95, and the SETUP utility will destroy the OS/2 Boot Manager. Once Windows 95 SETUP is complete, run the OS/2 FDISK tool from the OS/2 boot disk to restore the Boot Manager.

Uninstalling Windows 95

Uninstalling Windows 95 usually refers to returning the computer to the state it was in immediately before the installation of Windows 95. If you installed Windows 95 onto a computer without an existing OS, then your only uninstall option is to FDISK the drives and install something else. Uninstalling Windows 95 requires one of two situations:

➤ An upgrade installation was performed, and uninstall information was elected to be saved.

➤ A full installation was performed into a directory other than that used by Windows 3.x.

To uninstall Windows 95, just run the UNINSTAL.EXE utility from the startup disk. This utility will restore the boot sector and return the system to its pre-95 state (or nearly so). Some Windows 95 files may be left on your drive, including those that the utility could not confirm were used only by Windows 95.

Installation Troubleshooting

The installation of Windows 95 is fairly straightforward and automatic. Little can go wrong that the SETUP utility itself cannot work around or correct. However, a handful of problems can occur in Windows 95 installation. The following sections describe these problems and their solutions.

SETUP Utility Hang

The SETUP utility itself can hang, freeze, or stop responding. Knowing when and why this occurs can help determine the action to take to solve the problem.

If the SETUP utility hangs while creating the Windows 95 startup disk:

1. Cycle the power.

2. Restart the SETUP utility, but don't select Create Startup Disk.

3. After SETUP is complete, create the startup disk through the Add/Remove Programs applet in the Control Panel.

Alternatively, you could remove the "device=symevnt.386" line from the [386enh] section of the SYSTEM.INI file, then rerun SETUP.

If the SETUP utility hangs during ScanDisk's routing check on your system, you can try one of the following:

➤ Run a virus detection tool on your system.

➤ Run ScanDisk by itself.

➤ Use the /IS switch to skip the ScanDisk portion of the installation.

If SETUP hangs during the reboot phase, it may be due to an old swap file. Look for entries in the SYSTEM.INI file that point to previous Windows 3.x swap files, and remark them out by placing a semicolon (;) in front of them (i.e., as the first character on the line).

If SETUP fails to complete the installation for whatever reason, cycle the power, and if necessary, manually restart the SETUP utility. If prompted, select the Safe Recovery option. This will enable the SETUP routine to skip the last activity, which may have caused the failure.

Hardware Detection Failure

Setup can fail during the hardware detection phase when two devices are in conflict or when devices not compatible with Windows 95 are present. You should first check the Windows 95 Hardware Compatibility List (www.microsoft.com/isapi/hwtest/hcl.idc) to verify that the components are supported by Windows 95. Next, investigate the DETLOG.TXT file for abnormalities or incorrect configuration settings for devices.

If problems persist in this phase, you may need to use the Custom installation type and deselect any component that uses the suspect hardware component (e.g., the modem in Microsoft Fax is causing problems). Then, after installation is complete, use a manufacturer-supplied driver to install and configure the device. Finally, use the Add/Remove Programs applet in the Control Panel to install those components you previously avoided.

The final option is to remove components from the computer and install Windows 95 in their absence. Then, reinstall them using the manufacturer-supplied drivers.

Post-Installation Boot Problems

If Windows 95 fails to boot after SETUP is complete, only a few solutions are available other than inspecting your hardware and reinstalling:

➤ Remove any third-party memory managers, and use only HIMEM.SYS and EMM386.EXE.

➤ Boot into Safe Mode by selecting F8 when "Starting Windows 95" appears. If this is successful, something in the CONFIG.SYS file, TSRs, or Real Mode drivers may be causing the problem.

➤ If Safe Mode fails, run ScanDisk to test drive integrity.

Registry Corrupt Or Missing

The Windows 95 Registry is stored in two files: SYSTEM.DAT and USER.DAT. Both files are automatically backed up by Windows 95 into files with the extensions .DA0 or .DAT. If the SYSTEM.DAT file is missing, Windows 95 will restore it from the DA0 file or will boot into Safe Mode and prompt you whether to restore the Registry.

If both the DAT and the DA0 files are missing, or if the WinDir= parameter in MSDOS.SYS is not set, a warning appears on bootup that the Registry is missing. At this point, you must restore the Registry from a backup or re-launch the SETUP utility and select to use the Safe Recovery option.

Exam Prep Questions

Question 1

> What improvements does Windows 95 boast over Windows 3.x?
> [Check all correct answers]
>
> ❏ a. Compatibility
> ❏ b. Reliability
> ❏ c. Price
> ❏ d. Networking

Windows 95 is more compatible and more reliable, and it has native networking support—all significant improvements over Windows 3.x. Therefore, answers a, b, and d are correct. Windows 95 costs more than Windows 3.x (not an improvement). Therefore, answer c is incorrect.

Question 2

> Which of the following are differences between Windows 95 and Windows NT Workstation? [Check all correct answers]
>
> ❏ a. Preemptive multitasking
> ❏ b. 16-bit applications in separate memory space
> ❏ c. Secured logon
> ❏ d. User profiles
> ❏ e. Multiple CPUs
> ❏ f. Can be a client for Microsoft or NetWare networks
> ❏ g. Plug and Play

Windows NT supports 16-bit applications in separate memory space, has a secured logon, and supports multiple CPUs. Windows 95 does not. Therefore, answers b, c, and e are correct. Windows 95 supports Plug and Play. Windows NT does not. Therefore, answer g is also correct. Both Windows 95 and Windows NT use preemptive multitasking and user profiles, and both can be clients for Microsoft or NetWare networks. Therefore, answers a, d, and f are incorrect.

Question 3

> Which of the following activities occur during the Real Mode portion of setup? [Check all correct answers]
>
> ❏ a. File system integrity check
>
> ❏ b. Windows 95 startup disk creation
>
> ❏ c. Hardware detection and identification
>
> ❏ d. TSR management
>
> ❏ e. Building the Help system

During the Real Mode portion of SETUP, the file system's integrity is checked, and TSRs are managed. Therefore, answers a and d are correct. Windows 95 startup disk creation, hardware detection, and Help system building all occur in the Protected Mode portion of SETUP. Therefore, answers b, c, and e are incorrect.

Question 4

> Installing Windows 95 into the same directory as Windows 3.x will save user settings and program groups.
>
> ○ a. True
>
> ○ b. False

This is called an upgrade installation, and all possible settings from Windows 3.x are saved and imported into Windows 95. Therefore, answer a is correct.

Question 5

> Which utility can be used to convert Windows 3.x groups into Windows 95 Start menu items if an upgrade installation is not performed?
>
> ○ a. SETUP
>
> ○ b. CONVERT
>
> ○ c. GRPCONV
>
> ○ d. NETSETUP

GRPCONV is the utility used to convert Windows 3.x GRP (group) files to Windows 95 Start menu entries. Therefore, answer c is correct. SETUP is the installation utility, CONVERT is an NT utility for file systems, and NETSETUP is used to create network installation scripts. Therefore, answers a, b, and d are incorrect.

Question 6

> Which of the following are or can be involved in automating Windows 95 setup? [Check all correct answers]
>
> ❑ a. NETSETUP
>
> ❑ b. GRPCONV
>
> ❑ c. BATCH
>
> ❑ d. MSBATCH.INF
>
> ❑ e. INFINST
>
> ❑ f. SETUP

NETSETUP, BATCH, MSBATCH.INF, INFINST, and SETUP can all be involved in automating the installation of Windows 95. Therefore, answers a, c, d, e, and f are correct. GRPCONV is not an automated install tool. Therefore, answer b is incorrect.

Question 7

> If you have a Logitech series C mouse, a hard drive that fails ScanDisk checks, and a special temporary directory for the SETUP files, which of the following parameters should you use if you launch SETUP from a DOS prompt? [Check all correct answers]
>
> ❑ a. /IS
>
> ❑ b. /T:<path>
>
> ❑ c. /ID
>
> ❑ d. /IL
>
> ❑ e. /IM

The parameters needed for this situation are /IS, /T:<path>, and /IL. Therefore, answers a, b, and d are correct. /ID skips the hard drive space check, and /IM skips the memory check. Therefore, answers c and e are incorrect.

Question 8

Which file is used by the SETUP utility to record crashes?

○ a. DETLOG.TXT

○ b. MSBATCH.INF

○ c. CRASH.DMP

○ d. DETCRASH.LOG

DETCRASH.LOG is where SETUP records crashes that occur during installation. Therefore, answer d is correct. DETLOG.TXT stores the configuration details of identified devices. Therefore, answer a is incorrect. MSBATCH.INF is the script file for automated installations. Therefore, answer b is incorrect. CRASH.DMP is a fictional file name. Therefore, answer c is incorrect.

Question 9

Windows 95 can be configured in a dual boot with which other operating systems without additional software? [Check all correct answers]

❑ a. DOS

❑ b. Linux

❑ c. Windows 3.x

❑ d. Macintosh System 7.5

❑ e. Windows NT

❑ f. OS/2

Windows 95 can be in a dual boot with DOS, Windows 3.x, Windows NT, and OS/2 without additional software. Therefore, answers a, c, e, and f are correct. Additional software is required for dual boot with Linux (therein lies the "trick"), and dual boot is not possible with Macintosh System 7.5. Therefore, answers b and d are incorrect.

Question 10

> The most common recovery method to solve problems with the
> SETUP process is to cycle the power.
>
> ○ a. True
> ○ b. False

Cycling the power will often enable SETUP to reinitiate itself and bypass the activity that caused the error. This is a fault-tolerance feature built into the SETUP routing of Windows 95. Therefore, answer a is correct.

Need To Know More?

 Supporting Microsoft Windows 95. Microsoft Press, Redmond, WA, 1995. ISBN 1-55615-931-5. Chapter 1 contains a detailed discussion of the installation and setup issues of Windows 95.

 Mortensen, Lance and Rick Sawtell: *MCSE: Windows 95 Study Guide.* Sybex Network Press, San Francisco, CA, 1996. ISBN: 0-7821-2092-X. Chapter 1 discusses the basic features of Windows 95 and its comparison to Windows NT. Chapter 2 details the preparation and installation of Windows 95.

 Search the TechNet CD (or its online version through www. microsoft.com) and the *Windows 95 Resource Kit* using the keywords "install," "setup," "dual boot," and "uninstall."

Architecture
And Memory

Terms you'll need to understand:

√ Protected Mode

√ Real Mode

√ Virtual Machine (VM)

√ Virtual memory

√ Swap file

√ Demand paging

√ Preemptive multitasking

√ Cooperative multitasking

√ Process priority

Techniques you'll need to master:

√ Understanding the ring architecture of Windows 95

√ Knowing the purpose and function of Virtual Machines (VMs): System VM and DOS VMs

√ Understanding virtual memory, demand paging, and address space

√ Implementing a messaging system and message queues

√ Identifying core system components and device drivers

√ Understanding the concepts of multitasking and thread scheduling

The Windows 95 system architecture is vastly different from that of all previous Microsoft operating systems, including Windows 3.x and DOS. The material discussed in this chapter is essential for understanding the operation and use of Windows 95.

Base Architecture

Windows 95 was designed to take advantage of multiple levels (rings) of x86-protected privileges for execution code. The ring model of CPU-protected execution is defined with four rings, but most operating systems, including Windows 95, use only two (see Figure 3.1). The use of multiple rings identifies the software as a Protected Mode application. DOS failed to use the ring architecture and, therefore, was limited to Real Mode.

Ring 0 is controlled by the CPU and provides the highest level of component protection. Elements operating in Ring 0 are prevented from overwriting one another, have direct access to the hardware, and operate very quickly. Elements in Ring 0 cannot use the swap file as memory. A Ring 0 component failure can cause the entire system to fail. Ring 0 is where device drivers and critical (core) operating system components reside, including the kernel.

Ring 1 is controlled by the operating system, and no additional CPU protection is provided. Ring 3 elements must communicate with Ring 0 components

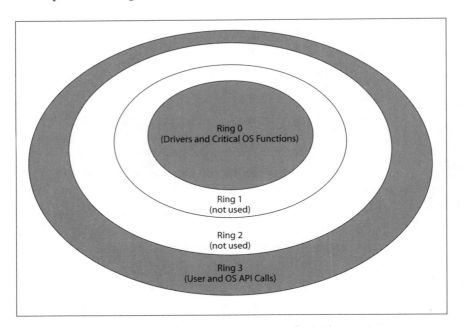

Figure 3.1 The protected ring architecture of Windows 95.

to gain access to hardware because Ring 3 is prevented from accessing hardware directly. A Ring 3 component failure usually does not cause the entire system to fail but can interfere with other Ring 3 components. Ring 3 is where user applications and noncritical system components and APIs reside. The elements here process at a much lower priority than Ring 0, and they can use the swap file as memory.

Virtual Machines

The multitasking environment of Windows 95 often demands that more than one program access the same resources. To solve this problem, Windows 95 uses Virtual Machines (VMs). A VM is simply a software construct within which applications are executed. From the application's point of view, a VM is the only program on the computer and has complete and direct access to all the computer's resources. Virtual Machines operate in Ring 3 and use a messaging technique with Ring 0 to access memory and hardware. Every application operates within a VM on Windows 95 (see Figure 3.2), which uses two types of VMs: a System VM and multiple DOS VMs.

The System VM has three components:

➤ System services and components (GUI, kernel, Windows management)

➤ 16-bit Windows shared address space

➤ 32-bit Windows individual/separate address spaces

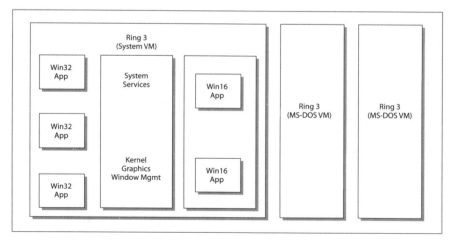

Figure 3.2   The VM structure of Windows 95.

All 16-bit Windows applications share a single address space and resource set in the System VM. This configuration enables Win16 applications to communicate with one another effectively, just as if they were operating on Windows 3.x. However, this arrangement also enables failed Win16 applications to interfere with other Win16 applications. A critical General Protection Fault (GPF) of one Win16 application can cause all other Win16 applications to fail. Unlike Windows NT, Windows 95 does not offer the ability to run Win16 applications in separate VMs.

Windows 32-bit applications are launched within the System VM, but each has an independent and separate address space and resource set. Thus, Win32 applications are not capable of interfering with one another, but are still able to communicate through the shared parent System VM.

 Multiple DOS VMs can exist within Windows 95 to accommodate finicky DOS applications. Many DOS applications assume that they are the only program in execution and have exclusive access to the entire computer. Thus, each DOS application is given its own DOS VM to fool it into thinking it has these benefits when executed under Windows 95.

Virtual Memory

Virtual memory is the feature of Windows 95 that enables a greater amount of memory to be available to programs than is physically present in RAM. The original memory architecture of DOS was limited to 640 KB. With a high-memory driver, such as HIMEM.SYS, the next 384 KB could be accessed, totaling 1 MB. To access memory above 1 MB, an Extended Memory Manager (XMS) or an Expanded Memory Manager (EMS) was required. Later versions of DOS employed EMM386.EXE to gain access to XMS and EMS. With Windows 95, these specialty memory drivers are no longer required.

 One of the core components of Windows 95 is the Virtual Memory Manager (VMM). The VMM is responsible for maintaining the 4 GB address space assigned to each VM. Address space is divided into segments called *pages;* each is 4 KB in size. Combining physical RAM with hard drive storage space makes available a larger amount of memory for applications.

However, even the best machines cannot offer 4 GB of memory to every application. Instead, the VMM maintains a page-mapping (linked) association between used pages of memory with actual memory spaces. As seen in Figure 3.3, each VM or application type is assigned 4 GB of memory address space.

The VMM associates these address spaces with available memory (the combination of RAM with storage space) through a page-mapping table.

When an application requests an area of memory from its address space, VMM pulls it from RAM and deposits it in the virtual address space of the application. If the request data is currently on the hard drive instead of in the RAM portion of memory, the VMM moves pages of memory from RAM to the hard drive and pulls the requested pages from the hard drive to RAM. This process is called "demand paging" and the hard drive storage file a "swap file." Demand paging is invisible to the application, which is fooled into seeing a full 4 GB of memory address space for its exclusive use.

Note: Because virtual memory relies on a hard drive to extend the physical RAM, the performance of the machine can be affected if too much paging takes place. Hard drive speeds are extremely slow when compared to RAM.

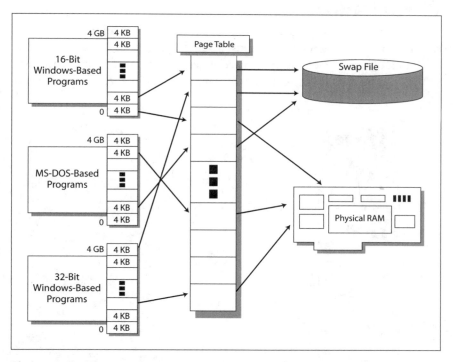

Figure 3.3   The memory mapping system maintained by the Windows 95 VMM.

Demand Paging

By default, Windows 95 will manage and maintain the swap file automatically, usually for the best. However, through the Virtual Memory button on the Performance tab of the Control Panel's System applet, you can:

➤ Set the drive where the swap file will be placed

➤ Set the minimum size of the swap file

➤ Set the maximum size of the swap file

➤ Disable virtual memory completely (i.e., not use a swap file)

If your CPU utilization is high and your hard drive is in a constant state of activity, you are probably experiencing excessive paging (disk thrashing). Generally, the only solution for this problem is to add more physical RAM to your computer. Otherwise, you must limit yourself to fewer applications to keep paging to a minimum.

Virtual Addresses

The memory address space assigned to each VM or application type has specific mappings that applications must abide by. Figure 3.4 shows the space allocation of the memory address space. These spaces are designated this way so they can be used by the components running within a VM to prevent the

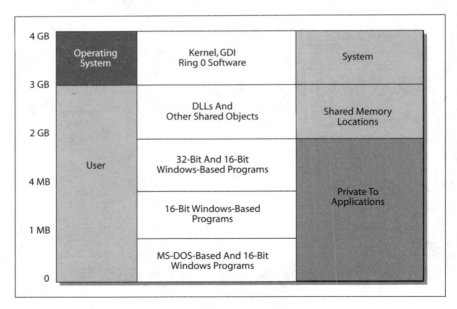

Figure 3.4 Windows 95 virtual memory addressing.

spaces from interfering with one another and to guarantee address space handles for them to grab.

The mappings of the Windows 95 address space are:

➤ **0 through 1 MB** Used by DOS and some Win16 applications. If a DOS VM is not in use, this area is not used by the application, but rather, is reserved for Real Mode drivers.

➤ **1 through 4 MB** Generally not used, but can be used by Win16 applications for backward compatibility.

➤ **4 MB through 2 GB** Used by Win32 and Win16 applications.

➤ **2 through 3 GB** Used by DLLs and other shared components.

➤ **3 through 4 GB** Reserved for exclusive use by Ring 0 components, usually virtual device drivers.

You should notice that the address space is divided into two main segments:

➤ **0 through 2 GB** User applications

➤ **2 through 4 GB** Operating system and core components

Internal Messaging Systems

Windows 95 controls the activity of applications and other components through an internal messaging system (see Figure 3.5). A message is generated each time an event occurs. An event can be just about anything, such as the movement of

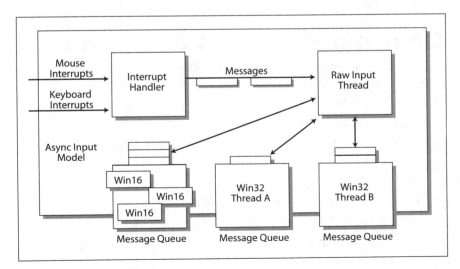

Figure 3.5   The Windows 95 messaging system.

a mouse or the pressing of a key on the keyboard. When an event happens, an interrupt occurs. An interrupt is simply a hardware-level request for services. The interrupt is converted into an internal message and sent to the operating system, which forwards the message to the appropriate application, where it is added to that application's message queue.

This messaging system is asynchronous; that is, each message queue is processed independently and at the speed that the application is able to handle. If one queue fails because of problems with Ring 0 or Ring 3, the other queues continue to operate.

All Win32 applications have separate and independent message queues. Actually, each thread of a Win32 application has its own message queue. This enables Win32 applications to operate quickly and efficiently and to not be affected by the speed or failure of other applications.

 All Win16 applications have a single shared message queue. As a message is read, the appropriate application accepts the message from the stack. If for any reason an application fails or stops reading its messages from the queue, all applications will be prevented from reading further messages. A *hung* program may resume normal operation, may cause a GPF, or may require manual termination. Depending on how the application was using resources and the message queue, other applications may be adversely affected or terminated.

DOS applications are not designed to use or accept messages of this type, so they do not have message queues.

Operating System Components

The Windows 95 operating system is not a single program, but rather, a conglomeration of cooperating components. These components are divided into three main sections, or job functions:

➤ **Kernel** Comprises KERNEL32.DLL and KERNEL.DLL; this section handles file I/O, program launching, thread execution, and memory management.

➤ **User** Comprises USER32.DLL and USER.DLL; this section handles user I/O (such as the keyboard, mouse, and sounds) and supports the Windows interface, dialog boxes, and icons.

➤ **GDI** Comprises GDI32.DLL and GDI.DLL; this section handles all graphic functions (such as the video screen and printing).

The operating system components are based around a 32-bit architecture, whereas the 16-bit versions are included only for Win16 backward compatibility. These components are dynamic link or modular code libraries that can be loaded or used multiple times by simultaneously operating applications.

Device Drivers

Device drivers are used by Windows 95 to communicate with and control hardware components. A device driver is simply a specialized language translator—it accepts the commands from the operating system and interprets them into the device-specific commands for the particular device. The use of device drivers removes Windows 95 from the responsibility of interacting directly with hardware and makes it more device-independent. In other words, the hardware constituting the computer can be changed without affecting the core operations of Windows 95.

Mode Type

We've already mentioned the difference between Real Mode and Protected Mode, and the same dichotomy applies to device drivers. Real Mode drivers are created to operate in a DOS environment. They are not as secure, robust, or fast as Protected Mode drivers, which are created to take advantage of the ring architecture of the x86 platform. A Protected Mode driver, also called a "virtual device driver" (VXD), is secure, robust, and fast. In addition, it allows shared simultaneous use of a device by several applications.

Driver Files

Windows 95 supports several types of device drivers:

➤ **SYS** DOS Real Mode drivers

➤ **DRV** Windows Real Mode drivers, usually loaded in the SYSTEM.INI

➤ **VXD or 386** Windows Protected Mode drivers

The setup utility will attempt, when possible, to use and install Protected Mode drivers in place of any Real Mode drivers found in the CONFIG.SYS file.

Most Windows device drivers are stored in the \Windows\System folder.

During the initial setup of Windows 95, VXD drivers that are always used are combined into a single driver file named VMM32.VXD. This single file is more efficient for loading device drivers than a large number of individual files. New drivers added to the system are placed in the \Windows\System\ VMM32 folder, where they remain until setup is used again, and then are combined into the VMM32.VXD file.

Multitasking

Windows 95 is a multitasking operating system, which means it can execute and support numerous applications and processes simultaneously. Two important concepts associated with multitasking are *processes* and *threads*. A process is a running application with the following characteristics:

➤ Initial code and data

➤ Memory address space

➤ System resources (such as files and display windows)

➤ At least one thread

A thread is a single, nondivisible unit of execution with the following characteristics:

➤ A stack used in user mode (Ring 3)

➤ A stack used in kernel mode (Ring 0)

➤ A processor state with the current instruction pointer (Register)

As you can see in Figure 3.6, the memory address space and system resources belong to a process, not to the threads. Each process can contain one or more threads, depending on how it was programmed. DOS and Win16 programs are only, and always, single threaded, but Win32 programs can be multithreaded. The resources of a process are shared by the threads of that process.

Windows 95 is touted as a multitasking environment, but it is really a single-CPU operating system. Therefore, multitasking is simulated through a technique called "time slicing," which is the process of dividing the computing cycles of the CPU (of which there are hundreds to millions per second) between more than one execution thread. Each thread is executed for a limited number of cycles before the next task is executed. This time-slicing and task-switching activity operates continuously. Although we perceive this activity as many applications operating simultaneously, we cannot perceive the small increments of each time slice. Therefore, the illusion of multitasking is created by our inability to distinguish milliseconds from picoseconds.

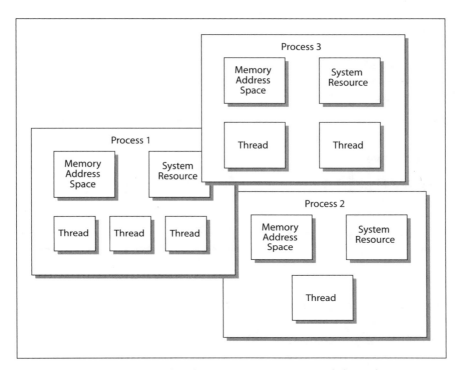

Figure 3.6   The relationship between processes and threads.

The two types of multitasking (see Figure 3.7) are:

➤ **Preemptive** The operating system has control over what process gets access to the CPU and for how long. Once the assigned time slice has expired, the current process is halted and the next process granted its computing time.

➤ **Cooperative** The operating system does not have the ability to stop a process. Once a process is given control of the CPU, it maintains control until its computing needs are satisfied. No other process can access the CPU until it is released by the current process.

Each thread of execution is assigned a priority that is used to determine how many CPU cycles are assigned to that thread and how often. There are 32 levels of priority (0 through 31). When a thread is activated, it is assigned a base priority. This assignment is made by the kernel and is determined by the type of thread. Core (central) threads are given higher priorities than user applications. This base priority can be raised or lowered by up to two levels by the scheduler to maintain system integrity and proper steward-ship of system resources.

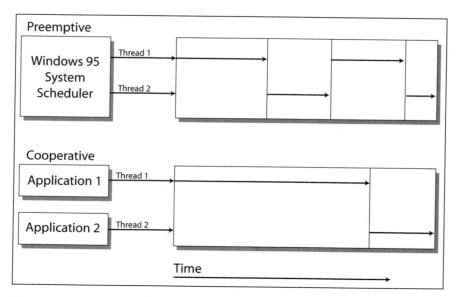

Figure 3.7 Preemptive and cooperative multitasking.

The *scheduler kernel* component of Windows 95 (see Figure 3.8) determines which thread is given access to the CPU and for how long. The scheduler actually comprises two components: the primary scheduler and the secondary scheduler. The primary scheduler evaluates the current priority level of all waiting threads and grants CPU access to the highest-priority thread. If more than one thread has the same priority, the primary scheduler gives each of these threads a turn on the CPU. As soon as each (or the only) high-priority thread is executed for a time slice, the primary scheduler reevaluates the priorities of the waiting threads. The secondary scheduler boosts the priorities of nonexecuted threads to give them a fighting chance to obtain a CPU time slice. Once a thread gains a CPU time slice, its priority is reduced one level.

This raising and lowering of thread priorities ensures that all threads eventually get a time slice (remember that "eventually" can mean one-quarter of a second). The high-priority core threads will gain enough time slices to complete their execution. The low-priority user threads will be completed at a slower rate, but because they usually depend on the core threads for system resources, this convention works well.

If a low-priority thread locks up a resource needed by a high-priority thread, the low-priority thread will be boosted so that it will execute faster and release the resource quicker. You should also remember that because all Win16 applications operate within a single resource area, they all operate by way of a single thread. This one thread is preemptively prioritized with all other threads in

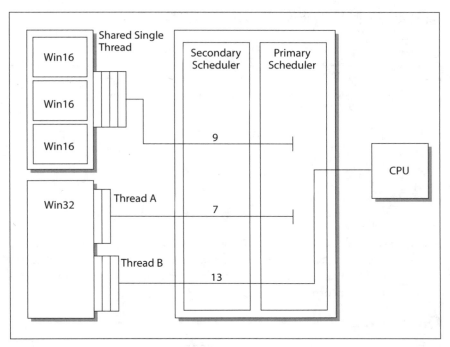

Figure 3.8   The scheduling system of Windows 95.

execution on the system. Within the thread, the Win16 applications are coop-eratively multitasked, meaning that one application must release control before another application can execute.

Exam Prep Questions

Question 1

At which ring level do the core (critical) components of Windows 95 function?

○ a. Ring 0

○ b. Ring 1

○ c. Ring 2

○ d. Ring 3

The core (critical) components of Windows 95 function at Ring 0; therefore, answer a is correct. Rings 1 and 2 are not used by Windows 95; therefore, answers b and c are incorrect. Ring 3 is where user applications function; therefore, answer d is incorrect.

Question 2

A Virtual Machine is a Windows 95 software construct that fools applications into seeing a large, exclusive address space and direct access to system resources when, in fact, the address space is mapped to real memory and the system resources are handled by proxy through Ring 0 components.

○ a. True

○ b. False

It is true that a Virtual Machine is a software construct used to fool programs into thinking they have full and exclusive use of an entire computer; therefore, answer a is correct.

Question 3

Which types of applications are executed within the System VM?
[Check all correct answers]

❑ a. Kernel

❑ b. Win16

❑ c. Win32

❑ d. DOS

The System VM houses the execution of the kernel, Win16, and Win32 applications; therefore, answers a, b, and c are correct. Each DOS application is executed within its own separate DOS VM; therefore, answer d is incorrect.

Question 4

Which applications share a common memory address space and system resource set?

○ a. DOS applications

○ b. Win16 applications

○ c. Win32 applications

All Win16 applications share a common memory address space and system resource set; therefore, answer b is correct. Each DOS and Win32 application has its own separate memory address space and system resource set; therefore, answers a and c are incorrect.

Question 5

Virtual memory combines what components to offer execution space to applications? [Check all correct answers]

❑ a. Time slices

❑ b. Physical RAM

❑ c. An Expanded Memory Manager (EMS)

❑ d. Hard drive storage space

Windows 95 virtual memory combines physical RAM and hard drive storage space to offer applications execution space; therefore, answers b and d are correct. Time slices are associated with CPU execution and not memory; therefore, answer a is incorrect. EMS is not used by Windows 95; therefore, answer c is incorrect.

Question 6

What is the size of a single memory page?

O a. 4 GB

O b. The size of physical RAM

O c. 4 KB

O d. 2 GB

A memory page is 4 KB in size; therefore, answer c is correct. 4 GB is the size of the address space assigned to each process, 2 GB is the portion of the address space assigned to user applications or system components, and the size of physical RAM is only part of the memory space used by Windows 95 through virtual memory; therefore, answers a, b, and d are incorrect.

Question 7

Which section of the address space assigned to a process can be used by Win32 and Win16 applications?

O a. 0 through 1 MB

O b. 1 through 4 MB

O c. 4 MB through 2 GB

O d. 2 through 3 GB

O e. 3 through 4 GB

The 4 MB through 2 GB range is used by Win32 and Win16 applications; therefore, answer c is correct. The 0 through 1 MB range is used by DOS and some Win16 applications. If a DOS VM is not in use, this area is not used by the application, but rather, is reserved for Real Mode drivers; therefore, answer a is incorrect. The 1 through 4 MB range is generally not used but can be used by Win16 applications for backward compatibility; therefore, answer b is incorrect. The 2 through 3 GB range is used by DLLs and other shared components; therefore, answer d is incorrect. The 3 through 4 GB range is reserved for exclusive use by Ring 0 components, usually virtual device drivers; therefore, answer e is incorrect.

Question 8

> If a Win16 application hangs, which of the following are true?
> [Check all correct answers]
>
> ❏ a. Other Win16 applications are prevented from reading the shared message queue.
>
> ❏ b. Win32 processes are temporarily halted.
>
> ❏ c. If the hung application terminates or GPFs, the other Win16 applications may also fail.
>
> ❏ d. The Ring 0 components halt operation.

Because of the shared message queue, address space, and resource set, a hung Win16 application will prevent other Win16 applications from reading messages and may cause them to fail; therefore, answers a and c are correct. Win32 processes operate independently of Win16; therefore, answer b is incorrect. Ring 0 components are protected from Win16 failures; therefore, answer d is incorrect.

Question 9

> Which of the following are not Protected Mode driver file types?
> [Check all correct answers]
>
> ❏ a. SYS
>
> ❏ b. DRV
>
> ❏ c. VXD
>
> ❏ d. 386

Both SYS and DRV are Real Mode driver types; therefore, answers a and b are correct. VXD and 386 are Protected Mode driver types; therefore, answers c and d are incorrect.

Question 10

> Win16 applications are preemptively multitasked as a group with other Win32 and DOS threads.
>
> ○ a. True
>
> ○ b. False

It is true that Win16 applications as a whole are preemptively multitasked with other Win32 and DOS threads, but within the Win16 process, each application is cooperatively multitasked; therefore, answer a is correct.

Need To Know More?

 Supporting Microsoft Windows 95. Microsoft Press, Redmond, WA, 1995. ISBN 1-55615-931-5. Chapter 1 contains a detailed discussion of the installation and setup issues of Windows 95.

 Mortensen, Lance and Rick Sawtell: *MCSE: Windows 95 Study Guide.* Sybex Network Press, San Francisco, CA, 1996. ISBN: 0-7821-2092-X. Chapter 1 discusses the basic features of Windows 95 and its comparison to Windows NT. Chapter 2 details the preparation and installation of Windows 95.

 Search the TechNet CD (or its online version through www. microsoft.com) and the *Windows 95 Resource Kit,* using the keywords "Protected Mode," "Real Mode," "Virtual Machine," "swap file," "multitasking," "process priority," "message queue," "thread scheduling," and "demand paging."

Windows 95
Boot Sequence

4

Terms you'll need to understand:

√ IO.SYS

√ MSDOS.SYS

√ Startup menu

√ LOGO.SYS

Techniques you'll need to master:

√ Understanding the Windows 95 boot process

√ Using the Startup menu

√ Modifying the MSDOS.SYS file

√ Creating a Startup disk and knowing its contents

Understanding the Windows 95 boot process is essential to troubleshooting many system failures and correcting faulty configurations. This chapter discusses the lengthy Windows 95 boot process and gives you several tips for troubleshooting.

The 95 Boot Process

The Windows 95 boot process takes place in five distinguishable segments, each of which is discussed in the following sections.

BIOS Bootstrap

The BIOS Bootstrap segment of the boot process is handled by the computer itself. Four distinct activities take place in this segment:

➤ **POST (Power On Self Test)** The computer powers all systems and tests them.

➤ **Plug and Play** If the system is Plug and Play-compatible (see Chapter 16), all Plug and Play devices are identified and configured.

➤ **Bootable partition** The bootable partition is located on the boot drive.

➤ **MBR (Master Boot Record) initialization** The MBR is loaded and executed.

Master Boot Record And Boot Sector

Once the MBR is loaded and executed, it looks for the bootable partition on the boot drive and passes control over to the boot sector on that partition. If the Windows 95 bootable partition contains IO.SYS, this program is executed. Basically, it is DOS.

This is the point in the boot process where boot viruses have the most effect. Most boot viruses either infect the MBR directly or attack the IO.SYS program. An Emergency Repair Disk (ERD, which will be discussed later) can be used to replace a failed IO.SYS, or the MBR can be repaired with the FDISK/MBR command.

Real Mode Boot

Once the IO.SYS is in memory and executing, the Real Mode portion of the boot process begins. The following activities occur during this segment:

➤ The boot parameters contained in MSDOS.SYS are read.

➤ "Starting Windows 95" is displayed, and the system waits for a function key to be pressed for two seconds (two seconds is the default though this is configurable; see the section titled "Modifying MSDOS.SYS" for details).

➤ The image of LOGO.SYS is displayed (the default Windows 95 splash logo). If this file is not found, the duplicate copy of the original image is pulled from IO.SYS. The display of this image is disabled by pressing the ESC key.

➤ DRVSPACE.BIN or DBLSPACE.BIN for compressed drives is loaded if DRVSPACE.INI or DBLSPACE.INI is present.

➤ The SYSTEM.DAT is verified.

➤ The Registry keys from the verified SYSTEM.DAT are loaded. If SYSTEM.DAT fails verification, SYSTEM.DA0 is loaded. Once the boot process is successful, the file not used to boot is updated.

➤ If double-buffering is turned on in MSDOS.SYS, it is enabled.

➤ A hardware profile is chosen by the system on the basis of detected hardware, or if multiple profiles are present, the user is prompted for a selection.

➤ CONFIG.SYS is read, and its entries are processed (if present).

➤ AUTOEXEC.BAT is read, and its entries are processed (if present).

Real Mode Configuration

Windows 95 does not require the CONFIG.SYS and AUTOEXEC.BAT files. However, support for them is maintained for backward compatibility with drivers, devices, and applications that require or use them. If these configuration files are not present, or if they fail to load HIMEM.SYS, IFSHLP.SYS, and SETVER.EXE, Windows 95 will automatically load these utilities. Any settings in CONFIG.SYS will override any defaults for these utilities.

Protected Mode Boot

Once the memory drivers are loaded, the Protected Mode boot segment begins. The following activities occur during this segment:

➤ WIN.COM is launched immediately after AUTOEXEC.BAT is processed, or if AUTOEXEC.BAT is not present, WIN.COM is launched after the loading of HIMEM.SYS, IFSHLP.SYS, and SETVER.EXE.

➤ The VMM32.VXD (the collection of virtual device drivers) and any additional drivers are loaded.

➤ The CPU switches to Protected Mode, and all virtual device drivers are initiated.

➤ The core components of Windows 95 are loaded, including kernel, GDI, and any user libraries. The shell (Explorer by default) and network support are loaded and enabled.

➤ All Startup group shortcuts are executed.

➤ Any programs listed in the Registry key, HKEY_LOCAL_MACHINE\ SOFTWARE\Microsoft\Windows\CurrentVersion\RunOnce, are launched and then removed from this key.

Once these steps are completed, control is released to the user, who may be prompted for a password to gain access to a user profile, a network account, or both.

Modifying The Boot Sequence

The boot process of Windows 95 is more or less automatic, self-healing, and sufficient for most purposes. However, you can use certain controls to alter the boot process.

Startup Menu

In previous versions of Windows, WIN.COM was either executed manually or was the last line in the AUTOEXEC.BAT, so it was easy to boot to DOS, correct problems, then boot into Windows. With Windows 95, WIN.COM is launched automatically, so you have to use the Startup menu to arrest Windows 95 launching. The Startup menu is reached by pressing F8 when "Starting Windows 95" appears on bootup. It appears with some or all of the following entries:

➤ **Normal** Launches Windows normally, including loading all startup files and Registry values.

➤ **Logged (\BOOTLOG.TXT)** Launches Windows and records a startup log file.

➤ **Safe mode** Launches Windows, bypasses all startup files, and uses only basic system drivers.

➤ **Safe mode without compression** Launches Windows. Does not load DRVSPACE.BIN, so compressed drives are not available (appears only on systems with compressed drives).

> **Safe mode with network support** Launches Windows and bypasses startup files using only basic system drivers and basic networking support (appears only on systems with network support installed).

> **Step-by-step confirmation** Launches Windows and requests user confirmation for each line of each startup file.

> **Command prompt only** Launches the DOS 7.0 command prompt using the normal startup files.

> **Safe mode command prompt only** Launches the DOS 7.0 command prompt and bypasses all startup files.

> **Previous version of DOS** Launches the previous version of DOS installed on this computer (appears only on systems where the previous DOS-based operating system was upgraded).

You can also use a single function key at the "Starting Windows 95" message to get to the same boot methods:

> **F4** Previous version of DOS

> **F5** Safe mode

> **SHIFT+F5** Safe mode command prompt only

> **CTRL+F5** Safe mode without compression

> **F6** Safe mode with network support

> **SHIFT+F8** Step-by-step confirmation

Modifying MSDOS.SYS

In DOS, MSDOS.SYS is an executable file that manages part of the operating system; in Windows 95, it is a text file in which boot details are defined and controlled. MSDOS.SYS is a read-only, hidden system file, so you need to reset these flags before and after editing the file. The MSDOS.SYS contains three mandatory entries (listed under [Paths]) and any number of options (listed under [Options]).

[Paths] section (these items are mandatory):

> **HostWinBootDrv=** Sets the boot drive root directory location.

> **WinBootDir=** Sets the directory that contains the startup files; this is usually the directory defined during Setup. C:\WINDOWS is the default.

➤ **WinDir=** Sets the Windows 95 directory; this is the directory defined during Setup with a default of C:\WINDOWS.

[Options] section (these items are optional):

➤ **BootDelay=n** Sets the delay in seconds (n) to await a function key when the "Starting Windows 95" message is displayed. BootDelay=2 is the default. BootKeys=0 disables the delay.

➤ **BootFailSafe=1** Forces boot to Safe Mode; this is the option typically used by hardware manufacturers for installation purposes. The default is 0.

➤ **BootGUI=1** Instructs Windows 95 to boot into GUI mode.

➤ **BootKeys=** Enables the use of function keys to determine the startup method. BootKeys=1 is the default. BootKeys=0 prevents the use of function keys and overrides the BootDelay=n value.

➤ **BootMenu=** Displays the Startup menu automatically, without requiring F8 to be pressed. BootMenu=0 (the default) does not display the menu; BootMenu=1 does.

➤ **BootMenuDefault=#** Sets the Startup menu item high-lighted by default. The defaults are BootMenuDefault=3 for a computer with no networking components and BootMenuDefault=4 for a networked computer.

➤ **BootMenuDelay=n** Sets the display delay in seconds (n) before the highlighted Startup menu item is used. BootMenuDelay=30 is the default.

➤ **BootMulti=** Enables dual-booting when BootMulti=1. BootMulti=0 is the default.

➤ **BootWarn=** Displays a warning when entering Safe Mode. BootWarn=1 is the default.

➤ **BootWin=1** Sets Windows 95 as the default operating system (this is the default setting). BootWin=0 disables Windows 95 as the default operating system.

➤ **DblSpace=** Loads DBLSPACE.BIN automatically. DblSpace=1 is the default.

➤ **DoubleBuffer=** Loads a double-buffering driver for a SCSI controller when DoubleBuffer=1. DoubleBuffer=0 is the default.

➤ **DrvSpace=** Loads DRVSPACE.BIN automatically. DrvSpace=1 is the default.

➤ **LoadTop=** Allows COMMAND.COM or DRVSPACE.BIN to be loaded at the top of 640 K memory. LoadTop=1 is the default.

➤ **Logo=** Displays the animated bootup logo. Logo=1 is the default.

➤ **Network=** Enables the Safe Mode with Networking selection in the Startup menu. Network=1 is the default for computers with networking installed. Network=0 should be used if networking components are not installed.

Emergency Boot Disk

The Emergency Boot Disk (EBD) is usually called the Startup disk. This floppy disk is created either during the initial setup of Windows 95 or through the Add/Remove Programs applet. It enables you to boot to a command prompt without using CONFIG.SYS, AUTOEXEC.BAT, or the Registry. The files that are present by default on a Startup disk are:

➤ **ATTRIB.EXE** File attribute utility

➤ **CHKDSK.EXE** Lightweight disk-scanning utility

➤ **COMMAND.COM** Command interpreter

➤ **DEBUG.EXE** System-level debugging utility

➤ **DRVSPACE.BIN** DriveSpace compression driver

➤ **EBD.SYS** Windows 95 startup disk flag/identifier

➤ **EDIT.COM** Text editor

➤ **FDISK.EXE** Disk partition utility

➤ **FORMAT.COM** Disk format utility

➤ **IO.SYS** System boot file

➤ **MSDOS.SYS** Boot setting information

➤ **REGEDIT.EXE** Registry editor

➤ **SCANDISK.EXE** Disk status and repair utility

➤ **SCANDISK.INI** ScanDisk configuration file

➤ **SYS.COM** System transfer utility

➤ **UNINSTAL.EXE** Windows 95 uninstall utility

You might want to add other files to this disk that are unique to your system or that you think might help in troubleshooting boot problems. These other files could include:

➤ DELTREE.EXE

➤ XCOPY.EXE

➤ SYSTEM.DAT (DA0)

➤ USER.DAT (DA0)

➤ CONFIG.SYS

➤ AUTOEXEC.BAT

➤ WIN.INI

➤ SYSTEM.INI

If you add files to your Startup disk, you'll need to change the names of CONFIG.SYS and AUTOEXEC.BAT or place them in a subdirectory if you do not want them to be used when you boot.

Exam Prep Questions

Question 1

> What is the last segment of the Windows 95 boot process?
>
> ○ a. BIOS Bootstrap
>
> ○ b. MBR and boot sector
>
> ○ c. Real Mode boot
>
> ○ d. Protected Mode boot

The last segment of the Windows 95 boot process is the Protected Mode boot. Therefore, answer d is correct. BIOS Bootstrap is the first segment, MBR and boot sector is the second segment, and Real Mode boot is the third segment. Therefore, answers a, b, and c are incorrect.

Question 2

> In which segment of the Windows 95 boot process is the VMM32.VXD loaded?
>
> ○ a. BIOS Bootstrap
>
> ○ b. MBR and boot sector
>
> ○ c. Real Mode boot
>
> ○ d. Protected Mode boot

VMM32.VXD are Protected Mode drivers that can be loaded only in the Protected Mode boot segment. Therefore, answer d is correct. Protected Mode drivers cannot be loaded during any other segment of the boot process. Therefore, answers a, b, and c are incorrect.

Question 3

Which methods are available to you to modify how Windows 95 boots? [Check all correct answers]

❏ a. Editing MSDOS.SYS

❏ b. Editing the MBR

❏ c. Using the Startup menu

❏ d. Editing BOOT.INI

Editing the MSDOS.SYS file and using the Startup menu are two methods for altering how Windows 95 boots. Therefore, answers a and c are correct. It is not possible to edit the MBR with any tools that are bundled with Windows 95, nor is this a valid method of altering how Windows 95 boots. Therefore, answer b is incorrect. BOOT.INI is a file that is present only on systems hosting Windows NT and is not used with Windows 95. Therefore, answer d is incorrect.

Question 4

If you need to determine which Real Mode driver was failing to load, which boot method should you use?

○ a. Safe Mode

○ b. Safe Mode without compression

○ c. Step-by-step confirmation

○ d. Previous version of DOS

Step-by-step confirmation allows you to watch as each Real Mode driver is loaded and see whether it fails or issues an error message. Therefore, answer c is correct. Safe mode bypasses most of the startup files and will not offer any information about which Real Mode drivers failed to load during a normal boot process. Therefore, answer a is incorrect. Safe mode without compression offers no more help than Safe Mode alone in terms of investigating Real Mode drivers. Therefore, answer b is incorrect. Booting to a previous version of DOS will not load (or attempt to load) the Real Mode driver in question because the previous operating system's startup files will be used. Therefore, answer d is incorrect.

Question 5

> If you needed to determine which Protected Mode driver was fail-
> ing to load, which boot method should you use?
>
> ○ a. Safe Mode
>
> ○ b. Logged (\BOOTLOG.TXT)
>
> ○ c. Step-by-step confirmation
>
> ○ d. Previous version of DOS

The Logged boot method stores information about Protected Mode drivers in the BOOTLOG.TXT file, which can be inspected to reveal errors with individual drivers contained in the conglomeration VMM32.VXD. Therefore, answer b is correct. Safe Mode bypasses most of the startup files and still loads the Protected Mode drivers found in VMM32.VXD, but no information about individual Protected Mode drivers will be available. Therefore, answer a is incorrect. Step-by-step confirmation will not offer you any useful information about the loading of Protected Mode drivers because they are loaded as a single entity in VMM32.VXD. Therefore, answer c is incorrect. Booting to a previous version of DOS will not load (or attempt to load) the Protected Mode drivers at all because the previous operating system's startup files will be used and the CPU will not enter Protected Mode. Therefore, answer d is incorrect.

Question 6

> Which of the following MSDOS.SYS options should be used to
> change the length of time the system waits for a function key
> when the "Starting Windows 95" message is displayed?
>
> ○ a. BootGUI
>
> ○ b. BootDelay
>
> ○ c. BootMenu
>
> ○ d. BootMenuDelay

BootDelay is the entry that should be changed to modify the waiting time for function keys. Therefore, answer b is correct. BootGUI determines whether Windows 95 boots into graphics mode. Therefore, answer a is incorrect. BootMenu determines whether the Startup menu is automatically displayed or whether F8 must be pressed. Therefore, answer c is incorrect. BootMenuDelay alters how long the Startup menu is displayed before automatically using the selected menu item. Therefore, answer d is incorrect.

Need To Know More?

 Supporting Microsoft Windows 95. Microsoft Press, Redmond, WA, 1995. ISBN 1-55615-931-5. Chapter 21 discusses the Windows 95 boot sequence.

 Mortensen, Lance and Rick Sawtell: *MCSE: Windows 95 Study Guide*. Sybex Network Press, San Francisco, CA, 1996. ISBN: 0-7821-2092-X. Chapter 3 contains information about the boot process of Windows 95.

 Search the TechNet CD (or its online version through www. microsoft.com) and the Windows 95 Resource Kit using the keywords "boot process," "IO.SYS," "MSDOS.SYS," "Startup menu," and "LOGO.SYS."

Customization
And Configuration

5

Terms you'll need to understand:

√ Desktop

√ Taskbar

√ Start menu

√ Objects

√ Control Panel applets

√ Shortcuts

√ Recycle Bin

√ Hardware profiles

Techniques you'll need to master:

√ Understanding the new desktop environment

√ Interacting with the taskbar and Start menu

√ Customizing the Start menu and taskbar

√ Understanding the purpose of the Control Panel applets

√ Creating and working with shortcuts

√ Using the Recycle Bin

√ Understanding hardware profiles

The look and feel of Windows 95 is one of the more noticeable changes from previous Windows versions. You need to be familiar with the look and feel of Windows 95 or you will have difficulty using the operating system. This chapter introduces most of the important aspects of the layout, the design, and several built-in utilities.

Desktop And Environment Introduction

Unlike Windows 3.x, Windows 95 no longer uses the Program Manager. Rather, it uses the desktop, a few icons on the left side of the desktop, and the taskbar (Figure 5.1). The desktop is the expanse that fills your monitor screen. Like the top of your physical worktable, the desktop is where your work takes place. The program icons that appear by default on the desktop vary, depending on the services installed and whether you have an OEM version of the OS. The four most common icons are:

➤ **My Computer** A multiwindow interface to all of the local and mapped storage devices, Control Panel, Printers folder, and Dial-Up Networking (Figure 5.2)

Figure 5.1 The desktop of Windows 95.

Figure 5.2   A typical My Computer.

➤ **Network Neighborhood** A multiwindow interface to all network resources

➤ **Inbox** The link to the Exchange client (see Chapter 15)

➤ **Recycle Bin** The interface to restore recently deleted files

The Taskbar

The bar at the bottom of the screen is the taskbar (see Figure 5.3). It replaces the functionality of the Task Manager from Windows 3.x and introduces many new features. The taskbar can be moved to any screen edge and its display resized. Clicking on the Start button on the taskbar reveals the main level of menus that are used to access applications, utilities, documents, and commands. An active application usually has an icon button on the taskbar (such as Paint Shop Pro in Figure 5.3). You can move among open applications by selecting the icon buttons on the taskbar or by pressing and holding Alt while pressing Tab. Another new feature is the icon tray, located on the right side of the taskbar, which contains the clock and may display small icons, such as volume, System Agent, and PCMCIA. Right-clicking over any of the icons in the tray gives you access to that item's pop-up menu. Also, right-clicking over any empty area of the taskbar reveals a pop-up menu with selections to tile all non-minimized applications horizontally, vertically, or cascaded, and to minimize all applications.

The Start Menu

Here is a list of some important items on the Start menu:

➤ **Start|Run** Launches programs using their pathname and file name (accepts both <drive>:\path\filename and UNC names); if supported by an application, command-line parameters can be specified.

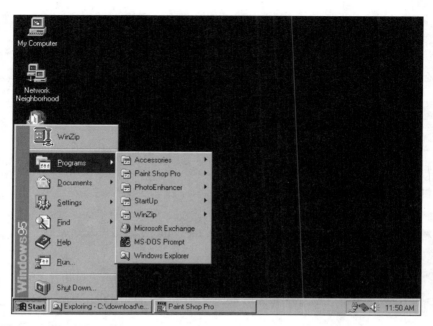

Figure 5.3 The Start menu and taskbar of Windows 95.

➤ **Start|Help** Opens the Windows 95 help system.

➤ **Start|Find|Files or Folders** Locates files and folders by name, date, and so on.

➤ **Start|Find|Computer** Locates computer names on a network.

➤ **Start|Settings|Control Panel** Opens the Control Panel.

➤ **Start|Settings|Printers** Opens the Printers folder (see Chapter 12).

➤ **Start|Settings|Taskbar** Opens the configuration dialog box for the taskbar (see the section "Start Menu/Taskbar Customization" that follows).

➤ **Start|Documents** Lists twelve of the most recently accessed documents and files.

➤ **Start|Programs** Contains multilevel groupings of programs, similar to Program Manager groups in Windows 3.x.

Start Menu/Taskbar Customization

The Start menu and the taskbar can be customized by using the Taskbar Properties, accessed by selecting Start|Settings|Taskbar, or by right-clicking the taskbar and selecting Properties. The Taskbar Options tab offers the following settings:

➤ **Always on top** Prevents other windows from hiding the taskbar (enabled by default).

➤ **Auto hide** Hides the taskbar as a thin line when not in use; the taskbar is restored when the mouse pointer is dragged over the line.

➤ **Show small icons in Start menu** Compacts the menu using smaller icons.

➤ **Show clock** Displays the clock from the tray area of the taskbar (enabled by default).

The Start Menu Programs tab allows you to individually add (Add button) or remove (Remove button) items from the Start menu or to manage the entire menu as a whole (Advanced button). You can also clear the Documents menu of all recently used items using the Clear button.

Objects

Everything within Windows 95 is an object. Each object can be opened, executed, addressed, or accessed, and each has properties that are dependent on the object's type. Some examples of Windows 95 objects include:

➤ Files

➤ Folders (directories)

➤ Programs, applications, and processes

➤ Printers

➤ Modems

To access and modify an object's properties, right-click over the object and select Properties from the pop-up menu. The available properties are dependent on the type of object. We'll look at several types of objects in subsequent chapters, including files, folders, printers, modems, applications, and more.

Control Panel Applets

The Control Panel is where you find most of the administration and configuration tools for Windows 95 (see Figure 5.4). The utilities collected in the Control Panel are generically called "applets." Most applets appear in all configurations of Windows 95, but some are hardware-, software-, or service-dependent and appear only if that particular item is installed on the system. The properties

Figure 5.4 The Control Panel of Windows 95.

and controls found in applets are usually self-explanatory, so take the time to open each applet in the Control Panel on your own and become familiar with it.

The most common Control Panel applets are:

➤ **Add New Hardware** Installs new drivers for hardware. Hardware can be detected automatically, selected manually from a list, or installed using third-party drivers.

➤ **Add/Remove Programs** Adds or removes software components of Windows 95, removes 32-bit applications, and creates a startup disk.

➤ **Date/Time** Sets and changes the date, time, and time zone.

➤ **Display** Alters the background pattern/wallpaper, enables screen savers with or without passwords, sets Energy Star-compliant monitor activities, sets the color and font scheme, sets screen color depth and resolution, defines the monitor type, and loads drivers for the video card.

➤ **Fonts** Adds, removes, and views fonts.

➤ **Internet** Sets Internet Explorer-specific settings (see Chapter 10).

➤ **Joystick** Sets joystick properties.

➤ **Keyboard** Sets keyboard functions and language used.

➤ **Mail and Fax** Adds, removes, and modifies information services (see Chapter 15).

➤ **Microsoft Mail Postoffice** Creates and administers postoffices (see Chapter 15).

➤ **Modems** Adds, removes, and configures modems (see Chapter 11).

➤ **Mouse** Sets mouse functions and pointer types.

➤ **Multimedia** Sets audio, video, MIDI, and CD functions (see Chapter 14).

➤ **Network** Manages network connectivity (see chapters 9-11).

➤ **Passwords** Sets and changes Windows 95 passwords (see Chapter 13).

➤ **PC Card (PCMCIA)** Manages removable PC Cards and drivers.

➤ **Power** Sets notebook power-saving features.

➤ **Printers** Opens the Printer folder, which is used to manage printers (see Chapter 12).

➤ **Regional Settings** Sets features, such as number system, currency designations, and time and date conventions.

➤ **Sounds** Associates sounds with system events (see Chapter 14).

➤ **System** Views installed devices, manages hardware profiles, and sets system performance.

Many of these applets are discussed in further detail in later chapters (where indicated).

Shortcuts

A shortcut is simply a logical pointer that can be placed in a folder, on the desktop, or in the Start menu to reference an application or file. A shortcut redirects a resource request or an application launch command to the actual location of that object. A shortcut can be defined with slightly different launching parameters from the original file. You configure these alternate parameters through the Properties of a shortcut (accessed by right-clicking on the icon for the shortcut and selecting Properties). Shortcuts can be assigned quick-launch keystrokes, command-line parameters, a startup directory, window size (minimized, maximized, or normal), and a unique icon (see Figure 5.5).

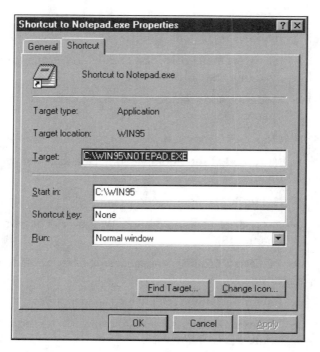

Figure 5.5   The Shortcut tab on the Properties dialog box.

Shortcuts can be created in several ways, including:

➤ Right-click over an empty area on the desktop, within My Computer, or within Windows Explorer and select New|Shortcut to launch the Shortcut Wizard. You will be prompted to provide the path to the original object.

➤ Right-click over an object on the desktop, within My Computer, within Windows Explorer, within Network Neighborhood, and so on, then select Create Shortcut. A shortcut for the selected object will be created in the same container (window, folder, or desktop) as the original.

➤ Drag and drop an object from one window or folder to another (e.g., My Computer, Windows Explorer, the Find utility, and Network Neighborhood) while holding CTRL+SHIFT to create a shortcut in the drop location. You can also perform this action by right-clicking over the object, dragging and dropping it to a new location, then selecting Create Shortcut Here from the pop-up menu that appears.

Shortcuts are managed like any other file. When you delete shortcuts, only the shortcut is moved to the Recycle Bin; the original object is not affected.

Windows Explorer

Windows Explorer is the underlying shell of Windows 95. As a user, you will interact with local resources mainly through Explorer. My Computer and Windows Explorer are simply different views of the same set of resources. Typically, My Computer displays less complicated information and uses images to access items; most novices use this interface. Windows Explorer is a more complex display. It has many levels and types of information; more experienced users tend to use this interface.

My Computer can use a single window to view resources or a separate window for each folder. The option is set on the Folder tab of View|Options.

The other two View|Options tabs—View and File Types—apply to all Explorer windows. The View tab determines whether all files are shown or whether certain types are hidden (.DLL, .SYS, .VXD, .386, and .DRV), whether the full path is displayed in the title bar, and whether registered file extensions are shown. File extensions are registered in the File Types tab. Once an extension is known, Windows 95 will understand how to handle the file type when it is accessed (i.e., when a file is double-clicked, if its extension is known, Windows 95 will launch the associated application and load the file into that application).

Recycle Bin

The Recycle Bin is a temporary storage space for deleted files. Instead of removing a deleted file from the directory listing as in DOS, Windows 95 moves deleted files to this folder/utility. The Recycle Bin can be configured to use a specified percentage of hard drive space to store deleted files. You can recover a deleted file as long as it is in the Recycle Bin. However, when the Recycle Bin is full, the deleted file that has been in the Recycle Bin the longest is permanently removed to make room for newly deleted files (you can also purge the Recycle Bin manually). You can access all the configuration and command properties of the Recycle Bin by right-clicking over the icon on the desktop or within a Windows Explorer window.

Once a file is removed from the Recycle Bin, either by manual or automatic purging, it cannot be recovered using any tool native to Windows 95.

Hardware Profiles

A hardware profile is a collection of configuration settings that correspond to a specific set of devices attached to a computer. Hardware profiles are typically employed on notebook computers that are used in conjunction with docking stations or on other removable devices (hot swappable hard drives, swappable CD-ROM and floppies, PC Cards, and so on).

Each time Windows 95 boots and determines that a significant change has occurred in the hardware configuration of the system, it automatically creates a new hardware profile and prompts you for a name. Each time Windows 95 encounters a known hardware configuration, it automatically selects the appropriate profile. You can create your own profiles manually on the Hardware Profiles tab of the System applet. Simply copy an existing profile, reboot into the new profile, then disable devices you do not wish to have active. If Windows 95 cannot determine which profile to use (for example, if it finds two very similar profiles), you will be prompted to indicate which hardware profile to use.

Exam Prep Questions

Question 1

> When a file is purged from the Recycle Bin, it can still be recovered using the RESTORE command from a Command Prompt or Start|Run.
>
> ○ a. True
>
> ○ b. False

Files that are purged from the Recycle Bin are unrecoverable in Windows 95. Therefore, answer b is correct.

Question 2

> Which options can be configured to modify how Windows Explorer displays its information? [Check all correct answers]
>
> ❑ a. Reveal or hide file extensions
>
> ❑ b. Use a single or multiple windows
>
> ❑ c. Hide common system files
>
> ❑ d. Show the full DOS path

Windows Explorer can be configured to reveal or hide file extensions, hide common system files, and show the full DOS path. Therefore, answers a, c, and d are correct. My Computer, not Windows Explorer, can be modified to use a single-window or multiple-windows setting. Therefore, answer b is incorrect.

Question 3

> Which improvements have been made to Windows 95 over Windows 3.x? [Check all correct answers]
>
> ❑ a. Taskbar
>
> ❑ b. Control Panel
>
> ❑ c. My Computer
>
> ❑ d. Start menu

The taskbar, My Computer, and Start menu are improvements to Windows 95 and are not found in Windows 3.x. Therefore, answers a, c, and d are correct. The Control Panel, although it contains many new applets, is not significantly different in Windows 95. Therefore, answer b is incorrect.

Question 4

> Which is the fastest method of regaining access to a document you edited earlier?
>
> O a. Use My Computer to scroll down through the file system to locate it, then double-click to open it.
>
> O b. Select it from the Start|Documents menu.
>
> O c. Launch the editing application from the Start menu, then use the application's File|Open command to locate and open the document.
>
> O d. Use the Start|Find|Files and Folders utility to locate the document, then double-click to open it.

The fastest method of regaining access to a recently used document is to select it from the Start|Documents menu. Therefore, answer b is correct. The other actions listed will work, but they are much more difficult and time consuming. Therefore, answers a, c, and d are incorrect.

Question 5

> Which commands are available to you when you right-click over an empty area of the taskbar? [Check all correct answers]
>
> ❏ a. Arrange horizontally
>
> ❏ b. Minimize all applications
>
> ❏ c. Cascade
>
> ❏ d. Properties

All of these commands are available in the taskbar pop-up menu. Therefore, answers a, b, c, and d are correct.

Question 6

> Which Control Panel applets handle some type of password con-
> figuration? [Check all correct answers]
>
> ❑ a. Date/Time
>
> ❑ b. Display
>
> ❑ c. Password
>
> ❑ d. System

The Display applet uses a password for screen savers, and the Password applet
manages all other Windows 95 passwords. Therefore, answers b and c are correct. Date/Time and System do not contain password configuration options.
Therefore, answers a and d are incorrect.

Question 7

> Which of the following can be set or configured for all shortcuts?
> [Check all correct answers]
>
> ❑ a. Command-line parameters
>
> ❑ b. Window launch size
>
> ❑ c. Memory usage
>
> ❑ d. Quick launch keystroke

A shortcut can be configured with command-line parameters, window launch
size, and a quick-launch keystroke. Therefore, answers a, b, and d are correct.
Only DOS PIF shortcuts can have their memory usage configured. Therefore,
answer c is incorrect.

Question 8

> Which feature of Windows 95 enables a notebook computer to
> dock and undock with a docking station without reconfiguring
> drivers?
>
> ○ a. User profiles
>
> ○ b. System policies
>
> ○ c. Hardware profiles
>
> ○ d. Devices applet

Hardware profiles define various hardware configurations for the same computer and enable docking station use without manual reconfiguration. Therefore, answer c is correct. A user profile stores desktop and environment settings, not hardware configurations. Therefore, answer a is incorrect. A system policy, even one for a computer, is used to restrict or limit the functionality of the operating environment for users and does not enable the use of docking stations. Therefore, answer b is incorrect. The Devices applet is a Windows NT Control Panel component and is not found in Windows 95. Therefore, answer d is incorrect.

Need To Know More?

 Supporting Microsoft Windows 95. Microsoft Press, Redmond, WA, 1995. ISBN 1-55615-931-5. Chapter 2 discusses the Windows 95 new environment of the desktop, Control Panel, and more.

 Mortensen, Lance and Rick Sawtell: *MCSE: Windows 95 Study Guide.* Sybex Network Press, San Francisco, CA, 1996. ISBN: 0-7821-2092-X. Chapter 5 contains information about the desktop environment and the Control Panel applets of Windows 95.

 Search the TechNet CD (or its online version through www. microsoft.com) and the *Windows 95 Resource Kit* using the keywords "profiles," "Recycle Bin," "taskbar," "desktop settings," "Start menu," "shortcuts," "objects," and "Control Panel applets."

Windows 95 Registry

. . . .

Terms you'll need to understand:

√ Registry

√ .INI file

√ REGEDIT

√ SYSTEM.DAT, USER.DAT

√ SYSTEM.DA0, USER.DA0

√ HKEY_LOCAL_MACHINE

√ HKEY_CURRENT_CONFIG

√ HKEY_CLASSES_ROOT

√ HKEY_DYN_DATA

√ HKEY_USERS

√ HKEY_CURRENT_USER

Techniques you'll need to master:

√ Understanding the Registry's purpose and structure

√ Knowing why editing the Registry is dangerous

√ Editing the Registry properly

√ Backing up and restoring the Registry

The Registry is a method of collecting and organizing system configuration data. It was first introduced in Windows 95 and has since been added to the Windows NT operating system as well. Nearly all the configuration settings, environmental variables, and device drivers are controlled, defined, and loaded through the Registry. Familiarity with and knowledge of the Registry are key to a successful deployment and maintenance of Windows 95 in a production environment.

Role Of .INI Files

In previous versions of Windows, the operating system and most applications stored information about users, environmental parameters, and necessary drivers in .INI files. Unfortunately, .INI files have several limitations, including:

➤ All settings are stored in a single file that does not designate by user (i.e., no user specific configurations)

➤ A size limitation of 64 KB

➤ No standard method of remote or local administrative troubleshooting

➤ Inconsistent use of .INI files from vendor to vendor

Windows 95 has moved most of this information into a new hierarchical database called the Registry, while continuing to support and use .INI files for backward compatibility with older applications or with those applications that do not save their information in the Registry. Several files, such as SYSTEM.INI, WINDOWS.INI, WINFILE.INI, CONTROL.INI, and PROGRAM.INI, are still present under Windows 95 and still have control over how the system functions. If Windows 95 is installed as an upgrade from Windows 3.x, most settings previously stored in these files migrate to the Registry, but some settings and the files themselves remain intact.

You can quickly gain access to six of the most common .INI files through a utility called SYSEDIT (System Configuration Editor), which is simply a multiple-window notepad. When launched from a command prompt or the Start|Run command, SYSEDIT brings up text-editing windows for the following files: WIN.INI, AUTOEXEC.BAT, CONFIG.SYS, SYSTEM.INI, PROTOCOL.INI, and MSMAIL.INI.

Registry Intro

The Registry is a multilayered database in which details about every aspect of the computer, applications, and users are stored. Most users will never need to interact with the Registry directly and even should avoid administrator interaction if possible. Why?

> The Registry is mainly a collection of exceptions. Most processes will function using their defaults unless settings in the Registry tell them otherwise. It is possible to change a single value in the Registry and stop Windows 95 in its tracks. *Never* edit something you don't understand, and *always* try to find a supplied GUI utility, tool, or applet to modify settings.
>
> Most of the applets in the Control Panel are interfaces for elements in the Registry. The use of these interfaces ensures that illegal elements and values are not entered into the database. There is a higher probability of making a mistake if you edit the Registry directly.

The Registry has several benefits over .INI files, including:

➤ The ability to store separate settings and configurations for each user

➤ Unrestricted size

➤ The ability to manage and edit remotely

➤ A standardized method of storing data with which all vendors comply

Data can be stored in the Registry in one of two forms: binary or string (text). Another value type, DWORD, is listed in the Registry Editor menu, but this is simply another form of binary data.

Registry Editor

The Registry can be edited directly by using the Registry Editor (see Figure 6.1). This utility does not appear anywhere on the Start menu but can be launched from a command prompt or the Start|Run command by executing "REGEDIT."

The Registry Editor displays the six default top-level keys when it is first launched. From here, you can scroll down to locate specific entries, elements, and values. The interface acts much like that of Windows Explorer. You can use the Edit|Find command to locate information within the Registry by value or element name.

Important Components Of The Registry

> The Registry is divided into six main segments, or keys. Each key contains all the elements that fall under its type. The six keys are:
>
> ➤ HKEY_LOCAL_MACHINE
>
> ➤ HKEY_CURRENT_CONFIG

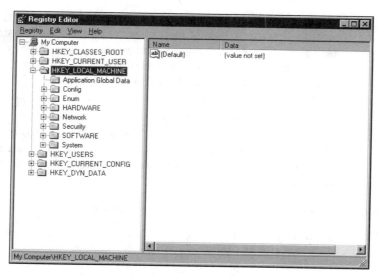

Figure 6.1 The Registry Editor of Windows 95.

> ➤ HKEY_CLASSES_ROOT
>
> ➤ HKEY_DYN_DATA
>
> ➤ HKEY_USERS
>
> ➤ HKEY_CURRENT_USER

The contents of each of these keys are detailed in the following sections.

HKEY_LOCAL_MACHINE

The HKEY_LOCAL_MACHINE key is where all the hardware settings for the computer are stored, including IRQs, I/O addresses, driver controls, and any other hardware-specific information. This information is machine-specific and user-independent.

This key has several subkeys:

➤ **Config** This subkey stores different hardware configurations that appear on the Hardware Profiles tab of the System applet. For example, a notebook may have several different states, including connected to the network, not connected to the network, and connected to a docking station.

➤ **Enum** This subkey contains technology-specific details about devices and bus types that enable Windows 95 to communicate effectively with the hardware and to build hardware driver trees.

➤ **Software** This subkey contains information from Registry-enabled applications. This includes both Win16- and Win32-type applications that register themselves with the Registry.

➤ **System** This subkey contains information used at startup to enable and configure the operational environment.

➤ **Hardware** This subkey holds details about the CPU and communication ports.

➤ **Network** This subkey holds details about the network, such as server name, user account name, and machine name.

➤ **Security** This subkey is where the details regarding user-level security are stored.

HKEY_CURRENT_CONFIG

This key is mainly a pointer to, or a copy of, the set of Registry settings stored in the HKEY_LOCAL_MACHINE key that pertain to the current configuration and setup of the hardware. This key is rebuilt or re-created each time Windows 95 boots so that it always reflects the existing status of functioning and present hardware.

HKEY_CLASSES_ROOT

The HKEY_CLASSES_ROOT key stores the mappings between file extensions and the applications that support them. It also stores other OLE-related data. Each time a file or a shortcut is accessed by double-clicking on it, this key is referenced to determine whether the file type is defined and which application to send it to for user interaction.

HKEY_DYN_DATA

The HKEY_DYN_DATA key contains details about hardware devices that can be altered while active, such as Plug and Play devices, PCMCIA cards, and removable media. This key is created dynamically each time the machine is booted.

HKEY_USERS

This key stores user-specific settings, such as desktop arrangements, drive mappings, Start menu configuration, and so on. A unique subkey is created for each enumerated user. A default subkey is used for each new user the first time the system is accessed.

HKEY_CURRENT_USER

The HKEY_CURRENT_USER key contains a copy of the subkey from the HKEY_USERS key that corresponds to the currently active user. Any and all changes made to the system are recorded in this key and transferred back to the HKEY_USERS key when the user logs off.

Backup And Restoration

The Registry is stored on the hard drive in two separate files: USER.DAT and SYSTEM.DAT. The USER.DAT file contains all user-specific settings. The SYSTEM.DAT file contains everything else (i.e., the system-specific settings). Both files are normally stored in the main Windows directory. However, the USER.DAT file can reside elsewhere, such as in a network share or a user's home directory, to enable roaming profiles (see Chapter 13).

By now, you should understand the importance of the Registry and that if the Registry is corrupted or deleted, your system will not function. To improve the chances that the Registry will survive from one computing session to another, the system automatically maintains a backup of the Registry each time the machine is booted. SYSTEM.DAT is copied to SYSTEM.DA0, and USER.DAT is copied to USER.DA0. Like their originals, backup copies are stored in the main Windows directory and have the attributes of hidden, read-only, and system files.

The SYSTEM Registry files, both the original and the backup, are about 1.3 MB each, whereas the USER files are about 300 KB each.

You can perform a manual backup of these files in two ways. One way is to reboot to a safe-boot command prompt only and then change the attributes and copy the files to floppies. The second manual backup can be performed inside Windows 95. The Registry Editor utility can be used from a command prompt or the Start|Run command to export the Registry to a text file. The syntax "REGEDIT /e filename.txt" will save the Registry to a single text file, and the syntax "REGEDIT /C filename.txt" will restore the contents of the file to the Registry.

If you have a copy of the .DA0 files on floppy or hard drive, you can restore the settings stored in them to the Registry by deleting the original files and changing the file extension of the backup copies to .DAT (this must be performed from DOS, not within Windows 95). Remember to remove the attribute settings before attempting to delete the files and restore them before rebooting.

Keep in mind that when you restore the Registry using either of these methods, you may not return the system to an optimal state if the hardware settings or devices have changed, the backup copies of the Registry are corrupted, or required files and drivers are no longer present on the system. Always make another backup of the Registry before restoring any copies of the Registry. Once you overwrite the existing Registry, there is no way to recover the changes without a backup.

In addition to protecting the Registry as a whole, you can also save and restore individual keys or subkeys through the Registry Editor utility. The Registry|Export and Registry|Import commands from the menu bar can be used to save and restore isolated keys of the Registry. Remember that all subcomponents of any level key are saved and restored at the same time.

Troubleshooting

Troubleshooting options for the Registry are fairly limited, as problems in the Registry can be corrected only one way: by restoring or replacing the corrupted or failed Registry with a working backup. Otherwise, the only option to restore the system to working order is to reinstall Windows 95.

Restoring backups of the Registry can be accomplished in several ways, some of which were discussed in the previous sections. Two other ways of restoring the Registry are with a Safe Mode boot and a startup disk.

Booting into Safe Mode is accomplished by pressing F8 when "Starting Windows 95" is displayed at the beginning of the boot sequence. From the menu that appears, select Safe Mode. If the original Registry files are corrupted but viable backups are present on the system, you may be prompted for permission to restore the Registry from backups. The system will copy the .DA0 files over the .DAT files and reboot.

The startup disk contains boot files, the Registry, and other important files needed to boot Windows 95 in the event of a system or boot failure. This disk can be created from the Startup Disk tab or the Add/Remove Programs applet. Just click on the Create Disk button and supply a floppy. The Registry files stored on the startup disk are used to boot Windows 95 and can be restored to the system through the Registry Editor utility once the system is booted.

The Registry Editor offers two additional features: printing and remote access. The Registry Editor can print one or all of the keys of the Registry, resulting in hundreds of pages of text.

The registries of other Windows 95 systems can be edited over the network by selecting the Registry|Connect Network Registry command from the menu bar. Select or provide the computer name you wish to administer remotely. This feature requires user-level security on both machines, and the remote machine must have the Remote Registry Services installed. The Remote Registry Services are installed via the Network applet, and the files are located in the \Admin\Nettools\Remotereg directory on the distribution CD.

Exam Prep Questions

Question 1

> Which key stores the hardware configuration details of the currently active session?
>
> ○ a. HKEY_LOCAL_MACHINE
>
> ○ b. HKEY_DYN_DATA
>
> ○ c. HKEY_CURRENT_CONFIG
>
> ○ d. HKEY_CURRENT_USER

The key that stores data about the current session's hardware configuration is HKEY_CURRENT_CONFIG. Therefore, answer c is correct. HKEY_LOCAL_MACHINE stores data on all possible and past configurations of hardware. Therefore, answer a is incorrect. HKEY_DYN_DATA stores OLE and file association information. Therefore, answer b is incorrect. HKEY_CURRENT_USER stores information about the currently active user. Therefore, answer d is incorrect.

Question 2

> Where are Plug and Play details stored in the Registry?
>
> ○ a. HKEY_LOCAL_MACHINE
>
> ○ b. HKEY_CURRENT_CONFIG
>
> ○ c. HKEY_CLASSES_ROOT
>
> ○ d. HKEY_DYN_DATA

HKEY_DYN_DATA is where all dynamic data is stored about hardware, including Plug and Play. Therefore, answer d is correct. HKEY_LOCAL_MACHINE, HKEY_CURRENT_CONFIG, and HKEY_CLASSES_ROOT do not store Plug and Play data. Therefore, answers a, b, and c are incorrect.

Question 3

> What is the name of the Registry's automatic backup file where user information is stored?
>
> ○ a. USER.DA0
>
> ○ b. USER.DAT
>
> ○ c. USER.BAK
>
> ○ d. SYSTEM.DAT

USER.DA0 is the automatically created backup file of the Registry's user settings file. Therefore, answer a is correct. USER.DAT is the original file where user settings are stored. Therefore, answer b is incorrect. USER.BAK can be a file name of the user portion of the Registry, but this is not the name of the automatically created file. Therefore, answer c is incorrect. SYSTEM.DAT is the name of the original Registry file that holds the system information. Therefore, answer d is incorrect.

Question 4

> Which types of information are stored in the Registry? [Check all correct answers]
>
> ❑ a. Binary
>
> ❑ b. Fractal
>
> ❑ c. Text
>
> ❑ d. Encrypted

The Registry stores binary and text data. Therefore, answers a and c are correct. The Registry does not store Fractal information. Therefore, answer b is incorrect. Unfortunately, the Registry of Windows 95 is not encrypted. Therefore, answer d is incorrect.

Question 5

If you suspect that the Registry has become corrupted, how can you restore the system to working order? [Check all correct answers]

- ❐ a. Boot into Safe Mode
- ❐ b. Copy the .DAO files over the .DAT files
- ❐ c. Use the startup disk
- ❐ d. Reinstall Windows 95

All these methods can return the system to working order. Therefore, answers a, b, c, and d are correct. The first three are the most promising; however, reinstalling Windows 95 is required if backups are unavailable or if corruption has spread to other files.

Question 6

What is the name used at a command prompt or the Start|Run command to access the Registry Editor?

- ○ a. REGEDT32
- ○ b. REGISTRY
- ○ c. REGEDIT
- ○ d. EDITREG

REGEDIT is the name used to launch the Registry Editor. Therefore, answer c is correct. REGEDT32 is the name of a Registry Editor in Windows NT. Therefore, answer a is incorrect. REGISTRY and EDITREG are fictional names of executables. Therefore, answers b and d are incorrect.

Question 7

A Windows 95 startup disk can be created by executing "rdisk /s" from a command prompt.

- ○ a. True
- ○ b. False

rdisk is the tool used with Windows NT to make an Emergency Repair Disk. Therefore, answer b is correct. A Windows 95 startup disk is created on the Startup Disk tab of the Add/Remove Programs applet.

Question 8

> What is the name of the Registry file that stores system information?
>
> ○ a. SYSTEM.INI
>
> ○ b. WIN.INI
>
> ○ c. SYSTEM.DAT
>
> ○ d. PROTOCOL.INI

SYSTEM.DAT is the name of the Registry file in which system information is stored. Therefore, answer c is correct. The other files are .INI files left over from previous versions of Windows or present for backward compatibility with applications that are not Registry-aware. Therefore, answers a, b, and d are incorrect.

Need To Know More?

 Supporting Microsoft Windows 95. Microsoft Press, Redmond, WA, 1995. ISBN 1-55615-931-5. Chapter 3, lesson 2, briefly discusses the Registry.

 Mortensen, Lance and Rick Sawtell: *MCSE: Windows 95 Study Guide.* Sybex Network Press, San Francisco, CA, 1996. ISBN: 0-7821-2092-X. Chapter 6 contains detailed and useful information about the Registry.

 Search the TechNet CD (or its online version through www. microsoft.com) and the *Windows 95 Resource Kit* using the keywords "Registry," "REGEDIT," "startup disk," "USER.DAT," "SYSTEM.DAT," or any of the HKEY... names.

File Systems, Storage Devices, And Utilities

Terms you'll need to understand:

√ File Allocation Table (FAT)

√ Virtual File Allocation Table (VFAT)

√ Long file names (LFNs)

√ Defragment

√ ScanDisk

√ Compression

√ Partitions, volumes, and clusters

√ Master Boot Record (MBR)

Techniques you'll need to master:

√ Knowing the Windows 95-supported drives and controller types

√ Comparing VFAT to FAT

√ Understanding LFNs and conversion to 8.3 equivalents

√ Implementing drive compression

√ Implementing disk defragmentation

√ Using ScanDisk

√ Understanding the process of data backup

√ Knowing how to tweak the file system for performance purposes

This chapter introduces Windows 95 file systems and several related topics. The details in this chapter are focused to help you study and may not be sufficient to fully understand or operate these utilities, services, or components in a production environment.

Disk Structure 101

Hopefully, you are already familiar with storage devices and the terminology used to describe their configuration and operation. But, just to be sure you're equipped with the bare minimum of such information, a short refresher follows.

Partitions

Hard drives are divided into partitions. A partition can contain one or more file systems, each of which enables an NOS or OS to store and retrieve files. Even though Windows 95 natively supports only FAT and VFAT, partitions that support other file systems can reside on a machine that runs Windows 95 (even if Windows 95 cannot access them). For instance, it's possible that a drive on a dual-boot machine running Windows 95 and Windows NT 4 could contain an NTFS partition. In that case, only Windows NT could access that partition; Windows 95 would not even see it.

In general, a hard drive can contain between 1 and 32 separate partitions. Thus, a single physical hard drive can appear as multiple logical drives. Hard drives should be partitioned to maximize their usage by the underlying NOS and its applications. If you attempt to change a partition, any information stored in that disk space will be destroyed. If there is free unpartitioned drive space, you may create new partitions without damaging existing partitions. Likewise, deleting any one partition does not affect other partitions on a drive.

A single drive may contain up to four primary partitions, or one to three primary partitions and a single extended partition. An extended partition can be subdivided further into multiple logical drives. The total number of primary partitions plus logical drives cannot exceed 32 on any one physical hard drive.

Partitions for Windows 95 are typically created using the DOS utility FDISK. This tool can be used to:

➤ Create and destroy primary and extended partitions and logical drives within the extended partition

➤ Mark a primary partition active

➤ View the current partition configuration

FDISK is able to see and delete several types of non-DOS partitions, such as HPFS and XENIX, but FDISK is unable to see and delete an NTFS extended partition or logical drive. (It is able to delete NTFS primary partitions.) It is recommended to use FDISK only from DOS 6.0 or greater. If you are unfamiliar with the FDISK utility and how to use it to create partitions, please read the *Windows 95 Resource Kit* material in Chapter 20.

Volumes

In general, a volume is an organizational structure imposed on a partition that supports file storage. Under Windows 95, volumes cannot span multiple drives or partitions; they are isolated within a single partition. Under Windows NT, volumes can span multiple drives or partitions.

Drive Letters

Every volume on a Windows 95 machine has an associated drive letter; in fact, Windows 95 cannot access a local volume unless it has an associated drive letter. Drive letters simplify the identification of an exact physical drive, partition, and volume for any referenced folder or file. Windows 95 can assign drive letters to storage devices using the letters C through Z (A and B are reserved for floppy drives).

Master Boot Record

The Master Boot Record (MBR), a BIOS bootstrap routine, is used by low-level, hardware-based system code stored in read-only memory (ROM) to initiate the boot sequence on a PC. This, in turn, calls a bootstrap loader, which commences loading the machine's designated operating system. The MBR directs the hardware to a so-called "active partition" where the designated operating system may be loaded. Only a primary partition can be made active.

Storage Devices And Drivers

The drive storage access system of Windows 95 has been enhanced and improved over previous versions of Windows. This system includes both 32- and 16-bit drivers: 32-bit for performance and size, and 16-bit for backward compatibility. Windows 95 supports several types of storage devices, including ESDI, IDE, IDE-LBA, MFM, SCSI, SCSI-2, and Hardcard. To support these drive types, Windows 95 also supports a wide range of bus adapter types for controller cards, including EISA, PCI, PCMCIA (PC Card), ISA, MCA, RLL, and VLB. In fact, most name-brand desktop computer storage hardware is supported by Windows 95. In addition to standard hard drive devices, Windows

95 supports floppy and other removable media drives (such as CD-ROM, Bernoulli, and optical cartridge devices).

Windows 95 includes a file system called CD File System (CDFS), which is a read-only driver set for accessing CD-ROMs.

The 32-bit file system drivers can be disabled on the Troubleshooting tab of the File System Properties dialog box (see Figure 7.1). You can access this dialog box through the File System button on the Performance tab of the Control Panel's System applet. Turning off the file system features should be necessary only for older motherboards, driver controllers, or storage devices. Changes to this dialog box should be carefully considered because disabling (i.e., marking a checkbox) will degrade the file system performance of Windows 95. The settings on this dialog box are:

➤ **Disable new file sharing and locking semantics** This setting changes how Windows 95 handles file sharing. This should be selected only when MS-DOS applications are unable to access Windows 95 shares.

➤ **Disable long name preservation for old programs** This setting turns off protection for LFNs. This should be selected only when legacy applications without LFN support fail to operate properly.

➤ **Disable protect-mode hard disk interrupt handling** This setting prevents Windows 95 from bypassing the drive controller by terminating interrupts. This should be selected only when legacy hardware requires the controller ROM to handle interrupts instead of the OS.

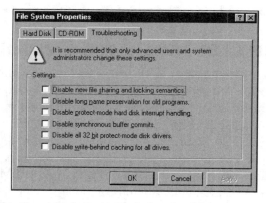

Figure 7.1   The Troubleshooting tab for the File System Properties dialog box.

➤ **Disable synchronous buffer commits** This setting allows Windows 95 to write buffer contents to disk and report to the applications of a completed action when the write may not be complete. This should be selected only when troubleshooting performance problems.

➤ **Disable all 32-bit, protected-mode disk drivers** This setting turns off all 32-bit drivers so that they are not loaded and forces the OS to use 16-bit Real Mode drivers. This should be selected only if hardware devices are malfunctioning with the 32-bit drivers.

➤ **Disable write-behind caching for all drives** This setting turns off write buffering, thus forcing all writes to occur directly to the storage device. This should be selected only when you expect a system failure that would interrupt the cache write-behind process and result in a loss of data.

VFAT Vs. FAT

The central file system of Windows 95 is the Virtual File Allocation Table (VFAT). VFAT, a 32-bit file system, has several improvements over DOS and Windows 3.x FAT. FAT (File Allocation Table) refers to a linear table structure used to represent information about files. Such information includes file names, file attribute information, and other directory entries that locate where files (or segments of files) are stored in the FAT environment. Windows 95 is designed around VFAT, but still supports, and is backward compatible with, FAT. In the next two sections, original FAT and VFAT are described and compared.

Original FAT

FAT is the original file system used with DOS. It represents a nearly unbroken chain of capability back to the earliest days of the first DOS-based PCs. The file allocation table from which FAT draws its name stores directory information in a simple table structure that must be searched from beginning to end, one entry at a time, when users access directories or the files that reside in them.

Although FAT is both primitive and simple, FAT implementations abound: Several versions are available for DOS, Windows 3.x, Windows NT, many flavors of Unix, and Macintosh. Many other, more exotic operating systems also support FAT file structures.

One of the most substantial characteristics of original FAT is its use of so-called 8.3 (pronounced "eight-dot-three") file names. These are file and folder names that can be up to eight characters long. All file extensions are preceded by a period and can be no more than three characters long. This latter specification has led to the proliferation of many common three-character file extensions, such as .TXT for text files, .DOC for word processing files, .XLS for Excel spreadsheet files, and so on. For many users, these file length restrictions are a defining characteristic of DOS, but they are really a requirement of the FAT file system.

Because the size of files and partitions that FAT can manage has grown with each new version of DOS, FAT uses two types of pointers in its allocation tables. Partitions smaller than 15 MB use 12-bit pointers, whereas larger partitions use 16-bit pointers (see Table 7.1). That's why you'll sometimes see FAT volumes labeled either "FAT12" (the volume's FAT uses 12-bit pointers) or "FAT16" (the volume's FAT uses 16-bit pointers). A FAT12 or FAT16 label appears in disk partition management utilities such as the FDISK command that ships with most versions of DOS. For DOS versions 3.0 through 6.22, all FAT drivers are 16-bit only (but this does not affect whether a volume is called FAT12 or FAT16—that's determined purely by the size of the FAT volume itself). Table 7.2 outlines the vital statistics for the FAT file system.

Table 7.1   Vital statistics of cluster size based on logical volume size.

Drive size (MB)	Sectors Per Cluster	Cluster Size (KB)
0 - 15*	8	4
16 - 127	4	2
128 - 255	8	4
256 - 511	16	8
512 - 1,023	32	16
1,024 - 2,047	64	32
2,048 - 4,096**	64	64

*Volumes less than 15 MB use 12-bit FAT; all others use 16-bit FAT.

**NT's implementation of FAT/VFAT only.

Table 7.2   Vital statistics for the FAT file system.

Feature	Capability/Maximum
Maximum volume size	2 GB
Maximum file size	2 GB
Maximum files in root directory	512
Maximum files in nonroot directory	65,535
Long file name (LFN) support	No

It's important to note that the type of data stored on a particular volume will affect how that data is stored and how much actual data can be stored on the given volume. The best way to explain this is to give you an example. Assume that you have a 300 MB partition on a drive used to store data files from a database application. These data files range from 1 to 4 KB each. On a 300 MB partition, each cluster is 8 KB. A cluster can hold data only from a single logical file. In addition, if you use only part of a cluster to store a file, the remaining space in that cluster cannot be used by another file. In addition, the 300 MB volume will be able to hold only 150 MB of data or less because the file sizes are so small. When storing lots of little files ("little" as in smaller than two clusters), you should opt to create smaller storage volumes to minimize the wasted space because of underused clusters. In other words, try to match the file sizes stored on a volume with multiples of the cluster size.

Virtual FAT (VFAT)

The Virtual FAT file system was first introduced with Windows for Workgroups 3.11 to process file I/O in Protected Mode. With the introduction of Windows 95, VFAT added support for long file names (LFNs). Nevertheless, VFAT remains backward compatible with original FAT, meaning that it supports access using 8.3 file names as well as LFNs. In fact, it maintains an equivalence mechanism that maps 8.3 names into LFNs and vice versa. This enables Windows 16-bit and DOS applications that lack LFN support to use files and data stored on VFAT volumes.

VFAT is the version of FAT that the original releases of Windows 95, Windows NT 3.51, and Windows NT 4 support. VFAT file systems require the use of file management utilities that understand VFAT in general and LFNs in particular. That's because earlier DOS file management utilities will reorganize what appears to them an original FAT structure and will often destroy any LFN information that the FAT table maintained by VFAT contains. Therefore, when working with VFAT volumes, you must use file management utilities that can understand and preserve VFAT file structures.

The 32-bit VFAT file system is the primary file system in the initial release of Windows 95. VFAT can use either 32-bit Protected Mode drivers or 16-bit Real Mode drivers. Actual allocation on disk is still 12- or 16-bit (depending on the size of the volume), so the FAT on the disk uses the same structure as earlier implementations of FAT. VFAT handles all hard drive requests and uses 32-bit code for all file access to hard disk volumes.

Table 7.3   Vital statistics for the VFAT file system.

Feature	Capability/Maximum
Maximum volume size	2 GB (4 GB for NT FAT)
Maximum file size	2 GB (4 GB for NT FAT)
Maximum files in root directory	512
Maximum files in non-root directory	No limit
Long file name (LFN) support	Yes

As Table 7.3 illustrates, the primary differences between VFAT and original FAT are an increase in maximum volume and file sizes, an increase in non-root-directory container size, and the addition of LFN support to 8.3 file names.

VFAT also supports both 16- and 32-bit calls, whereas original FAT supports only 16-bit calls.

LFNs

Long file names (LFNs) are a significant improvement over the 8.3 file name limitation of FAT. Windows 95 uses and supports LFNs by default. LFNs can contain up to 256 characters. Any path or path and file name is limited to 260 characters; fortunately, part of a path statement or an actual file name substituted with its 8.3 equivalent meets this length restriction.

> *Note: Some of the Microsoft documentation states that LFNs can be only 255 characters and that path names (or path and file names) can be only up to 259 characters. However, our tests with the OS show the true length to be 256 and 260.*

Other characteristics of LFNs are:

➤ They can include spaces and several characters that 8.3 names cannot, such as a plus sign (+), comma (,), period (.), equal sign (=), left bracket ([), and right bracket (]).

➤ They are not case sensitive, but case is preserved.

➤ They are preserved when copied to floppies.

An important issue relating to LFNs is converting them back to their 8.3 equivalents. The process is as follows:

1. Remove all spaces and special characters: plus sign (+), comma (,), period (.), equal sign (=), left bracket ([), and right bracket (]).

2. Use the first six remaining characters up to any periods.

3. Add a tilde (~) and any number from 1 through 9; if a unique name cannot be found, use the first five characters, a tilde, then numbers from 10 through 99, and so on.

4. For the extension, use the first three legal characters after the last period. If there is no period, no extension is used.

Each time an LFN is created, its 8.3 equivalent is automatically created by the file system. You should be adept at deciphering 8.3 equivalents of LFNs because this skill is called upon heavily when working with Windows 95.

LFNs should be used or manipulated only (and always) with utilities that support LFN (VFAT). The 8.3 (FAT) utilities (including backup utilities) can and do destroy the LFN information and will leave only 8.3 equivalents. LFNs can be used in DOS or through command lines, but quotation marks must be used to surround the LFN.

LFNs are stored by the file system using several directory entries. A single directory entry can contain 11 characters, so an LFN can use up to 24 entries. If several LFNs are used in a root directory, the number of files is reduced by the number of directory entries needed to store the LFN.

Disk Subsystem Management

Windows 95 has several built-in tools that help manage file systems, including compression, defragmentation, and drive integrity.

Compression

The compression tool is called DriveSpace 3. This is the latest version of the disk compression tool obtained from the Plus! package for Windows 95. Its predecessors include DriveSpace, which shipped as part of Windows 95, and DoubleSpace from MS-DOS 6.0 and 6.2. DriveSpace 3 supports compressed drives created by its predecessors. Drives compressed with these older tools can be upgraded to the new DriveSpace 3 format to obtain improved performance and reliability.

A short list of what you need to know about compression:

➤ Compression is performed on a drive or partition basis, not on a file-by-file basis.

➤ Compression results in a single large compression file that contains all the data (named DRVSPACE.000 or DBLSPACE.000). This file is a compressed volume file (CVF).

➤ Special bootstrap loading drivers are placed on the boot drive to map the compression file as a drive (usually C:) and hide the host drive (usually by assigning it the drive letter H).

➤ Both floppy drives and hard drives can be compressed.

➤ A compressed floppy drive contains the drivers, so even Windows 95 systems without compression enabled can read the floppies.

➤ Drives can be uncompressed, but if the uncompressed file size exceeds the storage capacity of the drive, either decompression will not occur or data will be lost.

➤ Never place a swapfile on a compressed drive.

DriveSpace gives you control over the compression level used to compact your data, which allows you to choose between optimized speed or optimized space. The higher the compression level, the greater the space, but the slower the read/write activity (and vice versa).

There are two controls within DriveSpace that are fairly important. The first, which appears in the Drive menu, is Adjust Free Space. The dialog box that this command reveals gives you the ability to adjust how much free or unused space is available within the compressed drive (typically C:) and on the host drive (typically H:). The slide bar on this dialog box is used to "shift" or move free space from the compressed drive to the host drive and back. The second important control, which appears in the Advanced menu, is Change Ratio. The dialog box that this command reveals enables you to change the estimated compression ratio used to estimate the remaining free space on the compressed drive. The actual compression achieved by DriveSpace when new data is added to this drive will fall significantly below this setting because most data cannot be compressed beyond a 2:1 ratio (in fact, 1.4:1 to 1.6:1 is typical). Therefore, setting this value to 8:1 will display a larger current free space, but you will probably not be able to store eight times the data on the drive, especially if you attempt to save dense data to that drive.

On a Windows 95 dual-boot system with Windows NT, you should be careful about using DriveSpace. Windows NT does not support DriveSpace compression. This means that when you boot into Windows NT, you will not be able to access any data stored on a compressed drive created by DriveSpace. However, if Windows 95 is a client of an NT network, a compressed drive can be shared over the network and accessed by Windows NT.

Fragmentation

The Windows 95 Disk Defragmenter is used to reorganize the storage patterns of files on a hard drive to reduce data segmentation. As files are written, deleted, changed, and altered on a storage device that holds more and more data, the patterns of that storage become more and more chaotic. Fragmentation is the state of a file when it is stored on a drive in a noncontiguous space. In other words, fragmentation is when a single file is broken into parts that are scattered across the disk. The greater the fragmentation of a drive, the more likely a read or write error will occur. Plus, the overall system performance is degraded because of the read and write time involved with a multipart, fragmented file. A defragmented drive performs better because the operating system does not need to search the entire drive for each part of a file—its files are stored contiguously. Defragmentation can be executed to maximize contiguous empty space, to defragment files, or to completely optimize the drive.

Disk Defragmenter should be used:

➤ If the drive is over 10 percent fragmented

➤ After deleting large or numerous files

➤ If the system is performing sluggishly

➤ When disk activity is high (not associated with demand paging)

ScanDisk

ScanDisk is a disk tool that checks and corrects disk errors. FAT and VFAT store files in blocks called "clusters." The location of the first cluster is stored with the file name in the directory. Each subsequent cluster's location is stored at the end of the previous cluster. Normal system activity or physical drive errors can cause clusters to be lost or to be cross-linked (see Figure 7.2). Lost (orphaned) clusters result from a corrupted or incorrect pointer. Cross-linked clusters occur when one cluster points to another file's cluster.

ScanDisk can often restore proper linkages to cross-linked files and orphaned files. If not, it can save the data to files where you can manually attempt to retrieve or salvage the data. ScanDisk should be used after system crashes and before using Disk Defragmenter. The unrecoverable clusters are stored in the root directory of the drive in files named file0001, file0002, and so on. Data from these files must be extracted manually, either with a text or hex editor.

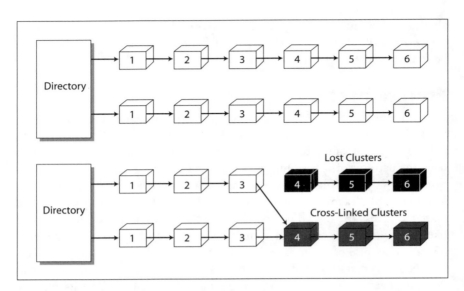

Figure 7.2   Cross-linked and orphaned clusters.

Backup And Restoration

Windows 95 includes a no-frills backup utility that creates backup copies of your important data. Microsoft Backup retains LFNs and can make backups to any local or network storage device, including tape, hard drives, or removable media (optical cartridges, floppies, and so on). Data is selected on a drive, folder or individual file basis. Other features of MS Backup include:

➤ File filtering—by date, type, or exclusions

➤ Drag and drop support

➤ Verification and compression

MS Backup can be used to restore files to their original locations or anywhere else within the file system. You can also compare files with their backup versions. The Backup utility is itself a Backup Wizard. By selecting the Backup, Restore, or Compare tabs from this utility, you can walk through the configuration and scheduling process step by step.

In addition to support for local and network hard drives, Backup includes support for the following types of tape devices:

➤ QIC 40, 80, 3010, and 3020 tape drives connected to the primary floppy disk controller, manufactured by Colorado Memory Systems, Connor, Iomega, and Wangtek (only in hardware phantom mode)

➤ QIC 40, 80, and 3010 tape drives, manufactured by Colorado Memory Systems, connected to the parallel port

Windows 95 Backup does not locally support:

➤ SCSI-based tape devices, typically DAT drives

➤ Devices connected to secondary floppy disk controllers

➤ Proprietary tape device controller cards (such as FC-10 and FC-15)

➤ QIC Wide, Summit, Travan, Irwin, or Mountain drives

Note: If these drives are located elsewhere on the network, they can be used as a network share.

Windows 95 Microsoft Backup will attempt to locate and enable any locally attached tape devices. Because the application is compatible with only a few devices, it loads any needed drivers automatically and does not require you to pre-install the drivers for these tape devices before launching Backup.

Backup supports only two types of backups—full and incremental. A full backup makes a copy of every file on or in the selected drives and folders, plus the archive bit on each file is cleared. An incremental backup copies only those files that have changed since the last backup (full or incremental), and the archive bit is cleared only on the changed files. To restore data after a drive failure, you will need to restore from the most current full backup and every incremental backup between the full backup and the failure. Windows 95 Backup does not support differential backups. A differential backup copies all files that have changed since the last full or incremental backup, but it does not reset the archive bit.

Windows 95 also includes two network backup agents. Backup agents enable Windows 95 to be included in networkwide backups. Windows 95 includes two agents—Cheyenne's ARCserve and Arcada's Backup Exec (now owned by Seagate)—that grant the network backup system access to the local Windows 95 files and Registry.

Other Tools

A handful of other tools and configuration utilities are useful for optimizing the file system. The first is a Microsoft Plus! add-on called "System Agent."

System Agent is a scheduling utility that can be used to automate the launching of compression, defragmentation, or ScanDisk utilities. When System Agent is installed, it is preconfigured to run the following tasks:

➤ Check for low disk space every hour; issue a warning if it is low

➤ Run a standard integrity test with ScanDisk daily

➤ Defragment the hard drive(s) daily

➤ Run a thorough integrity test with ScanDisk monthly

If you are using the DriveSpace compression tool, Compression Agent will be launched to compress new files. Any application that can be launched and controlled through a batch file or a command line with parameters can be routinely launched by System Agent.

Windows 95 offers a GUI to the old DOS FORMAT utility through the File|Format command of My Computer or Windows Explorer. This dialog box allows you to format floppies or hard drives and copy system files (i.e., make them bootable).

Earlier in this chapter, we mentioned that you can access the Troubleshooting tab of the File System Properties dialog box by pressing the File System button on the Performance tab of the Control Panel's System applet. Two other tabs of the File System Properties box are Hard Disk and CD-ROM. The Hard Disk tab allows you to set the role of the computer (desktop, server, or laptop). The CD-ROM tab allows you to set the size of the supplemental CD cache and the optimum access pattern (CD-ROM drive speed).

Exam Prep Questions

Question 1

> Which file systems are supported by Windows 95? [Check all correct answers]
>
> ❑ a. VFAT
>
> ❑ b. CDFS
>
> ❑ c. FAT
>
> ❑ d. NTFS

Windows 95 supports the VFAT, CDFS, and FAT file systems. Therefore, answers a, b, and c are correct. NTFS is the file system of Windows NT and is not supported by Windows 95. Therefore, answer d is incorrect.

Question 2

> Which characteristics do FAT and VFAT have in common? [Check all correct answers]
>
> ❑ a. Support 8.3 file names
>
> ❑ b. No limit of non-root directory entries
>
> ❑ c. Limit of 512 root directory entries
>
> ❑ d. Support volume sizes of 2 GB

Both VFAT and FAT support 8.3 file names, although VFAT also supports LFNs. Therefore, answer a is correct. Both VFAT and FAT are limited to 512 root directory entries. Therefore, answer c is correct. Both VFAT and FAT support volume sizes of 2 GB. Therefore, answer d is correct. FAT is limited to 65,535 non-root directory entries, whereas VFAT is unlimited. Therefore, answer b is incorrect.

Question 3

> What is the 8.3 equivalent of the following LFN? Sales Draft. 1997 [Sept.] Stock Report.doc
>
> ○ a. report.doc
>
> ○ b. salesd~1.doc
>
> ○ c. draft.199
>
> ○ d. Sept.

The 8.3 equivalent is salesd~1.doc. Therefore, answer b is correct. All other answers are incorrect.

Question 4

> If a DOS 5 XCOPY utility is used to duplicate a directory structure, all Windows 95 LFNs will be preserved.
>
> ○ a. True
>
> ○ b. False

DOS 5 does not support LFNs, so using the XCOPY utility will destroy the LFN information in the copied material. Therefore, answer b is correct.

Question 5

> Which of the following statements is true?
>
> ○ a. 512 LFN directory entries can be placed in the root directory, even if each file name is 50 characters long.
>
> ○ b. All backup utilities, including those built for DOS, preserve LFNs.
>
> ○ c. Windows 95 LFN-supporting utilities can reference files and paths using the 8.3 equivalents.
>
> ○ d. A complete LFN path and file name has no length restriction.

Windows 95 utilities can reference LFN files and paths with their 8.3 equivalents. Therefore, answer c is correct. Because directory entries are only 11 characters long and 50-character file names will use at least 5 entries per file, only about 100 such files can be placed in the root directory. Therefore, answer a is incorrect. Not all backup utilities, especially those built for DOS, support or preserve LFNs. Therefore, answer b is incorrect. LFN path and file names have a total length restriction of 260 characters. Therefore, answer d is incorrect.

Question 6

Which of the following statements are true? [Check all correct answers]

- ❑ a. Windows 95 compression is on a file-by-file basis.
- ❑ b. The CVF of a compressed drive is named DRVSPACE.000 or DBLSPACE.000.
- ❑ c. Both floppy and hard drives can be compressed.
- ❑ d. Compressed drives are not automatically mapped by the bootstrap routine.

The CVFs are named DRVSPACE.000 or DBLSPACE.000. Therefore, answer b is correct. Both floppy and hard drives can be compressed. Therefore, answer c is correct. Windows 95 compression is not on a file-by-file basis. Therefore, answer a is incorrect. Compressed drives are automatically mapped. Therefore, answer d is incorrect.

Question 7

When should the Disk Defragmenter utility be used? [Check all correct answers]

- ❑ a. If the drive is over 10 percent fragmented
- ❑ b. After deleting large or numerous files
- ❑ c. If the system is performing sluggishly
- ❑ d. When disk activity is high (not associated with demand paging)

All these answers indicate situations in which the defragmentation utility should be used. Therefore, answers a, b, c, and d are correct.

Question 8

ScanDisk is able to repair which of the following? [Check all correct answers]

❏ a. Overwritten files

❏ b. Orphaned clusters

❏ c. Deleted files

❏ d. Cross-linked files

ScanDisk can repair orphaned clusters and cross-linked files. Therefore, answers b and d are correct. ScanDisk cannot repair overwritten and deleted files. Therefore, answers a and c are incorrect.

Question 9

The Windows 95 MS Backup utility can be used to protect data by storing it on which media types? [Check all correct answers]

❏ a. Floppies

❏ b. Writeable removable cartridges

❏ c. Hard drives

❏ d. Tape drives

MS Backup supports floppies, removable cartridges, hard drives, and tape drives as backup destinations. Therefore, answers a, b, c, and d are correct.

Question 10

System Agent is a utility that can perform which function?

❍ a. Monitor overall system performance

❍ b. Maintain the security structure

❍ c. Format and create disk partitions

❍ d. Launch tasks at scheduled times

System Agent is a utility for launching tasks at scheduled times. Therefore, answer d is the only correct answer.

Question 11

> Your Windows 95 computer hosts a data drive for your workgroup.
> This data drive stores individual data files, which are 4, 8, 12, and
> 16 KB in size. What size partition would offer the most efficient
> use of space for this drive?
>
> O a. 250 MB
>
> O b. 500 MB
>
> O c. 750 MB
>
> O d. 2,000 MB

The most efficient partition for this data drive is 250 MB because this would offer 4 KB clusters and all of the files stored are integral multiples of four. Therefore, answer a is correct. 500 MB uses 8 KB clusters, which means both the 4 KB and 12 KB files would waste space. Therefore, answer b is incorrect. 750 MB uses 16 KB clusters, which means the 4, 8, and 12 KB files would waste space. Therefore, answer c is incorrect. 2,000 MB uses 32 KB clusters which means all of these files would waste space. Therefore, answer d is incorrect.

Question 12

> After installing a new Adaptec SCSI controller card and a Hewlett-
> Packard SCSI DAT tape backup drive on your Windows 95
> computer, you launch Microsoft Backup. Backup claims that no
> tape devices are present. Why?
>
> O a. You forgot to install the SCSI controller card's drivers.
>
> O b. You forgot to install the DAT device's drivers.
>
> O c. You forgot to configure the tape device from Backup's
>   Tools menu.
>
> O d. Windows 95 Microsoft Backup does not support SCSI
>   tape devices.

Windows 95 Microsoft Backup does not support SCSI tape devices. Therefore, answer d is correct. The drivers for the SCSI card and the DAT device are not helpful because the device type is not supported. Therefore, answers a and b are incorrect. There is no configuration command in the Tools menu; there is only a Redetect Tape Backup command that has no options. Therefore, answer c is incorrect.

Need To Know More?

 Supporting Microsoft Windows 95. Microsoft Press, Redmond, WA, 1995. ISBN 1-55615-931-5. Chapter 7 contains a detailed discussion of the file systems of Windows 95. Chapter 20 examines the Windows 95 disk utilities.

 Mortensen, Lance and Rick Sawtell: *MCSE: Windows 95 Study Guide.* Sybex Network Press, San Francisco, CA, 1996. ISBN: 0-7821-2092-X. Chapter 8 discusses the Windows 95 file system and disk utilities.

 Search the TechNet CD (or its online version through www. microsoft.com) and the *Windows 95 Resource Kit,* using the keywords "VFAT," "file system," "LFN," "compression," "defragment," "ScanDisk," and "backup."

Applications And Windows 95

8

Terms you'll need to understand:

√ Object Linking and Embedding (OLE)

√ Dynamic Data Exchange (DDE)

√ Non-reentrant

√ Win16Mutex

√ Thunking

√ Program Information File (PIF), DEFAULT.PIF, APPS.INF

√ MS-DOS mode

√ General Protection Fault (GPF)

√ Hung process

Techniques you'll need to master:

√ Working with application types supported by Windows 95: DOS, Win16, and Win32

√ Releasing resources when an application terminates

√ Using the Win16Mutex flag for 16-bit, non-reentrant code

√ Controlling DOS applications through a PIF

√ Working around and recovering from GPFs and hung processes

Windows 95 provides support for many applications. In this chapter, we examine how to implement application support for Windows 95. This discussion includes how Windows 95 handles application requests, how it interoperates with 16-bit applications, how you can control DOS applications, and how to recover from General Protection Faults (GPFs).

Application Support

Windows 95 supports three types of applications:

➤ DOS

➤ Windows 3.x 16-bit

➤ Windows 95 32-bit

To accommodate the needs of each application type, Windows 95 uses a Virtual Machine (VM) architecture. Recall from Chapter 3 that there is a main System VM and a separate VM for each DOS application. Both Win16 and Win32 applications are executed within the System VM. In addition to VM construction, there are two other components of application support: memory and message queues (also discussed in Chapter 3). All Win16 applications share a single address space and message queue. Each Win32 application has its own address space and message queue. Each DOS application has its own address space but does not use a message queue.

Support for these application types includes the ability to cut and paste text and nontext (except DOS) material, by way of OLE and DDE, between one application type and another.

OLE (Object Linking and Embedding) is a Windows process by which one application can include elements from another application, such as an Excel graph in a Word document. An OLE object in one application can be edited or modified by the program that created it simply by double-clicking on the object. *DDE (Dynamic Data Exchange)* is a Windows process by which two or more applications communicate with each other through the interprocess communications system of Windows 95. Two active applications that support DDE can exchange data and commands.

Applications And Resources

Windows 95 supports various program types through the use of VMs. Each VM manages the resources requested by applications that require that VM. When a DOS application terminates, its VM and all resources used by that

VM are returned to the system. Similarly, all Win32 applications return their resources to the system when they exit as part of the shutdown process. However, Win16 applications often share resources with other Win16 applications and can access resources without the operating system being aware of it. Therefore, when a Win16 application is closed, the resources it used may not be returned to the system, unless no other Win16 applications are active.

Even when all applications have exited and all resources have been returned to the system, the system resource level may not return to its original state. This is because Windows 95 uses a resource cache for frequently accessed resources. If the system doesn't require these cached resources, the operating system will clear the cache.

You can check and track resource usage through the Resource Meter (see Figure 8.1). This simple tool is located in Start|Programs|Accessories|System Tools|Resource Meter.

16-Bit System Code

To sustain backward compatibility, Windows 95 includes several portions of 16-bit system code. These are located throughout the system architecture: User, GDI, and Kernel (as mentioned in Chapter 3). Windows 95 also uses 16-bit code when speed and memory resources are critical because it has a smaller footprint than the 32-bit equivalent.

 The 16-bit code segments of Windows 95 are mostly non-reentrant, meaning they are unable to be used by more than a single thread at a time. When a thread uses a non-reentrant segment of code, the Win16Mutex flag is set. This flag indicates to the system that no other thread can make a call to this code segment until the flag has been unset.

To support DOS, Win16, and Win32 applications simultaneously, Windows translates 16-bit calls to 32-bit calls and vice versa. This translation process is called "thunking."

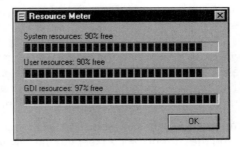

Figure 8.1   The Windows 95 Resource Meter.

DOS Control

Most Windows applications can manage their own environment and thus, co-exist with others because of parameter settings stored in the header of their executable. DOS applications do not have this header information, so they attempt to use all the resources found on the computer and assume that they are the only active application. To enable DOS applications to operate with other DOS and Windows applications, some parameter restrictions must be enforced. This is done through PIFs (Program Information Files). A PIF is essentially a header for DOS applications that defines and restricts their environment (i.e., the DOS VM).

 When a DOS application is launched, Windows 95 checks to see whether the application has a PIF defined for it. If it doesn't, the APPS.INF file is accessed. This file contains a master list of settings for common DOS applications. If the application is listed in the APPS.INF file, the defined settings are used to launch the application for the first time. If the application is not listed in the APPS.INF file, the DEFAULT.PIF file is used to launch the program. The first time a DOS application is launched, a PIF is created that stores the settings and parameters used. Any subsequent launch of the same application will use the settings stored in this PIF to control the program's operational environment.

When you attempt to view PIF file names through Windows Explorer, you will not see any file names with a .PIF extension. Instead, Windows Explorer displays only the first eight characters before the dot and will label the type "Shortcut to MS-DOS Program." However, if you view the directory from a Command Prompt, the .PIF extension will appear.

PIF files are not new to Windows 95 (Windows 3.x used them). However, unlike Windows 3.x, Windows 95 does not have a separate PIF editing utility. Instead, PIFs are edited by right-clicking over an EXE, a COM, or a PIF file and selecting Properties from the context menu. If a PIF file does not exist for a DOS application when you attempt to access its properties, a PIF file will be created. If a PIF file already exists, any changes you make will be stored in the existing PIF file.

 A newly created PIF file always has the same first eight characters as the application it controls, but with the .PIF extension. You can launch the application with the settings defined in a PIF by double-clicking either the original EXE or COM file or the PIF file itself.

You can create multiple PIF setups for a DOS application by renaming the current PIF file (keeping the .PIF extension) and creating a new one by the process described earlier or by simply

> copying the existing PIF and editing it. To use the alternate PIFs, you must double-click the PIF itself; otherwise, launching the EXE or COM file will load the PIF that matches its eight-character namesake.

The settings found on the multiple tabs of the Properties dialog box are detailed in the following sections.

DOS Application Properties: General

The General tab (see Figure 8.2) displays general information about the application being controlled, including:

➤ File type

➤ Location

➤ Size

➤ MS-DOS name

➤ Date created

➤ Date modified

➤ Date last accessed

➤ Attribute settings

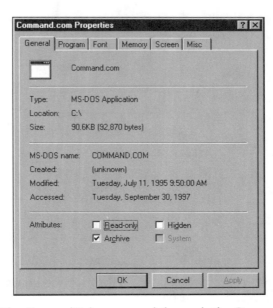

Figure 8.2   The General Tab, accessed through the Properties dialog box for a DOS application.

On this tab, the attributes are the only user-modifiable elements. The four attributes are as follows:

➤ **Read-only** A file can be read but not written to or deleted.

➤ **Archive** This instructs a backup utility whether this file should be backed up.

➤ **Hidden** A file will not be displayed in standard directory listings.

➤ **System** This file is required by the system for proper operation. This attribute is usually not available for change. System files are automatically hidden.

The icon associated with this file is displayed at the top-left corner of this tab.

DOS Application Properties: Program

The Program tab (see Figure 8.3) defines how the application will be launched. The top field box displays the modifiable name of the program or shortcut (PIF).

The options on this tab are as follows:

➤ **Cmd line** Lists the path and file name used to launch the program. Any required command line parameters can be added in this field box.

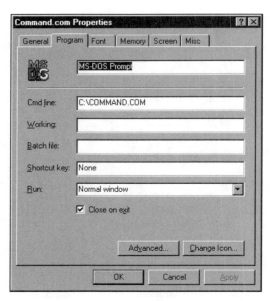

Figure 8.3 The Program tab, accessed through the Properties dialog box for a DOS application.

➤ **Working** Defines the working directory for the application. This can be the same or a different directory than the location of the executable. A DOS pathname or a Universal Naming Convention (UNC) can be used here.

➤ **Batch file** Defines a batch file to be run before launching the application. This can be used to load Terminate and Stay Resident (TSR) applications or to establish special network mappings.

➤ **Shortcut key** Defines a keyboard shortcut to launch the application. If a shortcut is defined, that keystroke combination will be reserved throughout the system, even if that key combination is defined for another purpose.

➤ **Run** Sets the size of the window of the application: normal, minimized, or maximized.

➤ **Close on exit** Instructs the DOS VM to close its interactive window when the application has exited. This needs to be unchecked for some applications that display important data and then exit, such as MEM.

➤ **Change Icon** Changes the icon associated with this application.

The Advanced button brings up the Advanced Program Settings window (see Figure 8.4), where MS-DOS mode is managed. In MS-DOS mode, Windows 95 reboots and enters into a DOS-only configuration to execute a single-demanding DOS application. Once the DOS application exits, Windows 95 automatically reboots. MS-DOS mode may be required by some applications for proper execution.

Figure 8.4 The Advanced Program Settings window.

The Advanced Program Settings window offers the following selections:

➤ **Prevent MS-DOS-based programs from detecting Windows** This selection prevents a DOS program from detecting Windows or, more specifically, the DOS VM in which it operates. Some DOS applications function differently if Windows is detected.

➤ **Suggest MS-DOS mode as necessary** This selection allows Windows to inspect the operation of the DOS application and recommend switching into MS-DOS mode if the application will perform better.

➤ **MS-DOS mode** This selection forces Windows to reboot into MS-DOS mode and reveals the bottom sections of this dialog box, where the parameters of the MS-DOS mode session can be defined.

➤ **Warn before entering MS-DOS mode** This selection displays a warning message before exiting Windows 95 and booting into MS-DOS mode. This warning gives you the opportunity to save and exit other applications.

➤ **Use current MS-DOS configuration** This selection launches MS-DOS mode using the current settings found in the existing AUTOEXEC.BAT and CONFIG.SYS files.

➤ **Specify a new MS-DOS configuration** This selection indicates that custom CONFIG.SYS and AUTOEXEC.BAT files (as defined in the text boxes) should be used to launch the MS-DOS mode.

➤ **Configuration** This button opens the Select MS-DOS Configuration Options dialog box (see Figure 8.5), where you can select the components to add to your custom CONFIG.SYS and AUTOEXEC.BAT files.

DOS Application Properties: Font

The Font tab (see Figure 8.6) is where the font type and size for the DOS application are defined. Because DOS applications are launched within a Windows 95-controlled VM, TrueType fonts are available, as are the standard bitmap fonts normally used by DOS. For convenience, this dialog box also displays a preview of the window size and the font, depending on your selections.

DOS Application Properties: Memory

The Memory tab (see Figure 8.7) is where the memory parameters for the DOS application are defined. All the pull-down selection boxes are set to Auto by default.

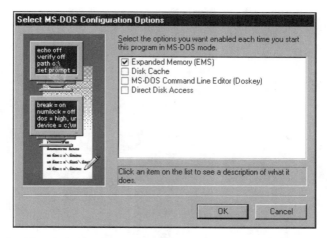

Figure 8.5   The Select MS-DOS Configuration Options dialog box from the Advanced Program Settings window.

The options on this tab are as follows:

➤ **Conventional memory** This selection defines how much conventional memory (640 KB) is used by the application, the size of the initial environment up to 4,096 KB (area used by COMMAND.COM), and memory protection (prevents the VMM from swapping this section of RAM).

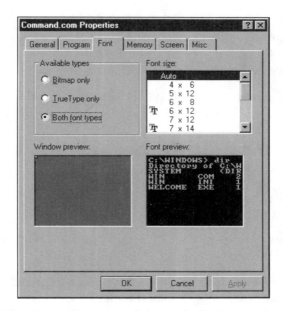

Figure 8.6   The Font tab, accessed through the Properties dialog box for a DOS application.

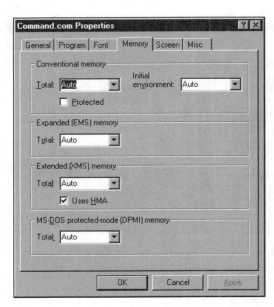

Figure 8.7 The Memory tab, accessed through the Properties dialog box for a DOS application.

➤ **Expanded (EMS) memory** This selection sets the amount of EMS memory for the application (up to 16 MB).

➤ **Extended (XMS) memory** This selection sets the amount of XMS memory for the application (up to 16 MB). There is also a checkbox to use HMA (High Memory Area). HMA is the first 64 K of high memory located just above the 640 K of conventional memory.

➤ **MS-DOS protected-mode (DPMI) memory** This selection sets the amount of DPMI memory for the application (up to 16 MB).

DOS Application Properties: Screen

The Screen tab (see Figure 8.8) is where the screen properties of the DOS application can be set.

The options on this tab are as follows:

➤ **Usage** Sets the display area to full screen, standard window, or a window with a specific number of text lines.

➤ **Window** Places display window options on a toolbar and restores all changes made to the display area after the DOS application exits.

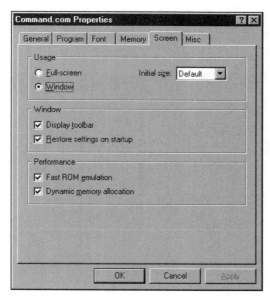

Figure 8.8   The Screen tab, accessed through the Properties dialog box for a DOS application.

➤ **Performance** Defines the performance parameters of the video driver for the DOS application. The parameters are fast ROM emulation and dynamic memory allocation.

DOS Application Properties: Misc

The Misc tab (see Figure 8.9) is where the remaining options and settings for DOS application control are located.

The options for this tab are as follows:

➤ **Allow screen saver** When selected, Windows 95 can switch to a screen saver, even when the DOS application is in the foreground.

➤ **Mouse** When selected, QuickEdit enables the mouse to select text within a DOS window. When selected, Exclusive mode restricts the mouse within the DOS window.

➤ **Always suspend** When selected, DOS applications are paused when minimized or in the background (i.e., not the foreground-active application).

➤ **Warn if still active** When selected, Windows 95 displays a warning if you attempt to close a DOS display window when the DOS application is still active. This enables you to exit the DOS application gracefully.

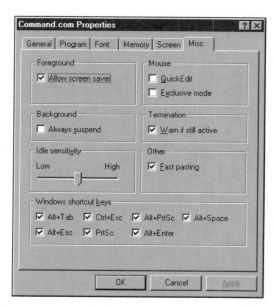

Figure 8.9   The Misc tab, accessed through the Properties dialog box for a DOS application.

➤ **Idle sensitivity** This sets the length of time before Windows 95 suspends a suspected inactive application (i.e., one that is waiting for user input or using the math coprocessor).

➤ **Fast pasting** When selected, this enables pasting into DOS from the Windows 95 clipboard buffer.

➤ **Windows shortcut keys** These key combinations are commonly used by Windows 95. When a keystroke is checked, the pressing of those keys will be passed to Windows 95, even if the DOS application is in the foreground. All the keystrokes are passed to Windows 95 by default (i.e., the box is checked).

GPFs

Windows 95 supports a variety of application types and has an architecture that adequately provides for resource access. However, applications, especially poorly written ones, still crash. These crashes are called General Protection Faults (GPFs).

 A GPF occurs when a process attempts to violate the integrity of the system, such as accessing the Ring 0 system components directly or attempting to access memory outside its assigned address space. A GPF is evidence that the system was able to detect and stop the application committing the violation.

When a DOS application causes a GPF, only that application is affected. Remember, each DOS application is launched within its own VM. When the GPF warning message appears, clicking OK terminates the application and the VM; clicking the Details button displays the stack dump. The information from the stack dump is generally useful only to the person who wrote the program or to a professional technician.

When a Win16 application causes a GPF, two GPF warning messages appear. The first is from Windows 3.x, and the second is from Windows 95 itself. All other Win16 applications are halted until the error is cleared. Usually, other Win16 applications continue to operate normally once the GPF is over; however, it is not uncommon for a GPFed Win16 application to prevent all others from continuing to operate normally.

When a Win32 application causes a GPF, only that application is affected. The isolation of the address space for each Win32 application protects it from all other active Win32 applications. Clicking OK on the GPF warning message terminates the failed application.

A device driver can also cause a GPF. When this occurs, the device accessing the driver is often no longer accessible or the entire operating system is unusable. If a device driver GPF occurs, it is highly recommended to reboot the system to attempt to restore the operating system to proper working order. The suspect device driver should then be inspected for corruption and replaced if necessary.

Hung Processes

A hung process is a program that has stopped responding to the system. Hung processes can occur for a variety of reasons, including:

➤ Inability to access the message queue

➤ A GPF that has not been cleared

➤ Inability to access a required resource

If a critical resource or code segment hangs, other programs or the entire system may stop responding as well. Usually, a hung process is cleared by terminating it (through the CTRL+ALT+DELETE key combination).

 Terminating a hung process can be attempted by pressing the keystroke combination for local restart (CTRL+ALT+DELETE). This causes Windows 95 to bring up the Close Program dialog box. This dialog box displays all active applications and offers the ability to end a task or shut down the system. Simply select a program listed and click End Task. DOS, Win16, and Win32 hung processes can be cleared through this method. In some cases, a warning message appears, stating that the application is not responding and asking you to verify the termination of the process.

Exam Prep Questions

Question 1

> Which application types are supported by Windows 95? [Check all correct answers]
>
> ❏ a. DOS
>
> ❏ b. Win16
>
> ❏ c. OS/2
>
> ❏ d. Win32
>
> ❏ e. POSIX

Windows 95 supports DOS, Win16, and Win32 applications. Therefore, answers a, b, and d are correct. Of the Microsoft product line, only Windows NT supports OS/2 and POSIX applications. Therefore, answers c and e are incorrect.

Question 2

> Which of the following application types release their resources when they exit, even if other applications of the same type are still active? [Check all correct answers]
>
> ❏ a. DOS
>
> ❏ b. Win16
>
> ❏ c. Win32

DOS and Win32 applications release resources when they exit, even if other applications of the same type are still active. Therefore, answers a and c are correct. Win16 applications release their resources only if no other Win16 applications are active. Therefore, answer b is incorrect.

Question 3

> Which process protects non-reentrant code so that only one ap-
> plication can use it at a time?
>
> ○ a. Thunking
> ○ b. Memory swapping
> ○ c. Setting the Win16Mutex flag
> ○ d. Ring 0 protection

Windows 95 protects 16-bit non-reentrant code from being used by more than
one application at a time by setting the Win16Mutex flag. Therefore, answer c
is correct. Thunking is the process of translating a system call between 16-bit
and 32-bit. Therefore, answer a is incorrect. Memory swapping and Ring 0
protection do not prevent non-reentrant code from being used by more than
one application at a time. Therefore, answers b and d are incorrect.

Question 4

> If a DOS application does not have a PIF specifically defined for it,
> what other files may be accessed to obtain startup parameters?
> [Check all correct answers]
>
> ❑ a. WIN386.SYS
> ❑ b. DEFAULT.PIF
> ❑ c. DOS.SYS
> ❑ d. APPS.INF

The system will consult APPS.INF to see whether the program is listed. If it is
not listed, the system will use DEFAULT.PIF. Therefore, answers b and d are
correct. The WIN386.SYS and DOS.SYS files are fictitious. Therefore, answers a and c are incorrect.

Question 5

How can you launch the same DOS application with two different environment configurations?

○ a. Edit the PIF to match the needed settings before launching the application each time.

○ b. Use the PIF editor to create a menu to select the launch type each time you access the application.

○ c. Create a PIF, make a copy of the PIF, and change the settings of the second PIF.

○ d. Windows 95 does not allow this type of configuration.

A single DOS application can be launched with different environment settings by creating a PIF, making a copy of the PIF, then changing the settings of the second PIF. Therefore, answer c is correct. Editing the PIF each time is very tedious and does provide two separate launch points. Therefore, answer a is incorrect. Windows 95 does not have a PIF editor, and a pop-up menu cannot be created with a PIF anyway. Therefore, answer b is incorrect. Windows 95 does allow multiple PIFs for the same application. Therefore, answer d is incorrect.

Question 6

Which tab of the Properties dialog box can be used to run a batch file before the DOS application itself is launched?

○ a. General

○ b. Program

○ c. Memory

○ d. Startup

The Program tab has the Batch File field area, where a batch file can be defined that is to be run before the DOS application is launched. Therefore, answer b is correct. The General and Memory tabs do not offer batch file options. Therefore, answers a and c are incorrect. The Properties dialog box does not have a Startup tab. Therefore, answer d is incorrect.

Question 7

> Which component or feature of Windows 95 enables DOS appli-
> cations to run if they are unable to function within a DOS VM?
>
> ○ a. Virtual Memory
>
> ○ b. MS-DOS mode
>
> ○ c. Ring 0 Protected Mode
>
> ○ d. Message queues

MS-DOS mode is the feature of Windows 95 that allows DOS applications
to be run even if they cannot function within a DOS VM. Therefore, answer b
is correct. Virtual Memory, Ring 0 Protected Mode, and message queues have
nothing to do with the ability of a DOS application to execute. Therefore,
answers a, c, and d are incorrect.

Question 8

> The Memory tab of the Properties dialog box for a DOS applica-
> tion enables you to configure or set the parameters for which types
> of memory? [Check all correct answers]
>
> ❑ a. Conventional
>
> ❑ b. XMS
>
> ❑ c. Virtual
>
> ❑ d. DMPI

The Memory tab enables you to set conventional, XMS, and DMPI memory
(plus EMS, not mentioned in this question). Therefore, answers a, b, and d are
correct. Virtual memory is controlled by the Virtual Memory Manager, not
the DOS properties dialog box. Therefore, answer c is incorrect.

Question 9

If the DEFAULT.PIF is used to launch a DOS application, what happens when you press CTRL+ALT+DEL?

- ○ a. The computer reboots.
- ○ b. The application terminates.
- ○ c. The Close Program dialog box appears.
- ○ d. Nothing.

When CTRL+ALT+DEL is pressed while a DOS application is in the foreground (which was launched using DEFAULT.PIF), the keystroke is passed to Windows 95, thus bringing up the Close Program dialog box. Therefore, answer c is correct. The computer would reboot if the DOS application were launched into MS-DOS mode. Therefore, answer a is incorrect. The application would not terminate with the CTRL+ALT+DEL keystroke. Selecting the application in the dialog box and clicking End Task is required to terminate the application. Therefore, answer b is incorrect. As already stated, the Close Program dialog box appears instead of nothing. Therefore, answer d is incorrect.

Question 10

If several Win16 applications are active and one of them GPFs, what occurs? [Check all correct answers]

- ❏ a. All the Win16 applications are paused until the GPF is cleared.
- ❏ b. The remaining Win16 applications should return to normal operation once the GPF is cleared.
- ❏ c. The entire system is corrupted, forcing a hard reboot.
- ❏ d. Win32 applications are paused if the Win16 applications are accessing a needed resource.

All the Win16 applications are paused until the GPF is cleared, the remaining Win16 applications should return to normal operation once the GPF is cleared, and Win32 applications are paused if the Win16 applications are accessing a needed resource. Therefore, answers a, b, and d are correct. A Win16 GPF rarely causes a complete system crash, which usually occurs only with device-driver GPFs. Therefore, answer c is incorrect.

Need To Know More?

 Supporting Microsoft Windows 95. Microsoft Press, Redmond, WA, 1995. ISBN 1-55615-931-5. Chapter 16 discusses application compatibility, GPFs, hung processes, and 16-bit system code. Chapter 17 details DOS PIF settings and controls.

 Mortensen, Lance and Rick Sawtell: *MCSE: Windows 95 Study Guide*. Sybex Network Press, San Francisco, CA, 1996. ISBN: 0-7821-2092-X. Chapter 7 contains material on GPFs, hung applications, resource usage, and editing PIFs for DOS applications.

 Search the TechNet CD (or its online version through www. microsoft.com) and the *Windows 95 Resource Kit*, using the keywords "DOS," "16-bit," "32-bit," "OLE," "DDE," "mutex," "PIF," and "GPF."

Networking
And
Windows 95

Terms you'll need to understand:

- √ Interprocess communication (IPC)
- √ Redirector
- √ Service
- √ NDIS (3.x and 2) and ODI
- √ Universal naming convention (UNC)
- √ Workgroup
- √ Domain
- √ Network Neighborhood
- √ TCP/IP, IPX/SPX-compatible protocol (NWLink), NetBEUI, DLC, NetBIOS
- √ Binding
- √ Browsing, Master Browser
- √ Browser election
- √ Frame type
- √ Service Advertising Protocol (SAP)

Techniques you'll need to master:

- √ Understanding the functions of redirectors and services
- √ Knowing the basics of supported NIC device drivers: NDIS (3.x and 2) and ODI
- √ Locating resources on a network using UNC names
- √ Understanding the differences between workgroups and domains
- √ Understanding when to apply supported protocols (TCP/IP, IPX/SPX, NetBEUI, DLC, and NetBIOS)
- √ Configuring network connections for Microsoft and NetWare networks
- √ Serving and accessing resources; creating and accessing shares
- √ Troubleshooting network connections
- √ Enabling remote administration

Unlike earlier Windows 3.x operating systems, Windows 95 was designed for networking. Microsoft built in several special components and features to make connecting Windows 95 to a network quick and easy. This chapter covers Windows 95 basics related to Microsoft NT and NetWare servers and several other important networking topics.

Networking Overview

Windows 95 was designed to connect to most existing networks or to be used to establish a peer-to-peer network on its own. To establish network compatibility, Windows 95 was constructed to support five key industry-standard network interfaces:

➤ **Windows Sockets** A transport-independent interface that is most often used to enable communication over TCP/IP links (RAS or network)

➤ **NetBIOS** A protocol that provides backward compatibility between redirectors and the transport protocol of a network

➤ **DCE-compliant RPC** A secure method of communication between clients and servers

➤ **Client-side named pipes** A communications mechanism for backward compatibility with LAN Manager (server-side named pipes are not supported)

➤ **Mailslots** A communications mechanism for backward compatibility with LAN Manager

In addition to these interprocess communication (IPC) mechanisms, Windows 95 boasts support for multiple protocols, multiple redirectors, and the Universal Naming Convention (UNC). These features enable Windows 95 to participate in several networks, such as:

➤ Banyan Vines 5.52 and later

➤ FTP Software NFS Client (InterDrive-95) DEC PATHWORKS version 4.1 and later

➤ Microsoft LAN Manager, Windows for Workgroups 3.x, and Windows NT

➤ Novell NetWare version 3.11 and later

➤ SunSoft PC-NFS version 5.0 and later

But even all this fails to encompass all the added features that enable Windows 95's robust and versatile network support. Other features include:

➤ GUI networking interfaces, controls, and configurations

➤ Automated networking setup

➤ LFN support for network resources, assuming that server supports it

➤ Automatic reestablishment of lost connections

➤ Multiple simultaneous network connections

➤ Conventional memory not used for networking components

➤ Plug and Play networking configuration

➤ Resource sharing between Protected Mode network clients and peers

➤ Control of remote access through Dial-Up Networking

➤ Single logon, script processing, and resource browsing

➤ Win32 WinNet interface support

Most of the books and reference materials that attempt to explain the Windows 95 networking system start with the OSI model of networking. Although such materials may be useful for network professionals and programmers, they contain complex and confusing terminology of behind-the-scenes operations (from the user's point of view). This terminology is typically not important and is irrelevant to productive use of Windows 95; thus, we focus only on issues relevant to your understanding and operation of networking.

Redirectors And Services

A redirector is a networking software component that acts as a traffic director for resource requests. Each time a user or application requests a resource, a redirector intercepts the request. The redirector inspects the request to determine whether the resource is local or found elsewhere on the network. Local requests are sent to the CPU for processing, whereas network requests are forwarded to the appropriate resource host. Redirectors perform this function for any type of resource request, from printing and file retrieval to security authentication. A redirector hides the complex process of retrieving a resource from the user, who is often unaware that the resource is located on the far side of the network instead of locally, because the actions required by a user to access either type of resource are the same.

A service is a fairly nebulous but important concept. A service is any activity or resource a computer can host for use by it or other computers on the network. A service can be an encryption protocol, a network application, a print server, a file server, remote network monitoring, remote Registry editing, or any number of information servers. Windows 95 ships with several installable services in addition to those installed automatically, and many third-party vendors offer services you can add to your system.

NIC Device Drivers

Windows 95 supports both NDIS (3.x and 2) and ODI network adapter drivers. NDIS is an industry-standard specification for how protocols and adapters should be bound. NDIS 2.0 drivers are Real Mode drivers, whereas NDIS 3.x drivers are Protected Mode drivers and support Plug and Play. ODI is a specification developed by Novell and is similar to NDIS 2.0. Both NDIS and ODI device drivers enable multiple protocols to be bound to multiple adapters.

A single instance of an NDIS 3.x driver can support up to eight adapters, whereas a separate NDIS 2.0 driver must be loaded for each adapter.

Universal Naming Convention

UNC is a method of addressing or locating resources on a network. A UNC name is constructed in the following manner:

*servername**sharename**path*

Therefore, the proper syntax is a double backslash, the name of the server, a single backslash, the share name, and then (if necessary) another single backslash and a path statement. The path can include several subdirectories and a file name. The server name used in UNCs is limited to 15 characters. The share name is usually also limited to 15 characters, but this ultimately depends on the network. UNC names can be used in place of the standard DOS pathnames (i.e., <drive>:\directory\ file name).

Windows 95 clients must have a unique computer name consisting of up to 15 characters. User names need not be unique within a Windows 95 network, but all users with the same name will receive any messages sent to that account. Therefore, it is always a good idea to make all names within a network unique (even if the network is a temporary peer-to-peer one).

Workgroup Vs. Domain

Windows 95 can participate in either a workgroup or a domain, but not in both simultaneously. A workgroup is a network of computers in which no single computer has any greater control or advantage over any other computer. Workgroups typically have the following characteristics:

➤ There are fewer than 10 computers.

➤ Each computer has full control of its local resources and requires a local administrator.

➤ There is no centralized control or security over the network as a whole.

➤ All computers must reside on a single subnet (even if TCP/IP or IPX/SPX is used).

A domain is a network of computers in which one or more computers maintain a security scheme and information services (known as servers) used by the other computers (known as clients). A domain typically has the following characteristics:

➤ Control and security are centralized over the network as a whole.

➤ A single administrator can maintain a moderate-sized network.

➤ Dedicated computers are required to host the security database and information servers.

➤ More administrative overhead must be maintained (e.g., user accounts, groups, and access permissions).

➤ Domains typically are more expensive than workgroups because of high-end computers and server software.

Network Neighborhood

Network Neighborhood is an integrated browser interface that can look at, locate, and use network resources just as if they were extensions of the local file system. Network Neighborhood (see Figure 9.1) can be accessed through its namesake icon on the desktop or through Windows NT Explorer. All NT Explorer controls and features are available through Network Neighborhood.

Supported Protocols

Windows 95 has native support for several protocols, including:

➤ **TCP/IP** This protocol is the most widely used protocol in the world, mainly because it is used on the Internet. TCP/IP is robust, reliable, and based on open standards. This protocol should be installed for Internet

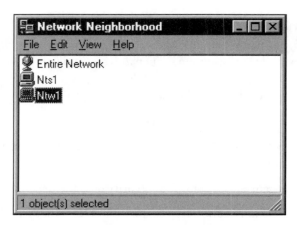

Figure 9.1 Network Neighborhood from Windows 95.

access. It can be used on small networks but, because of its overhead and system requirements, is more often reserved for larger networks. TCP/IP supports routing.

➤ **IPX/SPX** This protocol is a Novell IPX/SPX-compatible protocol, usually called NWLink. On an NT network, NWLink is good for small- and medium-sized networks, especially those requiring access to NetWare servers. NWLink supports routing.

➤ **NetBEUI** This protocol is a limited protocol that cannot be routed. It is small and fast but cannot be used on medium or large networks because it is limited to 254 nodes.

➤ **DLC** This is a protocol used in conjunction with TCP/IP, NWLink, or NetBEUI to access mainframes or network-attached printers.

➤ **NetBIOS** This is not an actual protocol. It is a communications interface between protocols and applications. Most of Microsoft's networking mechanisms use NetBIOS as a basis for communication.

During the initial installation of Windows 95, NetBEUI and IPX/SPX will be installed by default when a network adapter is present.

Network Configuration

The process of configuring Windows 95 to participate in a network involves several steps (see Figure 9.2), including:

➤ Licensing

➤ Network adapter installation

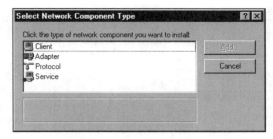

Figure 9.2   The Select Network Component Type dialog box of Windows 95.

➤ Protocol installation

➤ Service installation

➤ Client installation

Licensing

The basic issue of licensing involves determining which client access license type your network uses. Two schemes are used: per server and per seat. Per server enables a specific number of simultaneous client connections to a single specific server. Per seat enables a single specific client to connect to any server on the network. It is important to know the license scheme in use so that you don't violate your legal use of the operating systems involved in your network.

Network Adapter Installation

Installing a network adapter is accomplished in one of three ways (see Figure 9.3):

➤ Through Auto Detect during the initial installation of Windows 95 or a regular bootup

➤ Through Add New Hardware searching

➤ Through the Network applet in the Control Panel. Click Add, select Adapter, and then click Add again

Any one of these methods is sufficient. However, if you are adding a device unknown to Windows 95 or have an updated driver, using the Network applet is the most streamlined process (e.g., using the Have Disk option).

Once the drivers for an NIC are installed, you can access the configuration controls through the Network applet by selecting the NIC and clicking Properties. This should bring up a dialog box that offers you the ability to modify any Plug and Play or BIOS-controlled settings (usually IRQ, I/O port, and

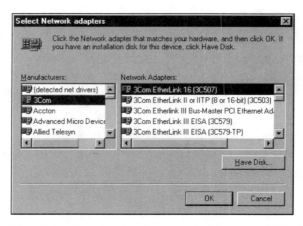

Figure 9.3 The Select Network adapters dialog box of Windows 95.

memory address). It is always a good idea to check that the settings known to Windows 95 reflect what you expected when you installed the device.

Protocol Installation

Protocol installation is performed through the Network applet of the Control Panel (see Figure 9.4). Click Add, select Protocol, and then click Add again. To install one of the native Microsoft protocols, select the Microsoft entry under Manufacturers and the appropriate protocol from the list of protocols. If configuration is required for the selected protocol, the appropriate dialog boxes will appear.

NetBEUI requires no additional configuration.

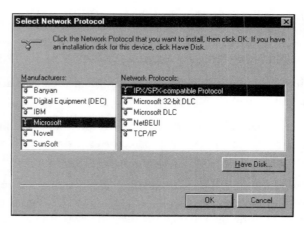

Figure 9.4 The Select Network Protocol dialog box of Windows 95.

IPX/SPX-compatible protocol (NWLink) configuration is discussed in the section "Windows 95 and NetWare Networks" later in this chapter.

TCP/IP configuration is detailed in Chapter 10.

DLC is discussed in Chapter 12.

Service Installation

Service installation is as simple as protocol and NIC installation. Simply use the Network applet, click Add, select Services, and then click Add again. Select the manufacturer and the service to install and click OK, or click Have Disk to install a third-party service (see Figure 9.5). Details on the File and Print Sharing services from Microsoft are discussed in the section "Windows 95 and NetWare Networks" later in this chapter.

Client Installation

Client services are also installed through the Network applet (see Figure 9.6). Click Add, select Client, and then click Add again. Select the manufacturer and the client to install and click OK, or click Have Disk to install a third-party client. Details on the Client for Microsoft Networks and the Client for NetWare Networks are discussed later in this chapter.

Binding

Binding is the process that links network components from various levels of the network architecture to enable communication between those components. In Windows 95 networking, each protocol, adapter, and service may offer a Bindings tab on the Properties dialog box to allow you to modify or change its

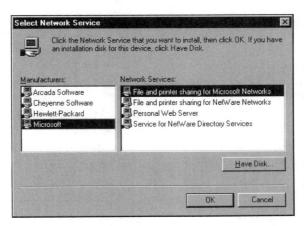

Figure 9.5   The Select Network Service dialog box of Windows 95.

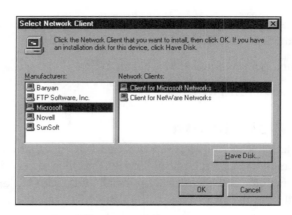

Figure 9.6 The Select Network Client dialog box of Windows 95.

binding orders and pairings. By default, Windows 95 enables all possible bindings among services, protocols, and adapters.

Binding should be ordered to enhance the system's use of the network. For example, if your network has both TCP/IP and NetBEUI installed (most network devices use TCP/IP), bindings should be set to bind TCP/IP first and NetBEUI second. In other words, the most frequently used protocol (or other network component) should be bound first. This speeds network connections.

Windows 95 As A Server

Windows 95 can participate in two types of networks: peer-to-peer and client/server. In either case, Windows 95 can act as a server in that it can host resources or an information service used by other computers on the network. File and Print Sharing is the most common service hosting performed by Windows 95. Installing this service for the appropriate network type (Microsoft or NetWare) allows locally attached files and storage devices to be served to the network. Unfortunately, Windows 95 is limited to acting as a server to only one network type at a time.

File and Print Sharing for Microsoft Networks and File and Print Sharing for NetWare Networks are installed and configured through the Network applet of the Control Panel. Click the Add button, select Service, and then select the appropriate service. Once installed, the configuration options accessed through the File and Print Sharing button on the Network applet can be used to turn on and off file sharing and print sharing by means of two checkboxes (see Figure 9.7).

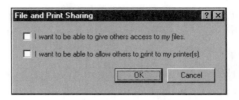

Figure 9.7   The File and Print Sharing dialog box of Windows 95.

Windows 95 As A Client

Once the appropriate NIC drivers, protocols, services, and clients are installed, you need to configure or verify the configuration of Windows 95 as a client. This involves the three tabs of the Network applet of the Control Panel: Configuration, Identification, and Access Control. You need to install and configure the Client service for the appropriate network type (Client for Microsoft Networks or Client for NetWare Networks). The procedures for this are discussed later in this chapter. Once installed, the remaining configurations required to join a network can be set.

On the Configuration tab, the pull-down box of the Primary Network Logon should be set to the appropriate logon type (see Figure 9.8):

➤ **Windows logon** To log in to only the local machine

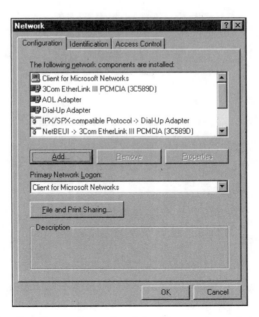

Figure 9.8   The Configuration tab of the Network applet of Windows 95.

➤ **Client for Microsoft Networks** To log in to a Microsoft domain or workgroup (this option is present only if the Client for Microsoft Networks service is installed)

➤ **Client for NetWare Networks** To log in to a NetWare domain (this option is present only if the Client for NetWare Networks service is installed)

➤ **Other clients** To log in to any other network type that is installed, e.g., Banyan Vines (this option is present only if the client service from the third-party vendor is installed)

On the Identification tab, you can change or set the following (see Figure 9.9):

➤ **Computer name** Up to 15 characters long (no spaces), unique to the network.

➤ **Workgroup** The name of the workgroup or the domain that will participate, up to 15 characters long. If you provide the name of an existing workgroup or domain to which you are currently cabled, this computer will attempt to join the domain on the next reboot.

➤ **Computer Description** A short blurb about this computer.

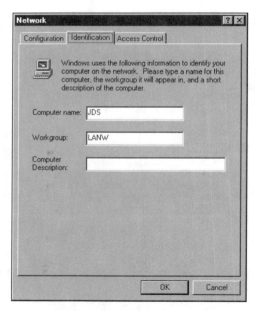

Figure 9.9 The Identification tab of the Network applet of Windows 95.

On the Access Control tab, you set the security model used to control access to local resources (see Figure 9.10):

➤ **Share-level access control** Access is controlled on a share-by-share basis, and each share is assigned a password through which a user can access the resource. Specific users cannot be blocked. This is the default selection, but it can only be used on systems in a peer-to-peer network or on a stand-alone machine.

➤ **User-level access control** Access is controlled by user authentication through a security scheme from an existing client/server network (such as Windows NT or NetWare). Individuals or groups can be granted or denied access. This selection requires you to provide the name of an existing domain/security controller or of an attached domain where a domain/security controller resides.

A valid user account (and sometimes a computer account) is required to join a domain. Be sure to create the required accounts on the domain before attempting to join the domain using a Windows 95 computer.

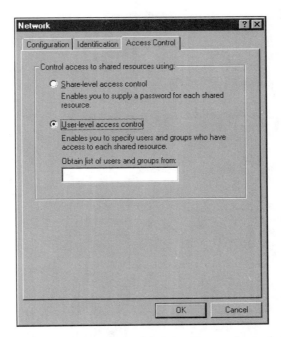

Figure 9.10 The Access Control tab of the Network applet of Windows 95.

Network Folders

Sharing a folder or accessing a share is easy with Windows 95, regardless of the type of network it is on. Sharing a folder, or even an entire drive, is accomplished by following these steps:

1. Open My Computer or Windows Explorer.

2. Scroll down to select (highlight) the drive or folder you wish to share.

3. Select File|Sharing from the menu bar or right-click and select Sharing from the pop-up menu. (Windows Explorer requires the highlighted entity to be in the right pane to access the Sharing command from the File menu.)

4. Select the Share As radio button.

5. Provide a name for the share, up to 15 characters (eight characters or fewer are required for non-LFN, or DOS, clients to access).

6. Provide a comment, if desired.

7. If share-level access is in use, define a password (see Figure 9.11).

8. If user-level access is in use, add users or groups and define their access levels (see Figure 9.12).

9. Click OK to close and save.

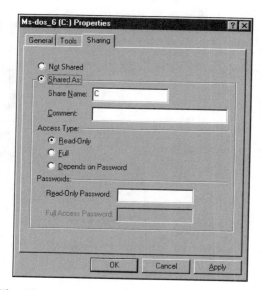

Figure 9.11 The Sharing tab with share-level security of a folder of Windows 95.

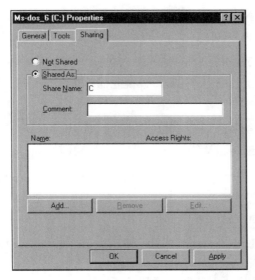

Figure 9.12   The Sharing tab with user-level security of a folder of Windows 95.

Now, this share is available to anyone on the network who has the proper access (based on security type).

To access a share, you can either work through the Network Neighborhood manually or map a drive for easy access from any application. To map a drive, you can use either Network Neighborhood or Windows Explorer.

Use the following steps to access a share with Network Neighborhood:

1. Open Network Neighborhood.

2. Scroll down to select (highlight) the share you wish to map.

3. Right-click and select Map Network Drive from the pop-up menu.

4. In the Map Network Drive dialog box, select a local drive letter from the pull-down box.

5. If required, type in a user account name to access the share.

6. Click OK. The share will now appear as a drive letter in all storage device browse lists.

Use the following steps to map a network drive with Windows Explorer:

1. Open Windows Explorer.

2. Select Tools|Map Network Drive from the menu bar.

3. In the Map Network Drive dialog box, select a local drive letter from the pull-down box.

4. If required, type in a user account name to access the share.

5. Click OK. The share will now appear as a drive letter in all storage device browse lists.

Use the following steps to disconnect a mapped drive:

1. Locate the drive in Windows Explorer or My Computer.

2. Right-click over the mapped drive and select Disconnect from the pop-up menu.

3. If asked, confirm the disconnect.

To discontinue sharing, return to the Sharing tab and select Do Not Share.

Network Printers

Working with network printers is similar to working with drive shares. Sharing a local printer can be accomplished in two ways: by selecting to share the printer during the installation (see Chapter 12) or through the Printers folder after a local printer is installed. The following steps are required to share an existing printer:

1. Open the Printers folder (Start|Settings|Printers).

2. Right-click over the printer to share and select Sharing from the pop-up box.

3. Select the Share As radio button.

4. Provide a name of up to 15 characters for the share (eight characters or fewer are required for non-LFN, or DOS, clients).

5. Provide a comment, if desired.

6. If share-level access is in use, define a password (see Figure 9.13).

7. If user-level access is in use, add users or groups and define their access levels (see Figure 9.14).

8. Click OK to close and save.

This printer is now available for other users on the network.

To access a network printer, you can map a printer locally by using the Add Printer Wizard from the Printers folder. Select network printer instead of local printer, locate the network printer to attach to, and then define a name to use locally. That's it. Now, all your applications can print to the network printer.

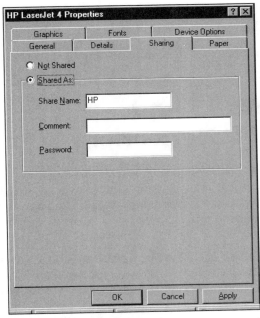

Figure 9.13   The Sharing tab with share-level security of a printer of Windows 95.

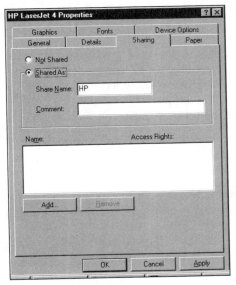

Figure 9.14   The Sharing tab with user-level security of a printer of Windows 95.

To disconnect from a network printer, simply delete the logical printer from the Printers folder.

To discontinue sharing of a local printer, return to the Sharing tab and select Do Not Share.

Windows 95 And Microsoft Networks

Connecting Windows 95 to a Microsoft network is amazingly simple and streamlined. In fact, once you set up Windows 95 for network access, everything else falls into place. To establish a connection to a Microsoft network, the following settings must be made:

➤ **Install Client for Microsoft Networks** This service is installed from the Network applet. Click Add, select Client, and then click Add again. Select Microsoft in the Manufacturers list and Client for Microsoft Network in the Network Clients list. Once the service is installed, select it in the installed component list of the Network applet and click Properties (Figure 9.15). If the network is a domain, select the Log on to a Windows NT domain checkbox, provide the domain name, and then set the logon options (Quick logon or Logon and restore connections).

➤ **Install the protocol used by the network** For details on configuring IPX/SPX, see the section "Windows 95 and NetWare Networks." For details on TCP/IP, see Chapter 10. NetBEUI requires no configuration. Other protocols, especially third-party protocols, may require special configuration.

➤ **Set the Primary Network Logon** Set the Primary Network Logon pull-down list on the Network applet to Client for Microsoft Networks.

➤ **Share resources** If you want to share resources with the network, install the File and Print Sharing for Microsoft Networks service, press the File and Print Sharing button, and then select the type(s) of resources to share (printers and/or storage devices).

Once these settings are made and the computer is rebooted, you will have access to the Microsoft network's resources.

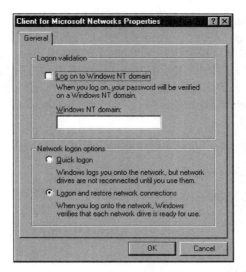

Figure 9.15   The Client for Microsoft Networks Properties applet of Windows 95.

Logon Scripts

When connected to a domain-based Microsoft network, logon scripts can be used to establish drive mappings, launch applications, or set environmental variables. Logon scripts require that a home directory be created for each user on a server within the domain. A home directory is typically where user profiles, logon scripts, and personal data files are stored. A user often has full exclusive control over the home directory to maintain privacy. Once a logon script is created and stored in a user's home directory, the user account hosted on the domain controller must be edited to include the path to the script, so it will be run each time the user logs in to the domain.

Browsing

Windows uses a service called Network Browsing that maintains a list of available resources. This list is consulted each time a dialog box needs to display printers, folders, shares, or any other type of network resource. Every computer within a domain participates in the Browser service. Each time a computer is brought up, it announces itself and the resources it has to share (if any). This is the most common level of participation for computers within a network. The most important role within the Browser service is that of the Master Browser, which maintains the main list of all available resources.

Two other important roles are the Backup Browser and the Potential Browser. The Backup Browser maintains a duplicate list of the resources and acts within the Browser service much the way the BDC does within domain control. The Backup Browser can serve lists of resources to clients. A Potential Browser is any machine capable of becoming a Backup or Master Browser. As needed, the Browser service changes the role of a machine from Potential Browser to Backup Browser. Within any domain, the Browser service attempts to maintain the maximum of three Backup Browsers, but any number of Potential Browsers can exist.

Only the following computer setups can serve as Potential Browsers:

➤ NT Server 3.5 or higher

➤ NT Advanced Server 3.1

➤ NT Workstation 3.1 or higher

➤ Windows 95

➤ Windows for Workgroups 3.11

Any of these computers can also be set up as non-Browsers so that they will not participate in supporting the Browser lists, except to announce themselves on bootup. A Windows 95 computer's participation in the Browser service is controlled through the Properties dialog box of File and Print Sharing for Microsoft Networks. The Browser Master can be set to:

➤ **Automatic** The default. The computer can be elected as a Master Browser if needed.

➤ **Enabled** The computer will always attempt to be a Master Browser.

➤ **Disabled** The computer will not attempt to be a Master Browser.

The second property of LM Announce determines whether a special announcement packet is sent to LAN Manager 2.x clients. The default is No.

Browser Election

When a Master Browser goes offline or when another machine that has the ability to claim the role of Master Browser comes online, an election occurs. The results of the election determine which machine becomes the active Master Browser. Once the Master Browser is no longer detected, an election packet is transmitted by the new computer or by a Backup Browser. This packet travels to each Potential Browser. The winner of the election is determined by the following hierarchy of criteria (presented in order of priority):

➤ **Operating system** NT Server, NT Workstation, Windows 95, Windows for Workgroups

➤ **Operating system version** NT 4.0, 3.51, 3.5, 95, 3.11, 3.1

➤ **Current Browser role** Master Browser, Backup Browser, Potential Browser

➤ **Alphabetical order** Further election is resolved through the alphabetical order of the computer names

When a computer comes online, it announces itself, initially once a minute, but increasing to once every 12 minutes. This repeated announcement is used by the Master Browser to determine whether a resource is still available. The Master Browser maintains the list of resources for any machine for three missed announcements to accommodate performance dips and communication bottlenecks. When a machine goes offline after having been up and running for a reasonable time, its resources can remain in the Master Browser's list for up to 36 minutes.

Backup Browsers poll the Master Browser every 15 minutes to request an updated version of the browse list. Therefore, a failed resource can remain in the Backup Browser's list for up to 15 minutes. If a Backup Browser requests an update from the Master Browser and receives no response, it initiates an election.

Connection Troubleshooting

The first step in troubleshooting is to locate or isolate the problem. This section lists several problems, causes, and solutions that you may encounter when using Windows 95 as a client of a Microsoft network.

➤ If any change was made (e.g., a new driver or hardware was added) and the network no longer functions, repeal the last change.

➤ If any component has been moved or bumped, check the cables, connectors, and terminators.

➤ If domain validation fails, check the client type and the Primary Network Logon selections.

➤ If domain validation fails, check the General tab of the Client for Microsoft Networks Properties applet to verify that logon validation is enabled and that the correct domain or server name is listed.

➤ If domain validation fails, double-check that the user account is still active.

➤ If domain validation fails, check the Identification tab of the Network applet to verify that the correct computer and domain/workgroup name are listed.

➤ If Network Neighborhood fails to display any resources, check the physical connection to the network and your domain validation.

➤ If Network Neighborhood displays only some resources, check to see that all systems are online and properly connected.

➤ If a resource is not accessible, check that it is shared properly and that its access permissions are correct.

➤ If network connection fails, check the NIC hardware settings, driver, and bindings.

You'll find that attempting one change at a time and performing a reboot between each change is the best course of action for solving a network communication problem.

Windows 95 And NetWare Networks

Connecting Windows 95 to a NetWare network is a bit more involved than the process of connecting to a Microsoft network. Unfortunately, unless you are already familiar with NetWare, you will need to memorize most of this material.

Microsoft has attempted to make connecting to NetWare networks as painless as possible. The following steps or components are required to establish a NetWare connection:

➤ **Install the protocol used by the network** This is IPX/SPX.

➤ **Install Client for NetWare Networks** Select the server name used for logon authentication, set the first drive letter for NetWare-specific drives, and select whether to enable logon script processing (see Figure 9.16).

➤ **Set Primary Network Logon** Select Client for NetWare Networks.

➤ **Share resources** If you want to share resources with the network, install File and Print Sharing for NetWare Networks, press the File and Print Sharing button, and select the type(s) of resources to share.

Once these settings are made and the computer is rebooted, you will have access to the NetWare network's resources.

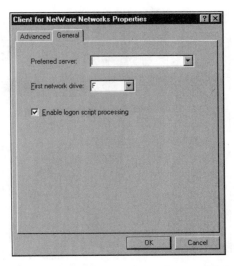

Figure 9.16   The General tab of the Client for NetWare Networks
Properties applet of Windows 95.

IPX/SPX Configuration

The most common protocol used by NetWare networks is IPX/SPX.
Microsoft has created its own protocol named IPX/SPX-compatible
protocol (also called NWLink) to interact with NetWare's protocol.
Usually, only two settings need to be changed when installing
IPX/SPX: frame type and enabling NetBIOS support.

The frame type is defined on the Advanced tab of the IPX/SPX-
compatible Protocol Properties dialog box (see Figure 9.17). The
following selections are possible:

➤ Ethernet 802.2

➤ Ethernet 802.3

➤ Ethernet_II

➤ Ethernet_Snap

Leave the default setting at Automatic to allow Windows 95 to
determine the frame type or set it to match the frame type used
on the network. Automatic will bind to the first frame type
detected, which may be the wrong one if multiple types are used.
Typically, Ethernet 802.2 is used as the industry standard and is
the default for NetWare 3.12 and higher. Ethernet 802.3 is used
by versions of NetWare earlier than 3.12.

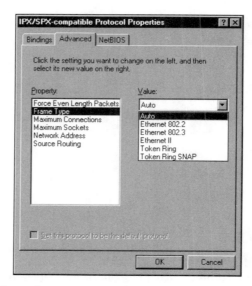

Figure 9.17 The Advanced tab of the IPX/SPX-compatible Protocol
Properties dialog box of Windows 95.

Enabling NetBIOS support is for backward compatibility with older
NetWare applications that used NetBIOS interprocess communications. This setting is made on the NetBIOS tab of the IPX/SPX-
compatible Protocol Properties dialog box (see Figure 9.18).

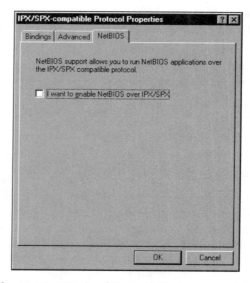

Figure 9.18 The NetBIOS tab of the IPX/SPX-compatible Protocol
Properties dialog box of Windows 95.

User Profiles, System Policies, And NetWare

Windows 95 user profiles can be stored on NetWare servers to enable either mandatory profiles or individual roaming profiles. When a user account is created on a NetWare server, a subdirectory for that user is created below the MAIL directory. Placing the user profile in this directory will enable NetWare Windows 95 client roaming profiles and mandatory profiles (see Chapter 13).

If you are using system policies (see Chapter 13) to enforce or restrict group-, user-, or computer-based access, you can store the CONFIG.POL file in the SYS:PUBLIC directory on each preferred NetWare server. Windows 95 will automatically search and download system policies stored in this manner.

NetWare Client Alternatives

The Microsoft Client for NetWare Networks is not the only choice for connecting a Windows 95 computer to a NetWare network. Other alternatives include:

➤ **Microsoft's MS-NDS Client** This client was not shipped with the original release of Windows 95, but it is available with Service Pack 1 and OSR2. This is a true Protected Mode NDS client.

➤ **Novell's VLM or NETX** NETX is a Real Mode DOS client used to connect to NetWare 2.x and 3.x servers. It is a bindery client and does not provide true NDIS support. VLM is a Real Mode NDS client released with NetWare 4.x. Both require ODI drivers and are loaded in the AUTOEXEC.BAT file.

➤ **Novell's Client 32** This is a 32-bit Protected Mode client with true NDS support. It is available from the Novell Web site (www.novell.com).

The Novell and Microsoft clients for NetWare are incompatible; you cannot install both on the same computer at the same time. Novell has an uninstall utility that you can download from www.novell.com, called UNC32.EXE. Novell claims that this tool will completely uninstall Novell's Client 32; however, in our experience, a reinstallation of Windows 95 has been required. Your mileage may vary.

NetWare logon scripts can be used with a Windows 95 client, but they must be edited to remove all commands loading TSRs (Terminate and Stay Residents). If these TSRs are required, they must be loaded via the AUTOEXEC.BAT or WINSTART.BAT files on the Windows 95 client. Because the Client for NetWare Networks gives Windows 95 the ability to use many NetWare utilities and command line tools, most standard NetWare logon scripts will function as is. Remember that there are two NetWare logon scripts. One is NET$LOG.DAT, the system logon script, which is stored in the PUBLIC NetWare server directory. The second is LOGON, which is stored in the user's MAIL subdirectory.

Shares And NetWare

Similar to the Browser service of Windows networks, NetWare networks use one of two advertising methods to inform clients of available resources. These advertisements can be configured through the Properties dialog box of the File and Print Sharing for NetWare Networks:

➤ **SAP advertising** Service Advertising Protocol (SAP) sends out a broadcast message to all NetWare and Windows 95 clients informing them of available resources. If this property is enabled (disabled by default), Novell Real Mode stack clients can reach resources hosted by Windows 95.

➤ **Workgroup advertising** This is the NetWare equivalent of the Master Browser. This can be set to Disable, Enabled: May Be Master, Enabled: Preferred Master, or Enabled: Will Not Be Master.

Sharing resources from a Windows 95 machine to NetWare clients forces you to use user-level security. Access permissions are determined by NetWare 3.x binderies or from NetWare 4.x servers with bindery emulation. Otherwise, sharing and attaching to shares for both printers and folders is the same for NetWare networks as it is for Microsoft networks.

Troubleshooting

NetWare troubleshooting can be extremely complex and time-consuming. If the connection fails to work, the most expedient method is to start over. The following are NetWare-related communication problems and some specific ways to correct them:

➤ **The network is unreachable** Through Windows 95, verify that Client for NetWare Networks is installed as well as the drivers and configuration of NIC, protocol, and other services.

➤ **A logon script fails to execute** Verify that the preferred server is set correctly and that Enable Logon Script Processing is checked (General tab of the Client for NetWare Networks Properties dialog box).

➤ **NetWare servers cannot be found** Check the frame type settings. Specify a frame type other than Automatic.

You'll find that attempting one change at a time and performing a reboot between each change is the best course of action for solving a network communication problem.

Common Network Activities

You need to be aware of some important network activities. User policies and system profiles are discussed in Chapter 13. The remaining sections of this chapter discuss common network activities and some administrative tools.

Change Passwords

One of the conveniences of Windows 95 is its ability to remember the passwords used to gain access to network resources. These passwords are stored and automatically used when the same resource or network is encountered again. You need to enter most passwords only once because Windows 95 will handle the authentication for each subsequent access. If you ever need to change your passwords or delete them entirely, use the Passwords applet of the Control Panel. Through this tool, you can change just the local Windows password to gain local access and any other passwords used to gain access to network resources (see Figure 9.19).

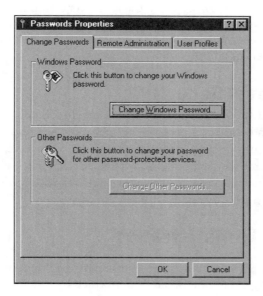

Figure 9.19   The Change Passwords tab of the Passwords Properties applet of Windows 95.

User-Level Security

User-level security offers you fine control over access to local resources. To use this method of access control, you must be on a network with access to a domain controller or security server. Access rights can be granted or denied for individual users or entire groups. Also, you can set various levels of access, including:

➤ **Read Only** Users can read and use but not manage, rename, or delete the resource.

➤ **Full Access** Users have full control over the resource.

➤ **Custom** Users can perform only those actions granted to them: read, write, create, delete, change attributes, list (get directory), and/or change access permissions.

These settings are chosen on the Sharing tab of an object's Properties (see Network Folders, Figure 9.12, and Network Printers, Figure 9.14, earlier in this chapter).

User-level security assumes that the domain controller or security server on the network will provide you with a list of users and a list of groups. Windows 95 does not have a native user and group administration tool, so these elements cannot be created on a Windows 95 client. The User Manager For Domains administration tool for Windows NT Server 4.0 can be installed onto Windows 95 (from the NT Server distribution CD, \Clients\Srvtools\Win95), but this provides only remote administrative control to the NT domain controller. It does not create users or groups within Windows 95.

Share-Level Security

Share-level security doesn't require access to a domain controller or security server; therefore, it can be used on peer-to-peer networks or stand-alone machines. This type of security simply assigns a password to a resource. Users enter the password each time they attempt to access that resource. The password is defined on the Sharing tab of an object's Properties (see Network Folders, Figure 9.11, and Network Printers, Figure 9.13, earlier in this chapter).

Remote Administration

Remote Administration, in the form of editing a Windows 95 Registry remotely, can be performed by system administrators using the System Policy Editor, Registry Editor, or other management tools. When a system administrator remotely manages a computer, the data seen on the remote computer screen is the same as if it is being performed directly on the client computer. To enable remote administration, you must perform three steps on each remote Windows 95 client:

1. Install the Remote Registry service via the Network applet. Click Add, select Service, click Add again, click Have Disk, and point the install wizard to \Admin\Nettools\Remotreg on the Windows 95 CD. Reboot when finished.

2. Launch the Passwords applet of the Control Panel, select the Remote Administration tab, then select Enable Remote Administration of this server (see Figure 9.20).

3. Also on the Remote Administration tab of the Passwords applet, define a password or assign users/groups to access remote administration, depending on your system's security type. Once again, it's a good idea to reboot.

To administer remotely, you must be on a Windows 95 computer connected to the same network. Locate the client to be administered in Network Neighborhood. Right-click over the computer name and select Properties. Select the Tools tab on the Properties dialog box. On this tab, three applications are available to manage the remote client:

➤ **Net Watcher** Enables you to manage shared resources (including remote creation of new shares) and the users accessing those resources. Two special shares are created by

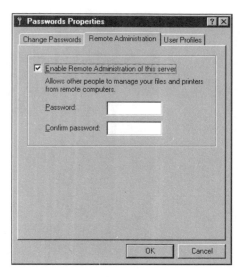

Figure 9.20 The Remote Administration tab of the Password Properties applet of Windows 95.

NetWatcher: ADMIN$, mapped to the Windows directory, and IPC$, an interprocess communication channel (for details, see Chapter 17).

➤ **System Monitor** Enables you to monitor network and disk use and performance on the remote client. This requires the Network Monitor Agent service on the client. Some of the items viewable through this tool are memory allocation and swap file usage (for details, see Chapter 17).

➤ **File System Administer** Enables the management of resources on the remote client. This requires the Remote Registry service on the client. This is not a separate utility or tool; rather, it is an extension of the Network Neighborhood that enables the manipulation of shared resources.

To edit the Registry of a remote client with the REGEDIT tool, select Registry|Connect Network Registry and enter the computer name of the remote client (see Chapter 6 about the Registry).

Note: The System Monitor requires the Remote Registry service, which in turn requires user-level security. If you do not need to use the System Monitor, you can forgo the installation of the Remote Registry service and stick with share-level security. This will still give you access to Net Watcher and the File System Administer.

Exam Prep Questions

Question 1

> If a single NDIS 3.x driver is installed on a Windows 95 computer, how many NICs can be supported?
>
> ○ a. 1
>
> ○ b. 2
>
> ○ c. 4
>
> ○ d. 8

A single NDIS 3.x driver can support up to 8 NICs. Therefore, answer d is correct.

Question 2

> If you wanted to access files from a shared folder named Sales on the server named Accounting1, what would the UNC name be for that resource?
>
> ○ a. [Accounting1]:Sales
>
> ○ b. \\Sales\Accounting1
>
> ○ c. \\Accounting1\Sales
>
> ○ d. D:\Accounting1\Sales

The correct UNC name is \\Accounting1\Sales. Therefore, answer c is correct.

Question 3

> During Windows 95 installation, which protocols are installed by default when a network adapter is present? [Check all correct answers]
>
> ❏ a. TCP/IP
>
> ❏ b. IPX/SPX
>
> ❏ c. NetBEUI
>
> ❏ d. DLC
>
> ❏ e. NetBIOS

NetBEUI and IPX/SPX are installed by default into Windows 95. Therefore, answers b and c are correct. All these protocols can be installed on Windows 95 because they are included in the distribution files.

Question 4

Which service is required to enable Windows 95 to share resources to other clients on a network hosted by Windows NT Server?

- ○ a. TCP/IP protocol
- ○ b. Client for Microsoft Networks
- ○ c. File and Print Sharing for Microsoft Networks
- ○ d. Interprocess communication (IPC)

File and Print Sharing for Microsoft Networks is the service required to share resources with clients on a network hosted by Windows NT. Therefore, answer c is correct. The TCP/IP protocol is not a service and is not the required protocol for all networks (IPX/SPX or NetBEUI can be used as the protocol, and resource sharing can still occur). Therefore, answer a is incorrect. The Client for Microsoft Networks is needed to communicate and connect to the network hosted by Windows NT Server, but it is a client, not a service, and it is not the component that enables resource sharing. Therefore, answer b is incorrect. Interprocess communication is a service that Windows 95 installs and uses independently of your configuration changes. Although IPC is used in the resource sharing process, it is not the service that enables resource sharing with Microsoft networks. Therefore, answer d is incorrect.

Question 5

If your Windows 95 client is unable to connect with a network hosted by NT Server, which of the following are configuration settings you should check? [Check all correct answers]

- ❑ a. Primary Network Logon
- ❑ b. Protocol installed and related settings
- ❑ c. Client for Microsoft Networks
- ❑ d. Workgroup name

All these are valid configurations to check when a Windows 95 client is unable to connect to a Microsoft network. Therefore, answers a, b, c, and d are correct. The workgroup name setting should list the name of the workgroup or the domain in which this client should participate. There is not a separate domain name box for Windows 95 as there is for Windows NT.

Question 6

> If you wish to control access to resources hosted by a Windows 95 client on the basis of group membership, which type of security should you set Windows 95 to use?
>
> ○ a. Share level
> ○ b. User level

User-level security enables you to control access to Windows 95 resources on the basis of user account and group membership. Therefore, answer b is correct. Share-level security protects resources with a single password and does not allow discrimination of access by user or group. Therefore, answer a is incorrect.

Question 7

> From which of the following utilities can you map a network share to a local drive letter? [Check all correct answers]
>
> ❏ a. My Computer
> ❏ b. Network Neighborhood
> ❏ c. Windows Explorer
> ❏ d. Net Watcher

My Computer, Network Neighborhood, Windows Explorer, and Net Watcher all have the function or ability of mapping a network share to a local drive letter. Therefore, answers a, b, c, and d are correct. You should remember that Net Watcher is used for performing this and other administration activities remotely if Remote Administration has been enabled on the client.

Question 8

> If Windows 95 has its Browser Master property set to Automatic, what roles can this computer play in the Browser service? [Check all correct answers]
>
> ❑ a. Non-Browser
>
> ❑ b. Backup Browser
>
> ❑ c. Potential Browser
>
> ❑ d. Master Browser

When the Browse Master property is set to Automatic, Windows 95 can play any role required of it, from that of non-Browser to that of Master Browser. Therefore, answers a, b, c, and d are correct.

Question 9

> When does a Browser election occur? [Check all correct answers]
>
> ❑ a. When a Backup Browser is unable to contact the Master Browser
>
> ❑ b. When the Master Browser goes offline
>
> ❑ c. When a computer boots into the network that is set to become a Master Browser
>
> ❑ d. When an administrator forces it

A Browser election occurs when a Backup Browser is unable to contact the Master Browser and when a computer boots into the network that is set to become a Master Browser. Therefore, answers a and c are correct. If a Master Browser goes offline, an election does not occur until a Backup Browser attempts to contact it and fails (which can be a delay of up to 15 minutes). Therefore, answer b is incorrect. There is no command that an administrator can give to force a Browser election. Therefore, answer d is incorrect.

Question 10

> If you are unable to connect to a NetWare network with your Windows 95 client, which of the following are valid configurations to check? [Check all correct answers]
>
> ❑ a. Browse Master setting
>
> ❑ b. Frame type IPX/SPX
>
> ❑ c. File and Print Sharing for NetWare networks
>
> ❑ d. Client for NetWare Networks

Frame type IPX/SPX and Client for NetWare Networks are two valid configurations that should be checked if a connection cannot be established with a NetWare network from a Windows 95 client. Therefore, answers b and d are correct. The Browse Master setting is a Microsoft network setting that is not relevant to NetWare networks. Therefore, answer a is incorrect. The File and Print Sharing for NetWare Networks service is used to share resources over an established connection and is not associated with establishing a connection with the NetWare network. Therefore, answer c is incorrect.

Need To Know More?

 Supporting Microsoft Windows 95. Microsoft Press, Redmond, WA, 1995. ISBN 1-55615-931-5. Chapters 8, 9, 10, and 11 contain detailed information about the process of and issues related to networking Windows 95 with Microsoft and NetWare networks.

 Mortensen, Lance and Rick Sawtell: *MCSE: Windows 95 Study Guide*. Sybex Network Press, San Francisco, CA, 1996. ISBN: 0-7821-2092-X. Chapters 9, 11, and 12 discuss basic networking issues, connection to Microsoft networks, and connecting to NetWare networks.

 Search the TechNet CD (or its online version through www. microsoft.com) and the *Windows 95 Resource Kit*, using the keywords "network," "workgroup," "domain," "protocol," "Microsoft networks," and "NetWare networks."

TCP/IP And The Internet

Terms you'll need to understand:

√ Dynamic Host Configuration Protocol (DHCP)

√ Windows Internet Naming Service (WINS)— LMHOSTS file

√ Domain Name Service (DNS)—HOSTS file

√ Serial Line Internet Protocol (SLIP)

√ Point-to-Point Protocol (PPP)

√ IP address

√ Subnet mask

√ Default gateway

√ Host ID, Network ID

Techniques you'll need to master:

√ Installing and configuring TCP/IP

√ Defining static IP properties or obtaining them dynamically

√ Understanding the meaning of an IP address

√ Working with subnets and subnet masking

√ Knowing the general purposes of TCP/IP tools

√ Understanding the functions of name resolution services: DHCP, DNS, and WINS

TCP/IP is the most widely used networking protocol in the world, mainly because of its use on the Internet. Windows 95 was designed with network capabilities to connect to LANs and to the Internet itself. This chapter discusses TCP/IP and its use with Windows 95.

TCP/IP Overview

Windows 95 interacts with and supports several useful TCP/IP services, such as:

➤ **Dynamic Host Configuration Protocol (DHCP)** This service enables the assignment of dynamic TCP/IP network addresses on the basis of a specified pool of available addresses. When a network client configured for DHCP logs on to the network, the DHCP service assigns the next available TCP/IP address for that network session. This greatly simplifies address administration. The DHCP server is available only on Windows NT Server. Windows 95 can request data from a DHCP server, such as IP address, subnet mask, and gateway address.

➤ **Domain Name Service (DNS)** This service is used to resolve host names into IP addresses. Host names are user-friendly conveniences that represent the dotted decimal notation of IP, which, unlike NetBIOS names, are not required for communication operations. A host name, such as www.microsoft.com, is much easier to remember than its corresponding IP address (207.68.156.51).

➤ **Windows Internet Naming Service (WINS)** This service enables the resolution of network names to IP addresses (similar to the Unix DNS). This means that you don't have to remember the IP address of the client with whom you are trying to communicate; you can enter the network name, and the network does the rest. If a TCP/IP-based network does not have a WINS server, each time one computer tries to access another, it must send a b-node broadcast message, which creates unnecessary network traffic and can slow a busy network to a crawl. WINS servers thus resolve these broadcast messages and improve network performance. The WINS server is available only on Windows NT Server; however, Windows 95 can use the WINS service to resolve network names.

➤ **Serial Line Internet Protocol (SLIP)** Originally developed for the Unix environment, SLIP is still widely used among Internet providers. Although SLIP provides good performance and has few system overhead requirements, it does not support error checking, flow control, or security features. SLIP is good for connecting to Unix hosts or Internet providers. This protocol is quickly being replaced by PPP.

➤ **Point-to-Point Protocol (PPP)** PPP addresses succeed in doing what SLIP cannot, providing the ability to encrypt logons as well as supporting additional transport protocols, error checking, and recovery. In addition, PPP is optimized for low-bandwidth connections and, in general, is a more efficient protocol than SLIP. PPP is the preferred WAN protocol for remote access connections.

Through these services, a Windows 95 client can participate in almost any TCP/IP-based network, be it a private intranet or the Internet.

IP Addressing Explored And Explained

An IP address is simply a number that uniquely identifies a TCP/IP host on the Internet or on an intranet. In TCP/IP terminology, a host is any machine with a network interface configured to use TCP/IP. For example, a host could be a Windows NT Server, a Unix workstation, or one of the many routers used to pass information from one network to another.

 Although the term "host" is used here to describe any device configured to access a TCP/IP network, it is also used when comparing DNS names to NetBIOS names. For example, www.microsoft.com is a host name, whereas SERVER2 is a NetBIOS name; however, both machines are considered hosts on a TCP/IP network. This can be confusing, but you can usually determine the meaning of the word "host" by the context in which it is used.

The Internet or IP addressing scheme is much like the addressing scheme used by the U.S. Postal Service to deliver mail to your home. An IP address comprises a network ID component and a host ID component. In this analogy, the network ID corresponds to the name of your street, and the host ID corresponds to your home's address.

The term "Internet" actually refers to not just one network, but a collection of interconnected networks. The boundaries of each of these networks are created by routers, which are used to segment and subdivide network traffic. Each interface on a router signifies a separate network (or subnet) and is therefore assigned a separate network ID. When the interfaces of two separate routers connect to the same physical network segment, they share the same network ID and are identified by unique host IDs.

The network ID identifies the particular network (or segment) on which a host physically resides, much like the name of a street identifies where a house is located. This address must be unique across the entire TCP/IP network, whether the network is a part of the global TCP/IP network called the Internet or a small company's LAN that has implemented TCP/IP. The network ID is used to forward information to the correct network interface on a router. Once the information reaches the correct network (or network segment), the data is delivered to the appropriate host using the host ID portion of the address. All hosts that share the same network ID must be located on the same physical network segment for information to reach them properly. If a host is moved from one network segment to another, it must be assigned a new network address.

 A unique network or subnet ID is required for each physical network segment. Network and subnetwork boundaries are created by using routers. Therefore, every interface on a router must have a unique network ID assigned to it. Two routers with interfaces connected to the same physical network segment share network IDs but have unique host IDs.

The host ID identifies a specific host on a particular network, much like a street address identifies a home from all others on the street. This portion of the address must be unique within each network (or subnet). Hosts are usually configured with a single network interface card (NIC), but some hosts, such as routers, are configured with multiple network interfaces. Each network interface on a host must be configured with a separate and unique IP address.

IP Address Formats

IP addresses can be represented in both binary and decimal formats. Because we tend to have a more difficult time with numbers than do computers, we usually prefer to deal with IP addresses in a decimal format.

A decimal format IP address comprises four groups of numbers called "octets," each separated by a period (.). This way of representing an IP address is called "dotted-decimal notation."

At first, you may not understand why a three-digit number would be referred to as an octet (eight digits), but when each of these numbers is converted to a binary format, the concept starts to make more sense.

Computers, unlike humans, see the world in binary terms; that is, everything is either on or off, true or false, or ones or zeros. This somewhat simplistic view of the world is a function of the computer's architecture, which is well suited to binary computation.

Computers see IP addresses as 32-bit numbers (or four bytes of eight bits each). Each octet in the decimal format ranges from 0 through 255 and can be represented by eight bits in the binary format (thus the name "octet").

Table 10.1 Binary versus decimal IP address formats.	
Binary IP Address	**Dotted-Decimal IP Address**
11000000 10101000 00000000 00000001	192.168.0.1

In Table 10.1, the number on the left represents the binary version of an IP address, and the number on the right represents its decimal counterpart. Perhaps now you can see why we would want to convert these binary numbers to a decimal format.

Where Do IP Addresses Come From?

Every IP address on the Internet or on an intranet must be unique. This is true whether the network has 1,000 or 1 million hosts. If a company has configured its network to use TCP/IP and it is not connected to the Internet, the allocation and use of nonduplicate addresses from the IP address space is not a big issue. IP addresses can be selected from the entire IP address space to suit particular needs. Depending on the size of the company, one or more people will be able to handle the task of assigning unique IP addresses to each subnetwork and host on the company's network. However, if the company needs to connect to the Internet, it becomes much more difficult to ensure that the IP addresses it is using are not also being used by someone else.

The InterNIC (Internet Network Information Center) is solely responsible for allocating and assigning IP addresses to those who wish to connect their networks to the Internet. Having one entity responsible for assigning IP addresses ensures that addresses are not duplicated and that they are properly distributed. However, the InterNIC does not keep track of every IP address that it allows an organization to use. Rather, it uses classes to assign to an organization a network ID that corresponds to the number of host IDs the organization desires. The organization is then free to assign the host IDs however it sees fit.

Address Classes

We have seen that IP addresses are numbers that uniquely identify every host or network interface on an IP network. These addresses comprise a network ID component and a host ID component that determine the network for which a packet is bound and the specific host on the network that the information needs to reach. We have also seen that IP addresses can be represented in dotted-decimal and binary formats. People prefer to work with IP addresses in a decimal format, whereas computers work with IP addresses in a binary format.

You can begin to see a relationship between the number of bits in an address space and the total number of addresses that can be created from those bits.

When the Internet was just beginning to emerge, the governing bodies decided that an address space composed of 32 bits was sufficient to handle all of the potential networks and hosts that would ever be connected to the Internet. This 32-bit address space can create about 4.3 billion (or 2^{32}) different addresses. The Internet founders never imagined the incredible growth the Internet would experience in subsequent years. Had they known, they could easily have added a couple of extra bits to the address space and thereby exponentially increased the number of hosts that could be supported.

Although the founders did not anticipate the need for additional addresses, they did devise a method for using address classes that allows the available address space to be allocated appropriately. Address classes range from Class A through Class E, although addresses in classes D and E are reserved for special use. These classes correspond to the number of network IDs and host IDs allowed within a range of the total IP address space.

Dividing the available address space into classes makes it possible to allocate blocks of address space to an organization according to the total number of hosts the organization needs to support.

Table 10.2 shows, from left to right, each class of the address, the value of the high-order bits (the first bits of the first octet), the range of decimal values allowed in the first octet of each class, and the number of networks and hosts supported by each class.

In a Class A address, the first octet represents the network ID component of the address. In a Class B address, the first two octets represent the network ID. In a Class C address, the first three octets represent the network ID. This subdivision of address space is shown in Table 10.3.

Class A addresses use only the first octet to designate the network ID and use the remaining three octets to designate the host ID. The high-order bit (first bit of the first octet) of this address class is always set to zero, indicating a Class A

Table 10.2   Address classes and corresponding network and host IDs.

Address Class	High-Order Bits	First Octet Decimal Range	Networks Available	Hosts Available
Class A	0	1-126.x.y.z	126	16,777,214
Class B	10	128-191.x.y.z	16,384	65,534
Class C	110	192-223.x.y.z	2,097,152	254

Table 10.3	Division of IP address component octets according to class.		
Address Class	IP Address	Network ID Component	Host ID Component
A	w.x.y.z	w	x.y.z
B	w.x.y.z	w.x	y.z
C	w.x.y.z	w.x.y	z

address. Because the high-order bit is always set to zero, there are only seven bits remaining to represent the network ID. These seven bits provide a maximum of 127 possible network addresses, but the 127 network ID is reserved for the network adapter loop-back function. Therefore, only 126 possible Class A addresses are available.

Class B addresses use the first and second octet to designate the network ID and use the remaining two octets to designate the host ID. The high-order bits (first two bits of the first octet) of this class are always set to 10 (one-zero), indicating a Class B address. Because the high-order bits of the first octet are always set to 10, only 14 bits remain to represent the network ID. These 14 bits provide a maximum of 16,384 network addresses.

Class C addresses use the first three octets to designate the network ID and use the remaining octet to designate the host ID. The high-order bits (first three bits of the first octet) of this class are always set to 110 (one-one-zero), indicating a Class C address. Because the high-order bits of the first octet are always set to 110, only 21 bits remain to represent the network ID. These 21 bits provide a maximum of 2,097,152 network addresses.

If an organization needs valid IP addresses to connect to the Internet, smaller blocks of addresses can usually be obtained from third parties such as ISPs (Internet Service Providers). ISPs usually receive larger portions of the IP address space with the intention of assigning those to customers who may need only a few IP addresses each.

Two other address classes you need to be aware of are D and E. Class D addresses are used for multicasting, which is a method of sending information to a number of registered hosts. Class E addresses are an experimental class reserved for future use.

It is important to avoid the use of restricted numbers in an IP address. The use of the numbers 0 (represented in an octet by all zeros) and 255 (represented in an octet by all ones) is restricted in host IDs. A host ID cannot comprise all ones or zeros. The use of all zeros in a host ID indicates that information is intended for a particular network without specifying a host, whereas the use of all ones in a host ID indicates that the information is intended for all hosts on a particular network.

Subdividing A Network: Subnets And Subnet Masks

Subdividing a range of addresses further into subnets is sometimes necessary because the block of addresses assigned to an organization by the InterNIC may not work well with the current network topology. Remember, each network ID corresponds to one physical segment of a network. If you receive a Class C address but already have two physical networks, further segmentation of the Class C address is desirable. Subdividing an existing network ID further is called subnetting.

Before continuing, recall that the entire IP address space is already subdivided into three address classes, each of which supports a predetermined number of hosts. The number of network IDs or host IDs that a class can support is a function of the number of bits available to each portion of the address. For example, in a Class B address, the two high-order bits are set to 10, leaving 14 bits available to the network ID and 16 bits to the host ID. Examining the high-order bits makes it is easy to determine which portion of the address indicates the network ID and which portion the host ID.

If you need to further subdivide the address space given to you by the InterNIC, you will need to borrow some of the bits assigned to the host ID and loan them to the network ID portion of your address. However, once you do this, you can no longer easily determine the length of the network ID simply by looking at the IP address. The subnet mask was designed to aid in this process.

Subnet Masks

A subnet mask is a 32-bit address that indicates how many bits in an address are being used for the network ID. The subnet mask indicates the length of the network ID by using all ones in the portion of its address that corresponds to the network ID of the address with which it is being used (see Table 10.4). The default subnet mask for a Class A address is 255.0.0.0 because only the first octet of the address is used to indicate the network ID. Similarly, a Class C address uses the first three octets to represent the network ID, so the default subnet mask for this type of address is 255.255.255.0.

Table 10.4   Default subnet masks for classes A, B, and C.

Address Class	Mask Decimal Value	Mask Binary Value
Class A	255.0.0.0	11111111.00000000.00000000.00000000
Class B	255.255.0.0	11111111.11111111.00000000.00000000
Class C	255.255.255.0	11111111.11111111.11111111.00000000

When a TCP/IP host is initialized, it compares its own IP address to its given subnet mask through a process called ANDing (see Table 10.5) and stores the result in memory. When the host needs to determine whether a packet is bound for a local network or a remote network, it compares the destination IP address of the packet with its own subnet mask and then compares the result to the original result it obtained during initialization. If these two results are the same, the packet is bound for a local host and is not routed from the network. If the results are different, the packet is bound for a remote host and is routed to the appropriate network.

During the ANDing process, corresponding ones and zeros are combined. The result of two ones is a one. The result of a zero and any number is a zero.

If you decide to subnet the Class C address into two separate networks, you must extend the subnet mask to indicate the bits that are being added to the network ID. To obtain two additional subnets from a Class C address, the mask 255.255.255.192 is most often used. The number 192 in the last octet of the subnet mask is obtained by borrowing the first two bits of the host ID. These two bits actually give a total of four networks, but because a network ID cannot comprise all ones or all zeros, two subnets remain (64 and 128). An example of the resulting subnet mask is shown in Table 10.6.

Table 10.5   The ANDing process.

IP Address	192.168.2.66	11000000.10101000.00000010.01000010
Subnet Mask	255.255.255.0	11111111.11111111.11111111.00000000
ANDing Result		11000000.10101000.00000010.00000000

Table 10.6   The ANDing process revisited.

IP Address	192.168.2.66	11000000.10101000.00000010.01000010
Subnet Mask	255.255.255.192	11111111.11111111.11111111.11000000
ANDing Result		11000000.10101000.00000010.01000000

Default Gateway

The default gateway is the IP address of a computer or device that serves as a router, a format translator, or a security filter for a network. The default gateway is used when the operating system determines that a requested resource or server is not located within the local subnet. All packets destined for hosts not in the local subnet are sent to the default gateway. The gateway is responsible for transmitting the packets to the host, if that host can be found. If the default gateway is not defined, the computer will be unable to communicate with machines outside its subnet. This detail can also be requested from a DHCP server.

TCP/IP Configuration

Installing and configuring TCP/IP on Windows 95 is much simpler than you might think. Before you install the TCP/IP protocol, you need to collect a few items for configuration purposes:

➤ **The workstation's IP address** This is the unique address that identifies a particular computer on a TCP/IP network. This number consists of four numbers separated by periods (e.g., 125.115.125.48). If you do not have a permanent IP address, Windows 95 can be configured to poll a DHCP server to request one.

➤ **The network segment's subnet mask** The subnet mask is a number mathematically applied to the IP address. This number determines which IP addresses are part of the same subnetwork as the computer applying the subnet mask. This detail can also be requested from a DHCP server.

➤ **The default gateway** The gateway is the computer that serves as a router, a format translator, or a security filter for a network. If the default gateway is not defined, the computer will be unable to communicate with machines outside its subnet. This detail can also be requested from a DHCP server.

➤ **The domain name server for the network** This is a computer that serves as an Internet host and translates fully qualified domain names (FQDNs) into IP addresses.

➤ **Any DHCP and WINS information about the network** These nonmandatory name resolution services can expand the range of reachable services from a Windows 95 client. You'll need the exact IP addresses of these servers if you plan to use them.

If you did not install TCP/IP when you first installed Windows 95, you must perform the following steps to install and configure this protocol:

1. Open the Control Panel (Start|Settings|Control Panel).

2. Double-click the Network icon.

3. Click the Add button.

4. Select Protocol, then click Add again.

5. Select Microsoft from the list of manufacturers and TCP/IP from the list of available protocols. You'll need to have local or network access to the Windows 95 distribution files.

6. Click OK to install.

The system may automatically prompt you to configure TCP/IP by bringing up the Properties dialog box once the required driver files have been copied. If it does not, you can select the TCP/IP protocol from the list presented to you on the Configuration tab of the Network applet and click Properties to configure TCP/IP.

Configuring TCP/IP involves the following steps:

1. On the IP Address tab, set the IP address and subnet mask, or if you are using a DHCP server, select the Obtain an IP address automatically radio button (see Figure 10.1).

2. On the WINS Configuration tab, select the Disable WINS Resolution or the Enable WINS Resolution radio button. If you select Enable, you'll need to select the IP address for the Primary WINS server (see Figure 10.2).

3. On the Gateway tab, define the default gateway. Note that multiple gateways can be defined, but that only the first gateway in the list will be used. The others are for fault tolerance if the first is unreachable (see Figure 10.3).

4. On the DNS Configuration tab, select the Enable DNS radio button. Define the host and domain names, one or more DNS server IP addresses, and one or more domain suffixes (see Figure 10.4).

5. On the Bindings tab, you probably won't need to make any changes. If you are worried about Internet users gaining access to your machine over your Internet link, deselect File and printer sharing for Microsoft Networks, if present (see Figure 10.5).

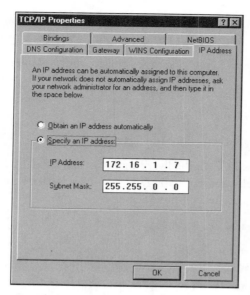

Figure 10.1 The IP Address tab of the TCP/IP Properties dialog box of Windows 95.

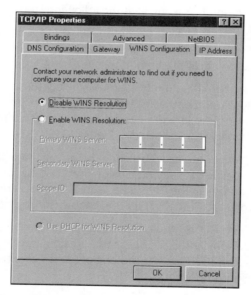

Figure 10.2 The WINS Configuration tab of the TCP/IP Properties dialog box of Windows 95.

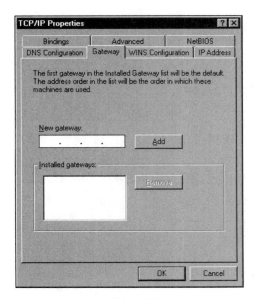

Figure 10.3   The Gateway tab of the TCP/IP Properties dialog box of Windows 95.

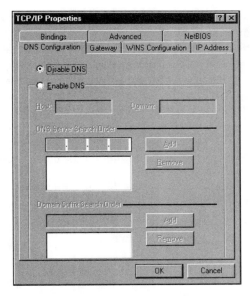

Figure 10.4   The DNS Configuration tab of the TCP/IP Properties dialog box of Windows 95.

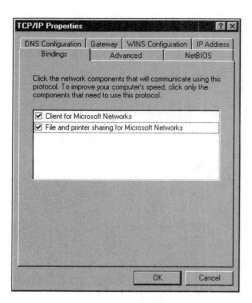

Figure 10.5 The Bindings tab of the TCP/IP Properties dialog box of Windows 95.

> The Advanced tab does not offer any settings to configure, although some nonstandard or third-party TCP/IP services or utilities may add configuration options to this tab. A NetBIOS tab may also be present, but you usually can't change its single setting of enabling NetBIOS communication over TCP/IP.

Always reboot the computer, even if you are not prompted, every time you modify the settings of a network component, especially a protocol. Once the system reboots, TCP/IP will be fully installed. You can always return to the Protocols tab of the Network applet to modify the configuration of TCP/IP.

TCP/IP Tools

Several utilities are installed with the TCP/IP protocol. These can help you set up, troubleshoot, and maintain IP connectivity:

➤ **WINIPCFG** A GUI display utility for listing the settings of an IP connection, such as IP address, subnet mask, default gateway, MAC address, and so on (see Figure 10.6)

➤ **PING** Verifies the existence of a remote host (see Figure 10.7)

➤ **TRACERT** Displays the route taken by an Internet Control Message Protocol (ICMP) to a remote host (see Figure 10.8)

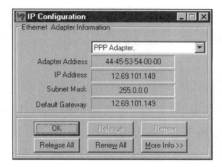

Figure 10.6   The WINIPCFG tool from Windows 95.

```
C:\>ping www.lanw.com

Pinging www.lanw.com [206.224.95.1] with 32 bytes of data:

Reply from 206.224.95.1: bytes=32 time=312ms TTL=112
Reply from 206.224.95.1: bytes=32 time=312ms TTL=112
Reply from 206.224.95.1: bytes=32 time=299ms TTL=112
Reply from 206.224.95.1: bytes=32 time=256ms TTL=112

C:\>
```

Figure 10.7   A PING result from Windows 95.

```
C:\>tracert www.microsoft.com

Tracing route to www.microsoft.com [207.68.143.193]
over a maximum of 30 hops:

  1   198 ms   187 ms   194 ms  192.168.255.253
  2   180 ms   195 ms   214 ms  199.70.147.97
  3   194 ms   182 ms   220 ms  12.127.13.233
  4   217 ms   237 ms   184 ms  br1-h10.wswdc.ip.att.net [12.127.15.153]
  5     *      245 ms   317 ms  gr1-a350.wswdc.ip.att.net [192.205.31.189]
  6   245 ms   196 ms   198 ms  903.Hssi9-0.GW2.DCA1.ALTER.NET [157.130.32.21]
  7   246 ms   211 ms   225 ms  105.ATM3-0-0.XR1.DCA1.ALTER.NET [137.39.64.34]
  8   299 ms   232 ms   183 ms  100.ATM10-0-0.TR1.DCA1.ALTER.NET [137.39.64.169]

  9   332 ms   268 ms   297 ms  101.ATM4-0-0.TR1.SCL1.ALTER.NET [137.39.104.1]
 10   273 ms   256 ms   286 ms  100.ATM4-0-0.XR1.SCL1.ALTER.NET [137.39.197.162]

 11   369 ms     *        *     195.ATM11-0-0.GW1.SCL1.ALTER.NET [137.39.197.29]

 12   438 ms   594 ms   586 ms  Dist1-SCL.MOSWEST.MSN.NET [137.39.100.58]
 13   301 ms   326 ms   309 ms  MN1-f0-0.moswest.msn.net [207.68.145.42]
 14     *        *
```

Figure 10.8   A TRACERT result from Windows 95.

➤ **ROUTE** Lets you view and edit local routing tables

➤ **NETSTAT** Displays protocol statistics and current TCP/IP network connections

➤ **FTP** Transfers files to and from an FTP server

➤ **TELNET** A terminal emulator for interacting with remote systems

All these utilities can be launched from a command prompt or the Start|Run command. For details on use and syntax, type /? as a parameter or consult the Windows 95 Help system.

Internet Access

To gain access to the Internet, you'll need to create a Dial-Up Networking entry, which contacts an ISP and establishes a PPP (or SLIP) connection. First, DUN must be installed on your computer through either the Internet Connection Wizard or the Control Panel.

The Internet Connection Wizard is located behind the Internet icon on the desktop. Double-click on the icon, and the Wizard will walk you through the connection process and install DUN. Otherwise, you can install DUN through the Add/Remove Programs applet of the Control Panel. Select the Windows Setup tab, select the Communications option, click Details, and then check the DUN box.

Setting up DUN is little more than defining a phone number with the appropriate TCP/IP settings. DUN and other RAS issues are discussed in more detail in Chapter 11.

Internet Explorer

Internet Explorer is the Web browser built for the Microsoft Windows platforms: Windows 3.x, Windows 95, and Windows NT (there is also a Macintosh version). This tool gives you the ability to access Web and FTP resources hosted within a TCP/IP intranet or on the Internet. More information about Internet Explorer can be found at www.microsoft.com/ie/.

Peer Web Services

Peer Web Services is a scaled-down version of Internet Information Server for Windows NT. This application allows you to host Web and FTP sites from your Windows 95 computer. However, it is limited to ten simultaneous connections. For details about IIS and PWS, please visit www.microsoft.com/iis/.

NT Names And Name Services

Computers interact with one another using long strings of complicated address numbers; fortunately, most of these numbers can be hidden behind easy-to-remember names. Name resolution is the activity of transforming a user-friendly name for a computer or network share into a computer-friendly network address. This process allows networks to quickly locate and request resources while shielding users from difficult-to-remember, hardware-level addresses. Windows 95 is able to interact with and use several name resolution services hosted by Internet and intranet servers.

Name resolution under TCP/IP is a complex but important issue. The resolution methods for IP include Dynamic Host Configuration Protocol (DHCP), Domain Name Service (DNS), and Windows Internet Name Service (WINS).

DHCP

DHCP (Dynamic Host Configuration Protocol) is available only on Windows NT Server. You need to be familiar with how DHCP works and with a few key terms.

DHCP is not exactly a name-resolution system. Rather, it is an IP address-leasing system that shares a limited number of IP addresses among numerous computers, usually clients. DHCP dynamically assigns IP addresses to clients on a local subnet.

When a client boots a computer, a message is sent requesting data from a DHCP server. The receiving DHCP server responds with an IP address assignment for a specified period of time. The client receives the data, integrates it into its configuration, and completes the boot process.

A DHCP server can also distribute subnet masks and default gateway addresses. Each assignment from a DHCP server is for a predetermined length of time, called a "lease period." When a lease expires, a DHCP server can reassign the address to another computer. An operating client can extend its lease simply by indicating that it is still using the address. When half a lease period is reached, a client requests a lease extension, if needed. The client continues to request extensions from the leasing DHCP server until 87.5 percent of its time period has expired, and then it broadcasts the extension request to all DHCP servers. If no server responds by the time the lease expires, all TCP/IP communications of that client cease.

A client can display its IP configuration and lease information by using the WINIPCFG utility. A client can release a lease by pressing the Release or Release All button and renew a lease by pressing the Renew or Renew All button.

DNS

Like DHCP, DNS (Domain Name Service) is available only on Windows NT Server. You need to be familiar with how DNS works and with a few key terms.

DNS is a Microsoft service that resolves host names into IP addresses. Host names are user-friendly conveniences that represent the dotted-decimal notation of IP, which, unlike NetBIOS names, are not required for communication operations. A host name, such as www.microsoft.com, is much easier to remember than its corresponding IP address (207.68.156.51). Early DNS consisted of a lookup table that was stored on every machine in a file called HOSTS. As networks expanded, maintaining an up-to-date and correct HOSTS file was increasingly difficult, so a centralized DNS was developed to ease administration. A single server hosts the DNS data for the networks it supports, a hierarchical table of domains, and a list of other DNS servers to which it can refer requests.

DNS operates on user-friendly FQDNs to determine the location (IP address) of a system. For example, ftp2.dev.microsoft.com could represent the server named FTP2 located in the .dev subdomain under the .microsoft domain within the .com top-level domain. This hierarchical structure enables DNS to quickly traverse its database and locate the correct IP address for the host machine.

DNS is essential on large networks, including the Internet. A client is configured to use a DNS server through the TCP/IP Properties dialog box. The DNS tab contains fields to define the host name of the client, the domain where the client resides, the IP addresses of DNS servers, and a search order of domains.

WINS

WINS is a name-resolution service for NT-based TCP/IP networks. Similar to DNS, WINS maps NetBIOS names to IP addresses. Unlike DNS, WINS dynamically maintains the mapping database. WINS main functions include:

➤ Mapping NetBIOS names to IP addresses

➤ Recognizing NetBIOS names on all subnets

➤ Enabling internetwork browsing

WINS reduces NetBIOS background tracking by eliminating the NetBIOS broadcasts. A WINS client communicates directly with a WINS server to send a resource notification, release its NetBIOS name, or locate a resource.

The original Microsoft solution to reduce NetBIOS broadcast traffic was the LMHOSTS file. This static file was stored on each client that associated IP addresses with NetBIOS names. Like the DNS HOSTS file, it had to be manu-ally maintained. Unfortunately, an LMHOSTS file is useless in a DHCP environment, where relationships between IP addresses and NetBIOS names change.

WINS and DHCP work well together. Each time a DHCP client goes online, it can inform the WINS server of its presence, so the dynamic relationships between IP addresses and NetBIOS names can be fully managed by these automatic services.

WINS clients are configured through the TCP/IP Properties dialog box of the Services tab of the Network application. The WINS Address tab enables you to configure two WINS servers. The second server is for fault tolerance.

WINS Vs. DNS

Although similar, WINS and DNS have significant differences that define when each should be used for name resolution. Table 10.7 highlights the dif-ferences between WINS and DNS.

Both DNS and WINS are installed within many private networks, providing support for both NetBIOS and FQDN resolution. Both DNS and WINS can be configured to pass resolution requests to the other resolution service if the referenced name is not listed in the respective database.

Table 10.7   Vital statistics for differences between WINS and DNS.

WINS	DNS
Maps IP addresses to NetBIOS names	Maps IP addresses to FQDNs
Automatic client data registration	Manual configuration
Flat database name space	Uses FQDN's hierarchical structure
Used on MS clients and networks	Used on TCP/IP-based hosts and networks
Only one entry per client	Each host can have multiple aliases
Enables domain functions, such as logon and browsing	N/A

Exam Prep Questions

Question 1

> Which of the following is a valid subnet mask for a Class C
> network?
>
> ○ a. 255.0.0.0
>
> ○ b. 255.255.0.0
>
> ○ c. 255.255.255.0
>
> ○ d. 255.255.255.255

255.255.255.0 is a valid subnet mask for a Class C network. Therefore, answer
c is correct. 255.0.0.0 is for Class A networks and 255.255.0.0 is for Class B
networks. Therefore, answers a and b are incorrect. 255.255.255.255 is an all-
node broadcast address and cannot be used as a subnet mask. Therefore, answer
d is incorrect.

Question 2

> What is an advantage of SLIP over PPP?
>
> ○ a. SLIP supports security, whereas PPP does not support
>   security.
>
> ○ b. SLIP supports error checking, whereas PPP does not
>   support error checking.
>
> ○ c. SLIP supports flow control, whereas PPP does not
>   support flow control.
>
> ○ d. SLIP requires less system overhead than PPP.

SLIP requires less system overhead than PPP. Therefore, answer d is correct.
SLIP does not support error checking, flow control, or security (these are features of PPP). Therefore, answers a, b, and c are incorrect.

Question 3

> Which of the following items must be defined to use a DHCP server? [Check all correct answers]
>
> ❑   a. Client IP address
>
> ❑   b. Client subnet mask
>
> ❑   c. Client default gateway
>
> ❑   d. IP address of DHCP server

The only item required for using a DHCP service is the IP address of a DHCP server. Therefore, answer d is correct. Although the other items can be provided by a DHCP server, they are not required. Therefore, answers a, b, and c are incorrect.

Question 4

> If a default gateway is not defined, a Windows 95 TCP/IP client can still communicate with other hosts in other networks simply by using the hosts' exact IP address instead of domain names.
>
> ○   a. True
>
> ○   b. False

If a default gateway is not defined, no traffic of any kind can pass outside the local network, even if an exact IP address is used. Therefore, answer b is correct.

Question 5

> You want to install TCP/IP on a Windows 95 client in a nonrouted network. You have already assigned an IP address manually to the computer. What other parameter must you specify to install TCP/IP on the client?
>
> ○   a. The subnet mask
>
> ○   b. The default gateway
>
> ○   c. The DHCP server IP address
>
> ○   d. The WINS server IP address

When installing TCP/IP on a nonrouted network, the IP address and subnet mask parameters must be specified. Therefore, answer a is correct. If a default gateway is not specified, the computer can communicate only with other machines within its subnet, and the gateway is not a mandatory element. Therefore, answer b is incorrect. DHCP and WINS are not mandatory fields to define. Therefore, answers c and d are incorrect.

Question 6

> With a subnet mask of 255.255.255.0, which of the following IP addresses are in the same network? [Check all correct answers]
>
> ❑ a. 172.16.3.6
>
> ❑ b. 172.16.4.6
>
> ❑ c. 172.12.3.6
>
> ❑ d. 172.16.3.254

Only 172.16.3.6 and 172.16.3.254 are in the same network when a subnet of 255.255.255.0 is used. Therefore, answers a and d are correct. The other two addresses lie in a different network. Therefore, answers b and c are incorrect.

Question 7

> If the use of the PING utility returns a timeout, what can you deduce from this? [Check all correct answers]
>
> ❑ a. The host is offline or not responsive.
>
> ❑ b. Your TCP/IP settings are wrong.
>
> ❑ c. The traffic on the network or Internet is preventing timely delivery of packets.
>
> ❑ d. You used the wrong IP address.

The PING utility's result of a timeout indicates that the host is offline or that there is too much traffic on the network. Therefore, answers a and c are correct. If your TCP/IP settings are wrong, the PING utility's responses would not inform you or even hint of this. Therefore, answer b is incorrect. If you use the wrong IP address to PING against, you'll get data only on the host you did contact instead of on the intended host. PING is not able to inform you that you used the wrong IP address. Therefore, answer d is incorrect.

Question 8

> Which of the following TCP/IP utilities are useful for troubleshooting connections between your Windows 95 client and a remote system? [Check all correct answers]
>
> ❑ a. WINIPCFG
>
> ❑ b. TRACERT
>
> ❑ c. PING
>
> ❑ d. Telnet

The TRACERT utility displays the route taken by packets to the remote system. Therefore, answer b is correct. The PING utility indicates whether a remote system is currently online. Therefore, answer c is correct. The WINIPCFG utility is useful only for identifying local TCP/IP configurations. Therefore, answer a is incorrect. The Telnet utility is used to establish a terminal emulation session with a remote system, and it does not offer connection diagnostics. Therefore, answer d is incorrect.

Question 9

> What are the functions of WINS? [Check all correct answers]
>
> ❑ a. Enable internetwork browsing
>
> ❑ b. Map FQDNs to IP addresses
>
> ❑ c. Map NetBIOS names to IP addresses
>
> ❑ d. Map NetBIOS names to MAC addresses
>
> ❑ e. Assign clients IP addresses

Enabling internetwork browsing and mapping NetBIOS names to IP addresses are two of the three functions of WINS. The third function is recognizing NetBIOS names on all subnets. Therefore, answers a and c are correct. Mapping FQDNs to IP addresses is a function of DNS. Therefore, answer b is incorrect. Mapping NetBIOS names to MAC addresses happens in both NWLink and NetBEUI. Therefore, answer d is incorrect. Assigning clients IP addresses is a function of a DHCP server. Therefore, answer e is incorrect.

Question 10

A DNS server links which types of information together? [Check all correct answers]

❏ a. NetBEUI names

❏ b. FQDNs

❏ c. Subnet masks

❏ d. IP addresses

❏ e. MAC addresses

DNS maintains a relationship between FQDNs and IP addresses in such a way that both forward and reverse lookups are possible. Therefore, answers b and d are correct. NetBEUI names are stored by WINS. Therefore, answer a is incorrect. Subnet masks can be distributed by a DHCP server, but a link table does not exist. Therefore, answer c is incorrect. MAC addresses are linked through NWLink and NetBEUI's cached name resolution. Therefore, answer e is incorrect.

Need To Know More?

Supporting Microsoft Windows 95. Microsoft Press, Redmond, WA, 1995. ISBN: 1-55615-931-5. Chapter 1 discusses Windows 95 and TCP/IP.

Hahn, Harley: *The Internet Complete Reference.* Osborne McGraw-Hill, Berkeley, CA, 1996. ISBN: 0-07-882-138-X. Covers numerous topics surrounding the Internet, including its history and technical aspects.

Levine, John R., Carol Baroudi, and Margy Levine-Young: *Internet For Dummies.* IDG Books Worldwide, Indianapolis, IN, 1996. ISBN: 0-76450-106-2. Discusses the basics of email, the Web, and FTP services.

Mortensen, Lance and Rick Sawtell: *MCSE: Windows 95 Study Guide.* Sybex Network Press, San Francisco, CA, 1996. ISBN: 0-7821-2092-X. Chapter 10 focuses on TCP/IP and its use in Windows 95.

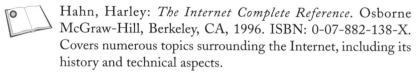

Search the TechNet CD (or its online version through www.microsoft.com) and the *Windows 95 Workstation Resource Kit,* using the keywords "TCP/IP," "name resolution," "Peer Web Services," "DNS," "WINS," "LMHOSTS," "HOST," and "DHCP."

Remote Communication

Terms you'll need to understand:

√ TAPI (Telephony Application Programming Interface)

√ DUN (Dial-Up Networking)

√ BRIEFCASE

√ PPTP (Point-to-Point Tunneling Protocol)

√ VPN (Virtual Private Network)

Techniques you'll need to master:

√ Installing and configuring a modem

√ Diagnosing a modem

√ Defining Dialing Properties

√ Installing DUN

√ Creating and configuring a Phonebook entry through DUN

√ Establishing a DUN connection

√ Using Dial-Up Server

√ Using a Direct Cable Connection

√ Troubleshooting remote communications

√ Using BRIEFCASE

Windows 95 clients use remote communication to connect to office LANs, Internet hosts, or Windows 95 peers using telecommunication lines. In effect, Windows 95 uses a modem and a phone line as if they were a network interface to connect to other computers. This chapter discusses dial-up networking, modems, remote administration, and other issues related to remote communication.

Overview

The Windows 95 communication system consists of five layers (see Table 11.1). The first (top) layer is the application requesting the remote-communication service. The next layer, UNIMODEM.VXD, is a virtual device driver that provides a standard interface between applications and VCOMM.VXD, the next layer. VCOMM is the central and irreplaceable component that manages access to all communication devices. The next layer contains the port or device drivers (also called miniport drivers) created by manufacturers for their particular device. (Some manufacturers also provide a replacement for UNIMODEM.VXD.) The last (bottom) layer is the hardware communications device itself.

The possible number of COM and LPT ports is defined by the hardware, not by the operating system, through this architecture. Note that when a device (such as a serial printer) is shared, the print *driver* is shared, not the port itself.

Modems

Remote communication typically requires a modem or similar device to establish a connection. You must install and configure a modem to establish a remote communication connection. Some ways to install a modem include:

➤ During the initial Windows 95 installation when detected by Setup

➤ During a boot sequence located through Plug and Play polling

➤ Through the Add New Hardware applet's autodetect or manual selection

➤ Through the Modem applet in the Control Panel

Table 11.1   The layers of Windows 95 communications.
Communication Application
UNIMODEM.VXD
VCOMM.VXD
Port drivers
Hardware

It is recommended that you use the Control Panel's Modem applet to install any modems not already installed and detected. If you do not already have a modem installed or if you attempt to install Dial-Up Networking or the Microsoft Network, the Install New Modem Wizard will appear. You can launch the Wizard by clicking the Add button on the General tab and let the Wizard poll the serial ports to automatically detect a modem (Figure 11.1). You can also select a modem manually from the list of manufacturers and models or install a new driver from a manufacturer-supplied diskette (Figure 11.2). The Wizard will prompt you to define or confirm the communications port used by the modem (Figure 11.3), after which the modem entry will appear in the main window of the General tab's Modem applet (Figure 11.4).

Once a modem is installed, you can modify its operational parameters through the Properties button. The port, speaker volume, and connection speed are defined at the General tab of Modem Properties (Figure 11.5). The Connection tab lets you set data bits, parity, stop bits, wait for dial tone, connection cancel timeout, and idle disconnect timeouts (Figure 11.6). This tab also offers access to the Port Settings and Advanced option dialog boxes. The Port Settings dialog box defines the size of the FIFO buffers for inbound and outbound traffic (Figure 11.7). Advanced controls include error control, compression, flow control, modulation type, the definition of any AT strings to use for special control over modem activities, and whether to record a modem log file (Figure 11.8).

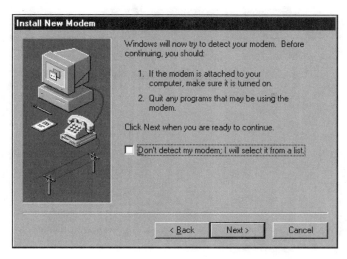

Figure 11.1   The first page of the Install New Modem Wizard.

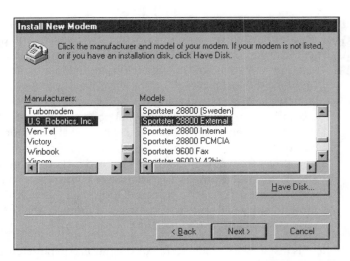

Figure 11.2 The manual modem selection page of the Install New
Modem Wizard.

If your modem is an ISDN interface, you can install it in almost the same
manner as any analog modem. The only exception is that to install an internal
ISDN adapter, you need to install the DUN upgrade 1.2 (covered later in this
chapter). In Windows 95, an ISDN adapter and a modem function almost the
same. The ISDN adapter just gives you significantly more throughput.

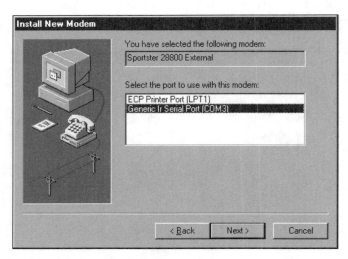

Figure 11.3 The port selection page of the Install New
Modem Wizard.

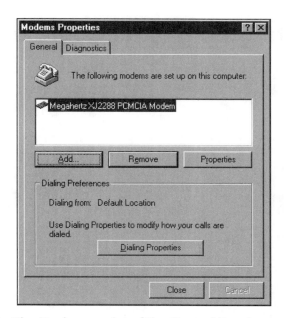

Figure 11.4   The Modem applet of the Control Panel.

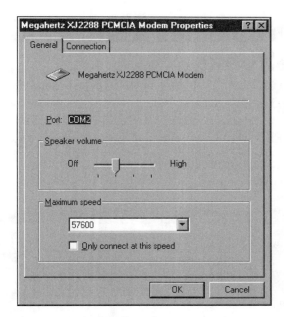

Figure 11.5   The General tab of Modem Properties.

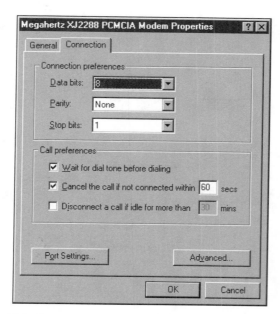

Figure 11.6 The Connection tab of Modem Properties.

TAPI Properties And Phonebooks

The Windows 95 TAPI (Telephony Application Programming Interface) provides a standard method of controlling communication over voice, data, or fax. Although the communication hardware is not provided, TAPI can be used to control many PBX systems and communication devices for automated activity.

TAPI is installed automatically when a modem is installed. Each time a dial-out connection is attempted, TAPI controls the modem and moderates the

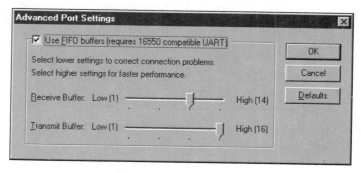

Figure 11.7 The FIFO buffer port settings.

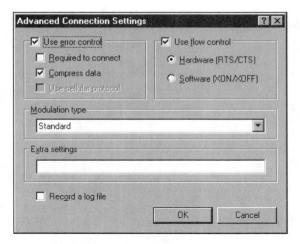

Figure 11.8 The Advanced Connection settings.

connection. Once the connection is established, TAPI continues to oversee the operation of the communication link.

 The Dialing Properties dialog box (Figure 11.9), which is reached through the Modem applet, controls how TAPI uses a modem to place calls. You can control long-distance dialing, calling card use, prefix numbers, and tone/pulse dialing. You can also define multiple configurations on the basis of physical location. For example, if you travel with a Windows 95 notebook, you can define a dialing property profile for each city you regularly visit.

TAPI is also the controlling entity for the Phonebook entries used to establish RAS connections. All the functions and features of the modem and the communication types established over a modem are configured through a TAPI-controlled interface.

DUN

Dial-Up Networking (DUN) is the remote-communications component that Windows 95 uses to establish a connection between a client and a remote system. Once a connection is established, any and all resources on the host system can be accessed—including printers, file shares, databases, network applications, mail, and scheduling—just as if they were connected locally. The only difference is speed; a serial connection over a POTS (Plain Old Telephone System)—which is also known as PSTN (Public Switched Telephone Network)—line is slower than a direct network connection using standard network media cables.

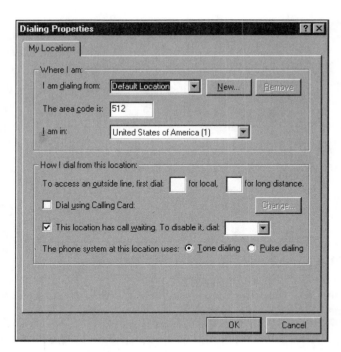

Figure 11.9 The Dialing Properties.

Using DUN, Windows 95 can establish a remote link over POTS, ISDN, and X.25 networks. You can use DUN to connect your client computer to the Internet via an ISP or to connect to an NT network via an RAS server (either hosted on a Windows NT Server, Windows NT Workstation, or Windows 95 computer).

Installing And Configuring DUN

DUN is installed automatically as part of the typical installation. If it is not currently on your system, add it through the Add/Remove Programs applet on the Windows Setup tab. To activate DUN, select Start|Programs| Accessories|Dial-Up Networking or open My Computer and double-click on Dial-Up Networking. If DUN is not fully installed, you will be prompted for the distribution files. If you have not used DUN before, the Phonebook Creation Wizard will help you establish the Phonebook entry to be used to connect to a remote system.

The first page of the Wizard is where you enter names for the connection and the modem (Figure 11.10). The second page sets the phone number to be dialed (Figure 11.11). The final page simply tells you that you have created a Phonebook entry (Figure 11.12). A new icon should appear in the Dial-Up Networking folder with the name of the connection below it (Figure 11.13).

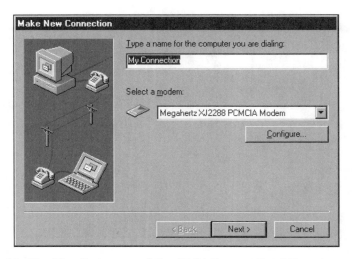

Figure 11.10   The first page of the DUN Connection Wizard.

To configure DUN further, right-click over the new icon and select Properties from the pop-up menu. From the Properties dialog box (Figure 11.14), you can change the phone number and modem being used for the connection; you will also see two buttons: Configure and Server Type. The Configure button takes you to a dialog box where modem-specific settings can be changed. The dialog box has a General tab and a Connection tab that are the same as those found through the Modem applet. There is also an Options tab, where you can choose operator assisted or manual dial and select to display a terminal window and modem status during connection establishment (Figure 11.15).

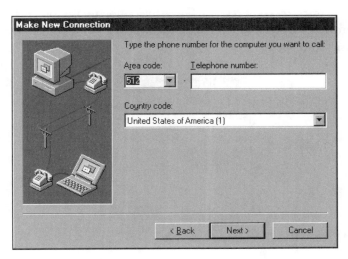

Figure 11.11   The second page of the DUN Connection Wizard.

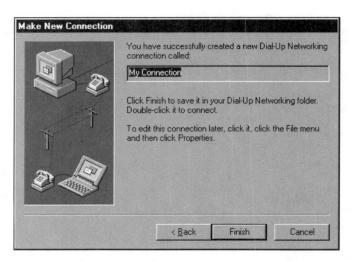

Figure 11.12 The final page of the DUN Connection Wizard.

The Server Types button brings up a dialog box where the DUN entry is configured to interact with a specific server (Figure 11.16). The settings include:

➤ **Type of Dial-Up Server** Allows you to choose the server being used: NRN (NetWare Connect); PPP (Windows 95, Windows NT 3.5+, Internet); or WFW/Windows NT 3.1. (SLIP appears in this list if it has been added through the Add/Remove Programs applet.)

➤ **Log on to network** Instructs DUN to attempt to log on to the network using the name and password supplied.

➤ **Enable software compression** Gives the option to use compression to improve the transfer rate if both ends of the connection share a compression protocol.

Figure 11.13 The DUN folder.

Figure 11.14   The DUN Phonebook entry Properties dialog box.

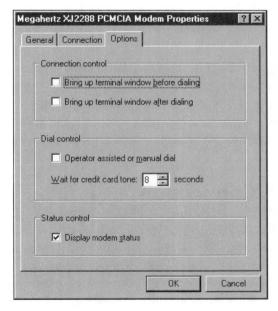

Figure 11.15   The Options tab of the Modem Properties.

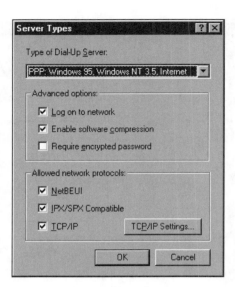

Figure 11.16 The Server Types dialog box.

➤ **Require encrypted password** Specifies that only encrypted passwords are transmitted over the link.

➤ **Protocols** Allows a choice of NetBEUI, IPX/SPX Compatible, or TCP/IP.

If you select TCP/IP as the protocol, you will need to use the TCP/IP Settings button to define how this DUN entry will use TCP/IP. The TCP/IP Settings dialog box (Figure 11.17) offers the options of automatically obtaining an IP address or defining a static address, using server assigned name servers or specifying them, using IP header compression, and using the remote network's default gateway.

Making A Connection

Once your DUN Phonebook entry is defined, double-click on it to bring up the Connect To dialog box (Figure 11.18). You can make any changes to the username and password, choose to store the password for future connections, change the phone number, and alter the dialing location. Once you press Connect, DUN will attempt to connect to the remote system. Configuring the Phonebook entry will bring up a terminal window where you can log in manually. Once the connection is established, the Connect To dialog box turns into the Connected To dialog box, which displays the speed and duration of the connection.

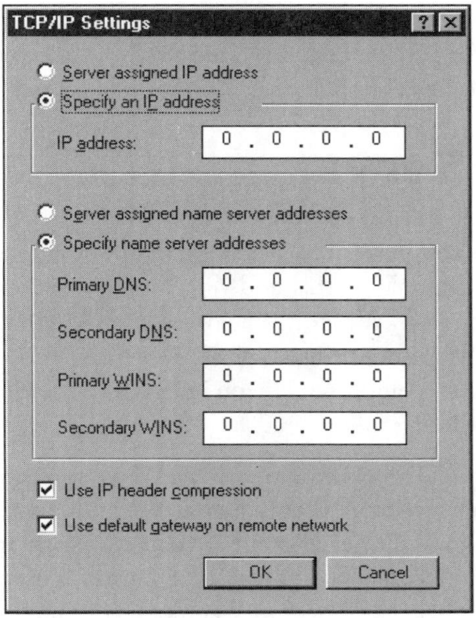

Figure 11.17   The TCP/IP Settings dialog box.

To disconnect, click Disconnect on the Connected To dialog box. For details on which protocols are being used over the connection, click Details.

Once you use a resource over a DUN link, the system remembers how to access that resource if you attempt to access it again. Thus, if you try to reach a remote resource that you've used before but do not currently have a DUN session

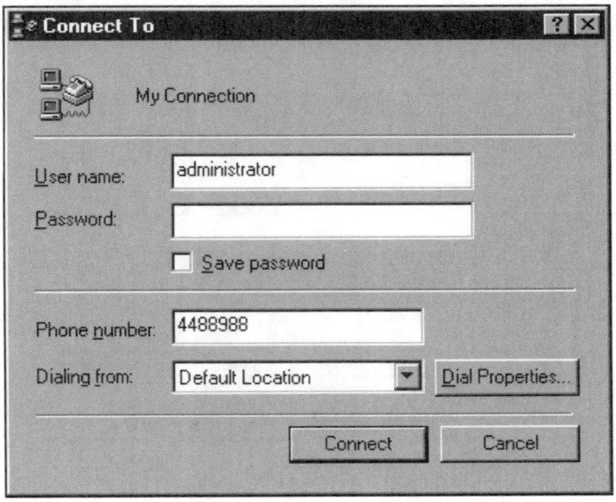

Figure 11.18   The Connect To dialog box.

active, the system will activate DUN automatically and attempt to make a connection to access the resource. In Windows NT this is called "autodial," in Windows 95 it is called "implicit connections."

Dial-Up Server

Dial-Up Server, an add-on component from Microsoft Plus!, lets you turn your Windows 95 computer into a host system that can accept inbound re-mote connection calls. With this add-on, Windows 95 can accept a single inbound connection from Windows 95, WFW, LAN Manager, Windows NT, or any PPP client. It cannot be used for SLIP or IPX/SPX connections. Dial-Up Server appears as an additional menu item under the Connection menu of the Dial-Up Networking folder.

The Dial-Up Server dialog box (Figure 11.19) is very simple to configure. Select the No caller access or Allow caller access radio button. Depending on the security type, you will need to either define a password or add users to whom you will grant access. The Server Type button is used to set the type of allowable connections, to enable software compression, and to require encrypted passwords (Figure 11.20). If a user is connected, the Disconnect User option will terminate their session.

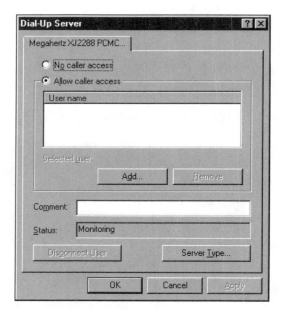

Figure 11.19 The Dial-Up Server dialog box.

Figure 11.20   The Server Types dialog box for Dial-Up Server.

DCC

The Windows 95 Direct Cable Connection (DCC) utility uses a null-modem cable to establish a network link between two Windows 95 computers. A null-modem cable can be connected to either a serial port or a parallel port, but both ends of the cable must be connected to the same type of port. DCC is installed by default but, if not present, can be added through the Add/Remove Programs applet on the Windows Setup tab.

 Setting up a DCC involves defining one system as the host and the other as the guest (Figure 11.21). The Connection Wizard (accessed by selecting Start|Programs|Accessories|Direct Cable Connection) is used on both machines. First set up the host, then set up the guest. Part of the setup process involves selecting the port to be used (Figure 11.22) and deciding whether to use a password. Once a connection is established, you should be able to interact over the cable as if it were a DUN or standard network connection.

PPTP And VPN

Since the original release of Windows 95, Microsoft has developed an improvement to the built-in Dial-Up Networking system. DUN Upgrade 1.2 is a downloadable upgrade package that improves and expands the remote access capabilities of Windows 95. ISDN and PPTP/VPN support are significant additions to Windows 95. DUN 1.2's ISDN support provides the ability to use internal ISDN adapter cards and multilink to aggregate both B channels for 128 Kbps throughput.

The addition of PPTP (Point-to-Point Tunneling Protocol) to Windows 95 has brought the ability to participate in Virtual Private Networks (VPN). PPTP, a communications protocol based on PPP, establishes a secure communication

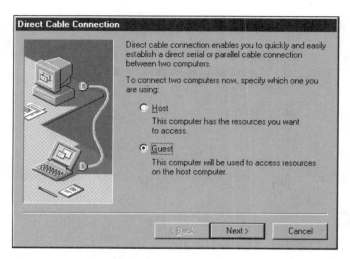

Figure 11.21 The Direct Cable Connection Wizard: Select host or guest.

channel between a client and a network (or a single server) over an existing Internet connection. This allows long-distance connections to be cost effective because inexpensive local connections to the Internet are used instead of long-distance, phone-line connections. Thus, the Internet acts as the long-distance carrier. PPTP connections, including the authentication process and all data transferred over the connection, are fully encrypted. As an extension of RAS and DUN, PPTP allows true network connectivity with reliable security. Thus, a PPTP DUN client is the same as a locally attached network client; only its communication speed is different.

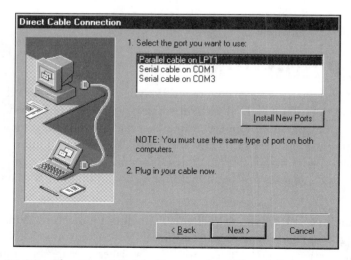

Figure 11.22 The Direct Cable Connection Wizard: Select port.

To configure a Windows 95 client as a VPN client using PPTP to connect to a network (or to a stand-alone server) over the Internet, you must have the following prerequisites:

➤ Windows 95 installed

➤ Any protocols to be used over the VPN installed and configured

➤ A modem, ISDN adapter, or other communication device installed

➤ A DUN phonebook entry to connect Windows 95 to the Internet using PPP

➤ DUN Upgrade 1.2 installed

A PPTP connection actually requires two DUN phonebook entries. One connects the client to the Internet; the second creates the PPTP tunnel over the PPP Internet connection between the client and the network (or the stand-alone server).

To create a PPTP DUN entry, follow these steps:

1. Open Dial-Up Networking (Start|Programs|Accessories|Dial-Up Networking).

2. Launch the Make New Connection wizard (MNCW) by double-clicking on the Make New Connection icon in the Dial-Up Networking window.

3. On the first page of the MNCW, define a name for this connection and select Microsoft VPN adapter as the device. Click Next.

4. On the next page of the MNCW, provide the host name of the IP address of the VPN RAS server that is connected to the Internet and awaiting the PPTP connection. Click Next.

5. Click Finish.

If you need to edit or change any part of the VPN entry, select it in the Dial-Up Networking window, then use the File|Properties command from the menu bar. This opens the configuration dialog box for a VPN entry. The General tab of this dialog box offers only the items for changing the host name/IP address of the RAS server to which you are connecting and the device used to make this connection. The Server Types tab allows you to log on to the network, use software compression, and encrypt passwords. Plus, you can select which protocol(s) (NetBEUI, IPX/SPX, and/or TCP/IP) to use over this connection.

Once your VPN entry is created, connecting to a network using PPTP is achieved as follows:

1. Establish your ISP connection by launching the DUN entry.

2. Launch the VPN entry to create the PPTP tunnel between your client and the remote network.

Once a PPTP connection is made, you will no longer have access to the Internet. VPN takes over full control of the connection so it can maintain a reliable and secure connection to the remote network. Internet access can be regained if the network you are connecting to provides Internet access itself or by using another communication device on your client to establish a separate link to an ISP.

Troubleshooting

Troubleshooting DUN problems is similar to solving standard network problems. Most often, the problem lies in mistakes made when configuring DUN's entry settings, such as typos, wrong selections, or not matching the parameters of the host system. Double-check all settings and try to connect again.

Monitoring Remote Access

You will find information about DUN's performance through the System Monitor, including whether server threads are Microsoft or Novell and, for Microsoft Clients, bytes read per second and bytes written per second.

Diagnostics

If you suspect problems with your modem or other communication hardware, you can use the built-in hardware diagnostics to help locate the problem. The Diagnostics tab of the Modem applet lists all communication ports and devices. Select one and click the Driver button to list the drivers or the More Info button to perform a simple diagnostic test. The diagnostic test is a sequence of standard AT commands that returns responses that you can compare with the device's documentation.

Modem Logging

Troubleshooting communication problems is much simpler when logging capabilities are used. The primary log that records modem-related activity is the MODEMLOG.TXT file, which is in the main Windows 95 directory. Logging is enabled through a modem's properties in the Modem applet in the Advanced Connections Settings area.

PPP Logging

Windows 95 DUN can also record a log file for events specifically related to PPP if enabled through the Network applet. Select the Dial-Up Adapter, click Properties, and select the Advanced tab. Select the Record a log file option and select Yes from the Value list. The name of the log file is PPPLOG.TXT; it is stored in the main Windows directory.

Port Contention

By default, DOS and Windows 16-bit applications are designed so that only one application can access one COM port at a time. To allow multiple applications to be active at once, a second application can use the port if the primary application is inactive (relative to port usage) for a specified time. This behavior is controlled through the SYSTEM.INI file. Under the [386enh] section, the COMxAutoAssign=y entry defines the time y in seconds for COM port x.

Windows 32-bit applications do not have this limitation; multiple Win32 applications can use the same COM port simultaneously.

BRIEFCASE

BRIEFCASE is a handy utility that provides two-way file synchronization. Although BRIEFCASE was originally developed as a means of keeping laptop files in sync with a corresponding desktop computer, it can be used in many situations where you want to keep two sets of files up-to-date. BRIEFCASE allows you to:

➤ Provide two-way data synchronization between Windows 95 computers.

➤ Sync a laptop to a desktop, a remote computer to a server, or a local computer to a server.

➤ Provide drag-and-drop simplicity to the data synchronization process.

To synchronize files using the BRIEFCASE program, you can:

➤ Drag-and-drop the files into the briefcase.

➤ Use the menu Copy command.

➤ Use the menu Send To command.

➤ Use cut-and-paste to place the files in the briefcase.

You can synchronize the files in the briefcase with the Update All command on the BRIEFCASE pull-down menu. As synchronization proceeds, whenever a question arises about how to sync two files, you will see a dialog box with the following four selections:

➤ **Replace** One of the files has changed; when you select Replace, the old file is overwritten by the new file.

➤ **Skip** Both files are already in sync; no changes are made to either file.

➤ **Delete** The original file has been deleted; the synchronized file will also be deleted once you click Delete.

➤ **Merge** Both files have changed, and the host application supports the data merge capabilities of BRIEFCASE.

Exam Prep Questions

Question 1

> Which protocols are supported by Dial-Up Networking? [Check all correct answers]
>
> ❑ a. PPP
>
> ❑ b. TCP/IP
>
> ❑ c. IPX/SPX
>
> ❑ d. NetBEUI

DUN supports all these protocols. Therefore, answers a, b, c, and d are correct. However, you should note that PPP is a WAN protocol and that the others are LAN protocols.

Question 2

> Which is the best way to increase security on a Windows 95 computer that is being used to dial out to another network?
>
> ○ a. Use share-level security
>
> ○ b. Enable modem logging
>
> ○ c. Encrypt all passwords
>
> ○ d. Enable software compression

Encrypting passwords is the best way to improve outbound security. Therefore, answer c is correct. Share-level security is less secure than user-level security, and resource security on Windows 95 as a client is usually not important. Therefore, answer a is incorrect. Modem logging will aid in troubleshooting but does not affect security in any way. Therefore, answer c is incorrect. Software compression will improve performance over a DUN connection but has no effect on security. Therefore, answer d is incorrect.

Question 3

When Windows 95 reestablishes a DUN connection automatically when a previously accessed resource is used again, _____ is being used. [Fill in the blank with the correct answer]

O   a. Autodial

O   b. Network connection

O   c. Implicit connection

O   d. A printer

An implicit connection is being used when Windows 95 automatically reestablishes a DUN connection to access a resource. Therefore, answer c is correct. Autodial is the name given to this process under Windows NT but is not used in Windows 95. Therefore, answer a is incorrect. A network connection would not initiate a DUN reconnect. Therefore, answer b is incorrect. A printer may have been a remote resource being accessed, but many other resource types cause implicit connections to be reestablished. Therefore, answer d is incorrect.

Question 4

Which is the central and irreplaceable component of the Windows 95 communication architecture?

O   a. UNIMODEM.VXD

O   b. A modem

O   c. Miniport drivers

O   d. VCOMM.VXD

VCOMM.VXD is the central and irreplaceable component. Therefore, answer d is correct. UNIMODEM.VXD is a common component but is often replaced by manufacturers. Therefore, answer a is incorrect. A modem is often used but is not a required or central component. Therefore, answer b is incorrect. The miniport driver is hardware-specific and is not central or irreplaceable. Therefore, answer c is incorrect.

Question 5

Which important communication log files are stored in the main Windows directory? [Check all correct answers]

❑ a. DUN.LOG

❑ b. MODEMLOG.TXT

❑ c. PPPLOG.TXT

❑ d. USERS.DAT

The communication log files stored in the Windows directory are PPPLOG.TXT and MODEMLOG.TXT. Therefore, answers b and c are correct. DUN.LOG is a fictitious file. Therefore, answer a is incorrect. USERS.DAT is the user-specific portion of the Registry stored in the Windows directory but has nothing to do with communication logging. Therefore, answer d is incorrect.

Question 6

Call waiting can be disabled through Dialing Properties.

○ a. True

○ b. False

Call waiting can be disabled through Dialing Properties. Therefore, answer a is correct.

Question 7

The Dial-Up Server for Windows 95 can support which types of clients? [Check all correct answers]

❑ a. PPP

❑ b. IPX

❑ c. SLIP

❑ d. Windows NT

Windows 95 Dial-Up Server supports PPP and Windows NT clients. In addition, Windows 95 can accept a single inbound connection from Windows 95, WFW, and LAN Manager. Therefore, answers a and d are correct. Dial-Up Server does not support IPX and SLIP. Therefore, answers b and c are incorrect.

Question 8

> BRIEFCASE can be used to carry out which functions? [Check all correct answers]
>
> ❏ a. Synchronize data between two Windows 95 computers.
>
> ❏ b. Carry printed documents between one workstation and another.
>
> ❏ c. Maintain version control between a desktop computer and a notebook computer.
>
> ❏ d. Create new Office documents.

BRIEFCASE can synchronize data between two computers and maintain version control between a desktop and a notebook. Therefore, answers a and c are correct. BRIEFCASE cannot store printed documents because it is a software product, not a physical carrying case. Therefore, answer b is incorrect. BRIEF-CASE cannot be used to create new Office documents, although it can be used to synchronize groups of existing Office documents. Therefore, answer d is incorrect.

Question 9

> Which is the simplest method of exchanging files between two Windows 95 computers? Assume they are in close proximity and the files to be exchanged are too big to fit on floppies.
>
> ○ a. Install NICs and create a network.
>
> ○ b. Use a Direct Cable Connection.
>
> ○ c. Install modems, dial into an Internet server, and use FTP.
>
> ○ d. Use a backup tape device.

The simplest method is using a Direct Cable Connection. Therefore, answer b is correct. Adding NICs or modems may not be easy, and creating or using system accounts and a directory share is not the easiest method. Therefore, answers a and c are incorrect. A tape backup device is the most difficult of all the solutions. Therefore, answer d is incorrect.

Question 10

> Which of the following communication media are supported by
> DUN in Windows 95? [Check all correct answers]
>
> ❑ a. X.25
>
> ❑ b. ISDN
>
> ❑ c. XDSL
>
> ❑ d. PSTN

DUN supports X.25, ISDN, and PSTN media. Therefore, answers a, b, and d are correct. Windows 95 DUN does not natively support XDSL. Therefore, answer c is incorrect.

Question 11

> If your modem requires a special AT command string to be sent
> to it each time a connection attempt is made, where can you de-
> fine this?
>
> ○ a. Through Dialing Properties
>
> ○ b. On the dialog box reached through the Advanced button
>   on the Connection tab of the Modem Properties
>
> ○ c. The Options tab of Modem Properties
>
> ○ d. By editing the MODEMLOG.TXT

An AT command can be defined on the dialog box reached through the Advanced button on the Connection tab of the Modem Properties. Therefore, answer b is correct. Dialing Properties does not offer an AT command option but is used to set the location, credit card, and line commands. Therefore, answer a is incorrect. The Options tab of Modem Properties is used to set a terminal window and operator-assisted or manual dial, and it has a checkbox for displaying modem status during connection establishment. Therefore, answer c is incorrect. The MODEMLOG.TXT records modem-related events. AT commands are not defined in this file, although the results of AT commands may be listed. Therefore, answer d is incorrect.

Question 12

> Which of the following TCP/IP items or options can be set through
> the TCP/IP Settings dialog box? Remember, the TCP/IP Settings
> button is located on the Server Type dialog box accessed from the
> Properties dialog box of a DUN Phonebook entry. [Check all cor-
> rect answers]
>
> ❏ a. Dynamically assigned IP address
>
> ❏ b. DNS name server
>
> ❏ c. The IP address of the default gateway
>
> ❏ d. Subnet mask

The TCP/IP Settings dialog box offers control over dynamically assigned IP
address and name servers. Therefore, answers a and b are correct. The IP address
of the default gateway and the subnet mask are not defined on the TCP/IP
Settings dialog box but through the Properties dialog box for TCP/IP in the
Network applet on the respective IP Address and Gateway tabs. Therefore,
answers c and d are incorrect.

Question 13

> A travelling salesman has an AT&T WorldNet account that allows
> him to connect to the Internet from all of the cities he frequents
> using a Windows 95 notebook computer. This is convenient be-
> cause it allows him to remain in contact by email. The home office
> has a network that stores all of the product inventory and cost
> statistics. The salesman currently connects with the network via a
> long-distance telephone call to retrieve the product details on a
> daily basis. What can be done with this notebook computer to
> reduce the cost and headache of communicating with the network?
>
> ○ a. Have a secretary email the product detail files each day.
>
> ○ b. Fax the product info to the salesman's hotel.
>
> ○ c. Use PPTP to create a VPN connection over the Internet.
>
> ○ d. This is already the best solution.

The use of PPTP to create a VPN connection is the best way to simplify and
decrease costs for the long-distance communication with the home network.
Therefore, answer c is correct. Emailing the files is inefficient and requires
someone to perform this task, which is not a cost- or time-effective solution.

Therefore, answer a is incorrect. Faxing the information is not only a waste of time, it costs money for long distance and does not get the data to the salesman in a useful form. Therefore, answer b is incorrect. The current method is not the best solution for this situation; PPTP can be used. Therefore, answer d is incorrect.

Need To Know More?

 Supporting Microsoft Windows 95. Microsoft Press, Redmond, WA, 1995. ISBN 1-55615-931-5. Chapter 13 discusses ports, modems, and TAPI. Chapter 24 discusses Dial-Up Networking and Direct Cable Connections.

 Mortensen, Lance and Rick Sawtell: *MCSE: Windows 95 Study Guide*. Sybex Network Press, San Francisco, CA, 1996. ISBN: 0-7821-2092-X. Chapter 17 focuses on the communications architecture of Windows 95, such as installing, configuring, and diagnosing modems. Chapter 18 discusses Dial-Up Networking.

 Search the TechNet CD (or its online version through www. microsoft.com) and the *Windows 95 Resource Kit* using the keywords "Dial-Up Networking," "DUN," "modem," "Dialing properties," "Direct Cable Connection," and "Briefcase."

Printing

Terms you'll need to understand:

√ Printer, logical printer

√ Print client, print server

√ Print device, print driver

√ Print job

√ Print spooler

√ Queue

Techniques you'll need to master:

√ Installing local and network logical printers

√ Sharing printers

√ Understanding the basics of print architecture

√ Understanding spooling and its controls and options

√ Configuring a printer

√ Using Point-and-Print

√ Administering print queues

√ Troubleshooting printers

Printing is one of the most common computer functions for both stand-alone and networked computers. This chapter focuses on the Microsoft approach to printing and defines a few Microsoft-specific printing terms to aid you in your studies.

Printing And Windows 95

Printing in Windows 95 introduced several new features, including:

➤ **Plug and Play** Automatically detects attached printers.

➤ **Bidirectional communication** Enables the printer and computer to communicate with each other to provide enhanced printer features and functions.

➤ **ECP (Extended Capabilities Port) support** A hardware add-on that improves print speed and transfer efficiency.

➤ **Color matching** Allows WYSIWYG device-independent color matching.

Windows 95 printing simplifies the process of attaching local printers and networked printers through the Add Printer Wizard. Previously, all client computers required that the print driver be installed on each client machine that needed to access a print device. Now, printing from a Windows 95 client requires that the driver be installed or upgraded only on the print server (whether it is Windows 95 or Windows NT), not on every client computer.

The Windows 95 Print Lexicon

The following list contains Microsoft-specific printing terminology. Pay close attention to these definitions since Microsoft has seen fit to alter their common usage.

➤ **Client application** This is a program that originates print jobs (this can be located on a print server or on a client computer on a network).

➤ **Connecting to a printer** To connect to a printer, you must attach to a network share that resides on the computer on which the logical printer was created (performed through the Add Printer Wizard accessed from Start|Printers).

➤ **Creating a printer** To create a printer, you must name, define settings for, install drivers for, and link a print device to a network. In Windows 95, this process is performed through the Add Printer Wizard.

➤ **Network interface printer** This comprises built-in network interface cards for print devices that are directly attached to a network (e.g., the Hewlett-Packard JetDirect).

Note: The DLC protocol must be installed to communicate with print devices that are directly attached.

➤ **Print client** This is a computer on a network (called a "client computer") that transmits the print jobs to be produced by the physical print device.

➤ **Print device** The print device is commonly referred to as the printer, which can be confusing. Just remember that the print device is the piece of hardware that actually outputs a printed product, so it can be a fax modem, a slide maker, or even a CAD plotter.

➤ **Print job** This code defines the print processing commands as well as the actual file to be printed. Windows 95 defines print jobs by data type, depending on the adjustments made to the file for it to print accurately (i.e., one data type can be printable as is, whereas another may need a form feed to conclude the data stream in order for the print job to be executed properly).

➤ **Print resolution** Pixel density is responsible for the smooth-ness of any printed image or text. Resolution is measured in dots per inch (DPI). The higher the DPI, the better the quality of the printed material.

➤ **Print server** This is the server computer that links physical print devices to the network and manages the sharing of those devices with computers on the network.

➤ **Print spooler** This is the collection of Dynamic Link Libraries (DLLs) that acquires, processes, catalogs, and disperses print jobs. A print job is saved to disk in a spool file. Print de-spooling is the process of reading what is contained in the spool file and transmitting it to the physical print device.

➤ **Print driver** Print drivers enable communication between applications and a specific print device. Most hardware peripherals, such as printers, require the use of a driver to process commands.

➤ **Printer/logical printer** The logical printer (Microsoft calls this "the printer") is the software interface that communi-cates between the operating system and the physical print device. The logical printer handles the printing process from the time the Print command is issued. Its settings determine the physical print device that renders the file to be printed as well as how the file to be printed is sent to the print device (e.g., through a remote print share or local port).

➤ **Queue/print queue** In printing terms, a queue is a series of files waiting to be produced by the print device.

➤ **Rendering** The rendering process in Windows 95 is as follows: A client application sends file information to the Graphics Device Interface (GDI), which receives the data, communicates that data to the physical print device driver, and produces the print job in the language of the physical print device. The device then interprets this information and creates a file (bitmap) for each page to be printed.

Printing Architecture

Windows 95 print settings are managed through the Printers folder, which is accessible from the Control Panel or the Start menu. (Note: The Printers folder replaces the old Windows 3.x Print Manager.) This approach is much more straightforward than that used by earlier versions of Windows and other network operating systems.

Windows 95 takes a modular approach to printing. Each component has a specific use and interfaces with the other components in the print architecture (see Figure 12.1).

The following list defines each component of the printing architecture:

➤ **Print driver** The software component that enables communication between the operating system and the physical print device.

➤ **Graphics Device Interface (GDI)** The component that provides network applications with a system for presenting graphical information. The GDI works as a translator between the application's print requests and the device driver interface (DDI) to make sure a job is rendered accurately.

➤ **Print router** The component that directs the print job to the appropriate print device.

➤ **Print spooler** (also called the **print provider**) The component that accepts print jobs from the router, calls the processor to make any needed changes to the print job, and transfers the jobs one at a time to the print monitor.

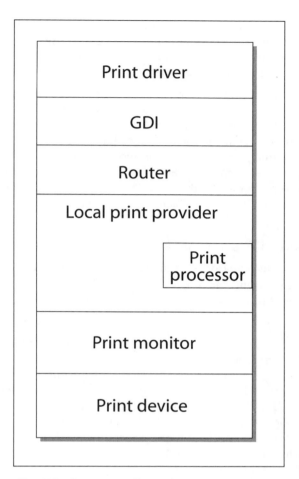

Figure 12.1   The Windows 95 print architecture components work together to render print jobs for the user.

➤ **Print processor** The component that makes any necessary modifications to the print job before passing the job to the print monitor.

➤ **Print monitor** The component that passes the print job, which has been translated to the print device's language, to the physical print device.

➤ **Print device** The physical hardware device that outputs a printed product.

The Windows 95 print architecture uses two types of drivers to control printing: universal drivers and minidrivers. A universal driver is a generic driver used for all printers. There are two types of universal drivers, one for regular printers and one for PostScript printers. Minidrivers are device-specific drivers supplied by the manufacturer that add sections of code needed to control the special features of a printer. The one exception to this two-part driver model is the HP Color InkJet, which uses a single, monolithic driver.

When a print job is spooled, it is stored in one of two data formats: EMF or raw. EMF (Enhanced MetaFile) format is the internal graphics language of Windows 95. It is a collection of commands used to create graphics images. Raw format, a printer's natural language, is device-specific. Typically, EMF is used because it is device-independent and produces more efficient spooling and network transfer. By default, all print jobs are spooled as EMF, except PostScript, which is spooled in PS format.

Printer Installation

Configuring or installing printers under Windows 95 is very simple, even if the drivers for the printer are not included with the shipping distribution files. The two types of printer setup are local and network.

A local printer is simply a print device that is physically attached to a computer. In such cases, the computer will act as the print server. Once the printer is physically connected, use the Add Printer Wizard from the Printers folder (Figure 12.2) to install the proper drivers. Select the Local printer option at the first prompt (Figure 12.3). You'll be asked for the printer make and model (Figure 12.4); if this is not listed, click the Have Disk option to load drivers from a floppy. Also select the port (Figure 12.5), a name for the printer (Figure 12.6), and whether to print a test page. To make the printer accessible to users over a network, you'll need to share it (see the section "Sharing" later in this chapter).

A network printer is simply a software redirector that guides print jobs from a client to the actual location of the print server

Figure 12.2 The Windows 95 Printers folder.

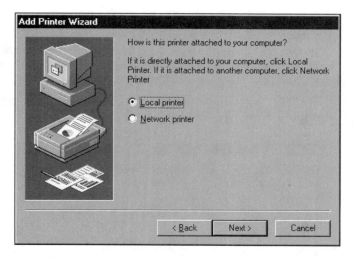

Figure 12.3   The Add Printer Wizard: Select local or network.

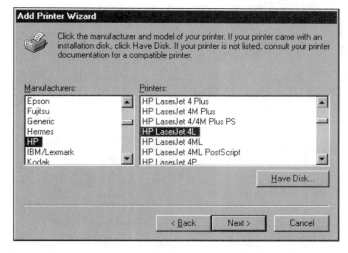

Figure 12.4   The Add Printer Wizard: Select printer make and model.

and, ultimately, to the printer itself. Attaching to a network printer is simple. Once again, use the Add Printer Wizard from the Printers folder, but select the Network printer option at the first prompt (Figure 12.7). Enter the UNC name of the printer or click Browser to locate a printer in the network name space (Figure 12.8). Select whether to allow DOS access to this printer. If you select Yes, you will be prompted to select an LPT to associate with this printer. Define a name for the printer, then print a test page. If the test document prints, you've been successful. Notice that you do not install a print driver when connecting to a network printer if you are working from a Windows 95 client. Instead, the driver is downloaded from the print server each time a print job needs to be created. However, when a Windows NT system is the print server, the Windows 95 driver must be installed on NT for Windows 95 clients to access the printer without installing a local driver.

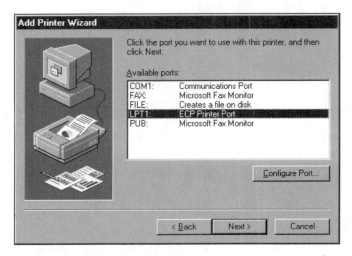

Figure 12.5 The Add Printer Wizard: Select port.

Figure 12.6 The Add Printer Wizard: Define printer name.

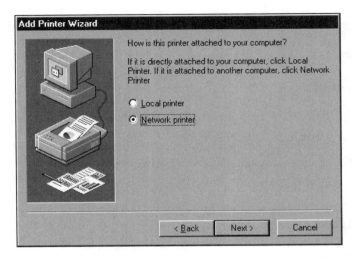

Figure 12.7   The Add Printer Wizard: Select local or network printer.

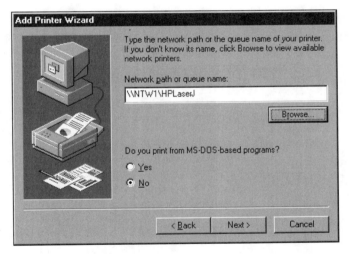

Figure 12.8   The Add Printer Wizard: Define network path to printer.

Printer Configuration

Once a printer has been installed, you can alter its configuration and setup to better suit your needs. The Properties dialog box of the printer has many tabs and options, including General, Details, Sharing, Paper, Graphics, Fonts, and Device Options. You should take the time to become familiar with the features and options presented on these tabs.

Note: These are the default tabs. Other tabs may be present or missing, depending on the printer. The layout and options on the tabs may differ as well.

General

On the General tab (Figure 12.9), you can do the following:

➤ Input a comment about the printer.

➤ Define a separator page that prints between print jobs.

➤ Print a test page.

Details

On the Details tab (Figure 12.10), you can do the following:

➤ Define the attached port or create/delete ports.

➤ Change the print driver.

➤ Capture (and terminate capture) a printer port (used for DOS printing).

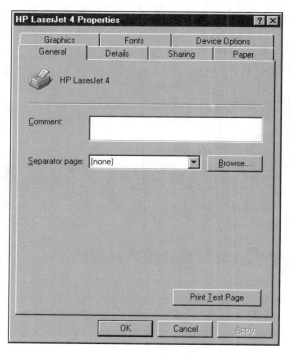

Figure 12.9   The General tab of Printer Properties.

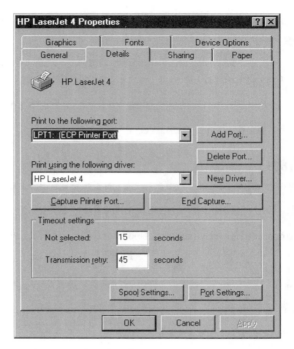

Figure 12.10   The Details tab of Printer Properties.

➤ Define timeout settings for online not operational and transmission retry.

➤ Change settings for Spool and Ports (see following sections).

Spool Settings

The Spool Settings dialog box (Figure 12.11) controls the spooling activities of the printer, including the following:

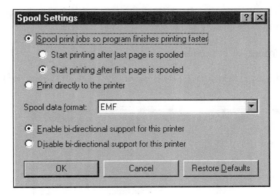

Figure 12.11   The Spool Settings dialog box.

➤ The logical printer can be set to use the spooler or to send print jobs directly to the physical printer.

➤ If the spooler is used, you can choose whether to begin printing immediately or to wait until the entire print job is spooled.

➤ The spooled data format can be changed between EMF and RAW.

➤ Bidirectional support can be enabled or disabled.

Port Settings

The Port Settings dialog box (Figure 12.12) has two checkboxes:

➤ **Spool MS-DOS print jobs** Forces DOS print jobs through the spooler.

➤ **Check port state before printing** Tests the port for inactivity before allowing a DOS application to attempt access.

Sharing

On the Sharing tab (Figure 12.13), you can do the following:

➤ Share or not share.

➤ Share a name.

➤ Define a password or users/groups to grant users access to the printer, depending on the security level.

Paper

On the Paper tab (Figure 12.14), you can do the following:

➤ Set paper size.

➤ Set to portrait or landscape.

➤ Define the paper source tray.

➤ Set the number of copies to print by default.

➤ Define the unprintable area of a page (i.e., .25 in. from each edge).

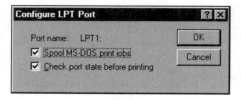

Figure 12.12 The Port Settings dialog box.

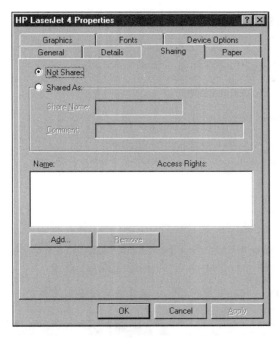

Figure 12.13 The Sharing tab of Printer Properties.

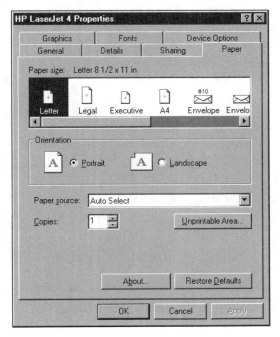

Figure 12.14 The Paper tab of Printer Properties.

Graphics

On the Graphics tab (Figure 12.15), you can do the following:

➤ Set resolution in dots per inch.

➤ Set dithering method.

➤ Set intensity level.

➤ Choose graphics mode: raster or vector.

Fonts

On the Fonts tab (Figure 12.16), you can do the following:

➤ Define installed font cartridges.

➤ Choose how to handle TrueType fonts: download as outline soft fonts, download as bitmap soft fonts, or print as graphics.

➤ Add fonts to the printer's memory through Install Printer Fonts.

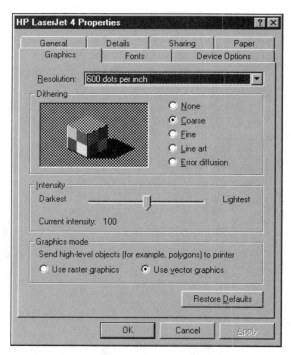

Figure 12.15 The Graphics tab of Printer Properties.

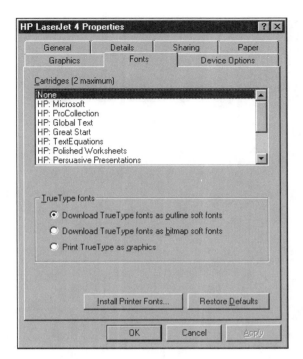

Figure 12.16   The Fonts tab of Printer Properties.

Device Options

On the Device Options tab (Figure 12.17), you can set printer-specific settings. There is a print quality selection list as well. Memory options are available here for some printers.

Network Printing

Another feature of Windows 95 network printing is called Point-and-Print. This feature automates the installation and use of network shared printers. If the print server is Windows 95 or a Windows NT computer with Windows 95 drivers installed, you can access or use a network-shared printer (a.k.a., Point-and-Print) in three ways:

➤ Locate the print share in Network Neighborhood; double-click to install the logical printer locally.

➤ Locate the print share in Network Neighborhood; drag-and-drop to your desktop or Printers folder.

➤ Drag-and-drop a document onto the printer icon in Network Neighborhood.

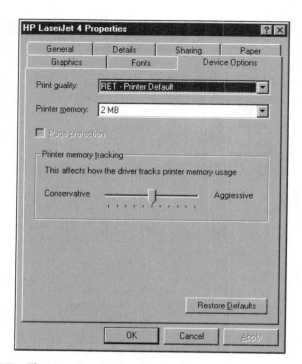

Figure 12.17 The Device Options tab of Printer Properties.

If the print server is a NetWare server, you'll need to do the following to use Point-and-Print. First, locate and select the print queue in Network Neighborhood. Right-click and select Print and Print Setup from the pop-up menu. This menu item reveals two other entries: Set Printer Model and Set Driver Path. Once you have defined both these items, you can use Point-and-Print with NetWare-hosted printers. Several tweaks and controls must be performed on the NetWare side, but those details are not imperative.

File And Printer Sharing For NetWare Networks

The File and Printer Sharing for NetWare Networks service enables Windows 95 to host printers and directories to be used by NetWare clients. This service, which must be used in conjunction with the Microsoft Client for NetWare Networks, enables Windows 95 printers to accept output from NetWare-hosted print queues and spoolers. The service adds another tab in Printer Properties, called Print Server, which allows you to enable or disable the Microsoft Print

Server for NetWare. You can then select the NetWare server, the print server object, and the polling timeout. Now, NetWare print servers can send documents to your local printer, and you can continue using your local printer normally.

Network Attached Printers

Windows 95 supports network attached printers via the Data Link Control (DLC) protocol. DLC was originally designed as a protocol for communicating with host mainframes (such as the IBM AS/4000). However, it can also be used to enable communications between a print server and a printer attached directly to the network. DLC is installed via the Network applet in the same fashion as any other protocol.

The Windows 95 distribution CD contains the drivers and applications for two network attached printer types, namely HP JetDirect interfaces and Digital's stand-alone PrintServer. Support for the HP JetDirect devices is installed as a Service through the Networking applet and is listed under the Hewlett-Packard Manufacturer as HP JetAdmin (Figure 12.18). This allows you to communicate, administer (through the new HP JetAdmin applet in the Control Panel), and print to printers equipped with HP's network interface. Digital PrintServer stand-alone devices are also directly attached to the network. They are installed like a normal local printer through the Add Printer Wizard, but you are prompted to provide TCP/IP address information for the network-attached print device.

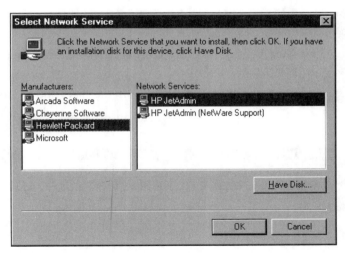

Figure 12.18   The Select Network Service dialog box from the Network applet.

Administration

Managing print jobs is fairly simple. You can manipulate a print job if it is listed in the print queue. Open the print queue window (see Figure 12.19) through the main Printers folder (see Figure 12.2). Select a print job and use one of the commands from the Document menu:

➤ **Pause Printing** Pauses the printing of this print job.

➤ **Cancel Printing** Deletes the print job from the print queue.

The Printer menu offers you three other administration commands:

➤ **Pause Printing** Pauses the entire printer.

➤ **Purge Print Jobs** Deletes all print jobs currently in queue.

➤ **Set as Default** Sets this logical printer as the default print device.

You can rearrange the order of print jobs by dragging-and-dropping. Remember that the jobs near the top of the window will be printed before those at the bottom.

Troubleshooting

A seemingly infinite number of issues must be resolved to return a printer to normal operation. Many printer problems are simple and obvious, so be sure to check the basics first.

➤ Always check the physical aspects of the printer: cable, power, paper, toner, and so on.

➤ Check the logical printer on both the client and the server.

➤ Check the print queue for stalled jobs.

Document Name	Status	Owner	Progress	Started At
Untitled - Notepad		administrator	1 page(s)	3:55:52 PM 10/16/97
Untitled - Notepad		administrator	1 page(s)	3:55:53 PM 10/16/97

HP LaserJet 4 - Paused

Printer Document View Help

2 jobs in queue

Figure 12.19 The print queue window of a logical printer.

➤ Reinstall the print driver to verify that it has not become corrupted.

➤ Attempt to print from a different application or a different client.

➤ Set the spool data type to raw.

➤ Print directly to printer instead of using the spooler.

➤ Check the hard drive space on the volume hosting the main Windows directory.

Exam Prep Questions

Question 1

You have an HP LaserJet attached to your Windows 95 computer that is acting as the print server for 20 other Windows 95 computers on your network. Hewlett-Packard has just released an updated printer driver. What must be done to distribute the updated driver to all the computers that print to this print server?

- ○ a. Install the updated driver on all client computers; there is no need to update the server.
- ○ b. Install the updated driver on the print server, and do nothing more.
- ○ c. Install the updated driver on the print server and on all client computers.
- ○ d. Create a separate logical printer with the updated driver on the print server and tell all your users to print to the new printer.

The best way to update a print driver is to update the driver on the print server. Therefore, answer b is correct. There is no need to update the driver manually on each client computer that is running Windows 95. Therefore, answer a is incorrect. When a client computer sends a print job to the print server, the updated driver is automatically copied to the client. Therefore, answers c and d are incorrect.

Question 2

During the printing of a 43-page document, your printer jams on the second page. You pause the printer through the Printers folder. After you remove the jam and reset the physical printer, what should you do? [Check all correct answers]

❏ a. Open the Printers folder for the printer and select Restart from the Document menu.

❏ b. Open the Printers folder for the printer, select the failed print job, select Cancel Printing from the Document menu, deselect Pause Printing from the Printer menu, then reprint the document starting on page 2.

❏ c. Open the Printers folder for the printer and deselect Pause Printing from the Printer menu.

❏ d. Open the Printers folder for the printer and select Purge Print Jobs from the Printer menu.

Printing a failed document in Windows 95 requires the following steps: Open the Printers folder for the printer, select the failed print job, select Cancel Printing from the Document menu, deselect Pause Printing from the Printer menu, then reprint the document starting on the failed page. By deselecting Pause Printing, the remaining portion of the job will print, but you will likely lose several pages and need to start the job over. Therefore, answers b and c are correct. Windows 95 printing does not have a Restart command, but Windows NT does. Therefore, answer a is incorrect. By Purging Print Jobs, you might delete print jobs sent by other users and will not be able to resend documents. Deleting only your print job is a better idea. Therefore, answer d is incorrect.

Question 3

You have just installed a new printer on your print server. You send a print job to the printer, but it comes out as pages of nonsense. What is the most likely cause of the problem?

○ a. The NetBEUI protocol is not installed.

○ b. The print spooler is corrupt.

○ c. An incorrect printer driver has been installed.

○ d. There is not enough hard disk space for spooling.

If an incorrect print driver has been installed, documents may print illegibly. Therefore, answer c is correct. A print job won't print if the wrong protocol is used. Therefore, answer a is incorrect. Likewise, nothing will print without the spooler. Therefore, answer b is incorrect. As in answer b, a print job won't print without proper spooling unless the option to print directly to the printer is selected. Therefore, answer d is incorrect.

Question 4

Which features are found in Windows 95 but not in earlier versions of Windows? [Check all correct answers]

❑ a. Plug and Play

❑ b. Bidirectional communication

❑ c. ECP (Extended Capabilities Port) support

❑ d. Color matching

All of these features are new to Windows 95. Therefore, answers a, b, c, and d are correct.

Question 5

Which of the following is not a part of the print architecture of Windows 95?

○ a. Print spooler

○ b. Print monitor

○ c. Print job

○ d. Print router

The print job is not part of the print architecture of Windows 95. Rather, it is the data sent through the print system. Therefore, answer c is correct. The print spooler, print monitor, and print router are parts of the Windows 95 print architecture. Therefore, answers a, b, and d are incorrect.

Question 6

The HP Color InkJet printer uses a universal driver and a minidriver to enable color printing within Windows 95.

○ a. True

○ b. False

False. The HP Color InkJet is the only exception to the universal driver/ minidriver architecture, as this printer requires a monolithic driver to operate within Windows 95. Therefore, answer b is correct.

Question 7

Which of the following settings, options, or parameters can be determined through the Add Printer Wizard? [Check all correct answers]

❑ a. Name of the printer

❑ b. Printer sharing

❑ c. Raw data for spooling

❑ d. Name of port used by the printer

The Add Printer Wizard can set the name of the printer and the port. Therefore, answers a and d are correct. Sharing and spool data type must be defined through Printer Properties, which can be accessed after the Add Printer Wizard has successfully installed the printer. Therefore, answers b and c are incorrect.

Question 8

If a print job fails to print properly or at all, which of the following are valid and useful steps to take to locate or eliminate the problem? [Check all correct answers]

❑ a. Start and stop the spooler service.

❑ b. Change the data type from EMF to raw.

❑ c. Change the spooling settings so that data is sent directly to the printer instead of being spooled.

❑ d. Resend the print job until it prints.

❑ e. Reinstall the printer driver.

Possible valid and useful troubleshooting steps include changing the data type from EMF to raw, changing the spooling settings so that data is sent directly to the printer instead of being spooled, and reinstalling the print driver. Therefore, answers b, c, and e are correct. Answers a and d are not valid or useful troubleshooting steps.

Question 9

Which components must be installed on Windows 95 to service NetWare-hosted print queues and spoolers? [Check all correct answers]

❑ a. File and Printer Sharing for NetWare Networks

❑ b. Microsoft Print Server for NetWare

❑ c. IPX/SPX

❑ d. Microsoft Client for NetWare Networks

The File and Printer Sharing for NetWare Networks Microsoft service and Client for NetWare Networks client must be installed to enable Windows 95 to service NetWare-hosted print queues. Therefore, answers a and d are correct. Microsoft Print Server for NetWare is a radio button selection on the Print Server tab of Printer Properties that can be used after File and Printer Sharing for NetWare Networks Microsoft has been installed. Therefore, answer b is incorrect. Remember that IPX/SPX is required only if that is the protocol being used on the NetWare system. If TCP/IP is being used, installing IPX/SPX is useless, so you must install whatever protocol is in use. Therefore, answer c is incorrect.

Question 10

Point-and-Print allows which of the following actions? Assume that the network print server is a Windows NT Server with Windows 95 drivers installed. [Check all correct answers]

❑ a. Double-click on the printer share in Network Neighborhood to automatically install.

❑ b. Drag-and-drop the printer share from the Network Neighborhood into the local Printers folder.

❑ c. Select network-shared printers without local logical printers in application print dialog boxes.

❑ d. Drag-and-drop documents onto the printer share in the Network Neighborhood.

Point-and-Print enables double-click on printer share in Network Neighborhood to automatically install, drag-and-drop the printer share from the Network Neighborhood into the local Printers folder, and drag-and-drop documents onto the printer share in the Network Neighborhood. Therefore, answers a, b, and d are correct. Point-and-Print does not enable applications to access printers that have not been assigned local logical printers. Therefore, answer c is incorrect.

Need To Know More?

Supporting Microsoft Windows 95. Microsoft Press, Redmond, WA, 1995. ISBN 1-55615-931-5. Chapter 14 discusses Windows 95 print architecture and the installation and configuration of local printers. Chapter 15 discusses network printing.

Mortensen, Lance and Rick Sawtell: *MCSE: Windows 95 Study Guide*. Sybex Network Press, San Francisco, CA, 1996. ISBN: 0-7821-2092-X. Chapter 13 contains information on local and network printing, troubleshooting, and many other printing-related issues.

Search the TechNet CD (or its online version through www. microsoft.com) and the *Windows 95 Resource Kit* using the keywords "print," "spooler," "print server," "print queue," "print folder," "Add Printer Wizard," and "Point-and-Print."

User Profiles
And System
Policies

. . . .

Terms you'll need to understand:

√ Profiles

√ System policies

√ Local profile, roaming profile

√ Mandatory profile

√ Default policy

√ Policy template, ADMIN.ADM

√ System Policy Editor

√ CONFIG.POL

Techniques you'll need to master:

√ Enabling user profiles

√ Managing roaming profiles on NT and NetWare servers

√ Forcing Mandatory profiles

√ Troubleshooting profiles

√ Installing System Policy Editor

√ Enabling system policies

√ Creating and modifying policies

√ Understanding the application procedure for overlapping policies

√ Storing the CONFIG.POL file in a network-accessible location

Windows 95 is a multi-user system. A multi-user system is an operating system that maintains separate secure environments for more than one person. Windows 95 is able to maintain separate environments for different users through user profiles. This chapter discusses profiles and system policies as they are addressed on the certification exam.

User Profiles

A user profile is a stored collection of details and configuration settings for a user. A profile includes the structure of the Start menu, the icons present on the desktop, the color and sound schemes, the font settings, wallpaper, screensaver, drive mappings, and more. Windows 95 is able to store a unique profile for each user. Profiles are stored in \WINDOWS\PROFILES\ <username> directories, where <username> is the name of the user. Each user's profile directory contains:

➤ **\Desktop** A directory containing the desktop layout (e.g., shortcut locations)

➤ **\Recent** A directory containing shortcuts to the last used documents

➤ **\Start Menu** A directory containing the Start menu structure

➤ **USER.DAT** A file containing all data about the environment not stored in the three directories; this is a copy of the Registry key HKEY_CURRENT_USER. (This is the portion of the Registry that stores user-specific data.)

➤ **USER.DA0** A backup of USER.DAT

Multiple profiles are enabled through the User Profiles tab of the Control Panel's Password applet (see Figure 13.1), where you can select the following:

➤ All users of this PC use the same preferences and desktop settings (i.e., no individual profiles).

➤ Users customize their preferences and desktop settings; Windows switches to your personal settings whenever you log in (i.e., individual profiles).

If you choose to use individual profiles, you have two further configuration choices:

➤ Include desktop icons and Network Neighborhood contents in user settings (\Desktop directory)

➤ Include Start Menu and Program groups in user settings (\Start Menu directory)

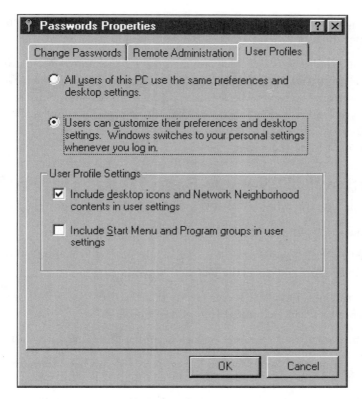

Figure 13.1   The User Profiles tab of the Password applet.

Once you've enabled profiles, each time a user logs in, he or she will be presented with a customized desktop. All the changes made to a user's environment are saved when the user logs off. Windows 95 copies the current USER.DAT to USER.DA0, then makes a new USER.DAT file from the current configuration settings as that user logs off.

 Mandatory profiles can be created and enforced by renaming the USER.DAT file to USER.MAN. This change prevents Windows 95 from saving any modifications to the environment, so you can force users to work with an organization-approved desktop look, feel, layout, and design.

Local And Roaming Profiles

Once a user profile has been created, it can remain a local profile only or be set so that it follows the user from machine to machine. By default, a profile is local only, meaning it is present only on the Windows 95 computer where it was created. A roaming or roving profile is simply a profile that can be loaded from a shared network drive, so it can be used no matter which Windows 95 computer the user logs on to.

Roaming profiles can be enabled on networks with Windows NT or NetWare servers. You should note that Windows NT has profiles as well; however, even though the environment looks similar, profiles from NT and 95 are incompatible. Thus, if users with a Windows 95 roaming profile log on to a Windows NT Workstation, they will not get their normal environment, but the default environment for that computer.

Windows NT Server-Based Roaming Profiles

To enable roaming profiles with a Windows NT Server, perform the following:

1. Enable user profiles on the Windows 95 clients.

2. Make sure Microsoft Client for Microsoft Networks is installed on Windows 95 and set as the Primary Network Logon.

3. On the Windows NT Server, ensure that the user has a valid user account and that a home directory has been defined.

4. Synchronize the Windows 95 clock with that of the Windows NT Server.

The next time a user attempts to log on to the Windows 95 computer, and ultimately the NT network, he or she will be prompted as to whether or not to use profiles. Answering no will result in the default profile being used. Answering yes will store the Windows 95 profile in the defined home directory. If a profile already exists locally for the user, the log of that profile will be copied to the home directory automatically.

NetWare Server-Based Roaming Profiles

To enable roaming profiles on a NetWare network, perform the following:

1. Enable user profiles.

2. Make sure Microsoft Client for NetWare Networks is installed on Windows 95.

3. Synchronize the Windows 95 clock with that of the NetWare server.

4. Make the NetWare client the primary network logon type.

5. Make sure the user has a defined directory under the Mail directory on the NetWare system (i.e., \Mail\User_Id).

6. Make sure the NetWare server supports long file names.

Once this is accomplished, the process is the same as with Windows NT Server.

Troubleshooting Profiles

If profiles are not functioning properly or at all, here are several steps you can take to eliminate the problem:

➤ Check to ensure that profiles are enabled on each Windows 95 machine.

➤ Check that the appropriate client is installed and set as the primary network logon.

➤ Check the time, date, and time zone of each client and make sure they are in sync with the network servers.

➤ Check that home directories have been assigned on NT.

➤ Check that Mail directories exist for each user on NetWare.

➤ Briefcases created prior to enabling profiles must be re-created to reflect the path changes made by the profile storage method.

System Policies For Users, Groups, And Computers

Windows 95 offers administrators a wide range of control over what a computer can access and what a user can do. System policies are tools used to restrict or limit the operational environment of users, groups, or computers. A system policy selectively edits the Registry each time a user logs in.

System policies are created through the use of two file types:

➤ **.ADM files** These are template files that are modified and transformed into actual policy files.

➤ **.POL files** These are the policy files.

You can think of template files as source code that can be edited and modified easily and of policy files as compiled code that is used by a computer.

The process of using policies requires the following steps:

1. Enable user profiles.

2. Decide on the policies required for your computer system.

3. Decide whether policies should be user- or group-based.

4. Install the System Policy Editor and the Group Policies (if group policies are required).

5. Load or create the desired template.

6. Create group policies (if required).

7. Configure the application order for group policies (if appropriate).

8. Create the default settings for the Default User profile.

9. Create the default settings for the Default Computer profile.

10. Create specific user profiles for any exceptions.

11. Create specific computer profiles for any exceptions.

12. Save the policy as CONFIG.POL in the appropriate location so Windows 95 can locate it.

The specifics on how to accomplish these steps are detailed in the following sections.

You should take care to establish policies that are not too restrictive; it is possible to restrict the Windows 95 environment so that nothing can be done. If you create a "DOA" type of default computer profile and place it on your network, every Windows 95 computer that boots with that profile will need to be reinstalled to restore it to an operational state.

Installing System Policy Editor

The tool used to create and modify system policies is the System Policy Editor (SPE). This utility is not installed by default; you must manually install it from the distribution CD. The System Policy Editor is installed through the Windows Setup tab of the Add/Remove Programs applet. Select Have Disk and point to \Admin\Aptools\Poledit. You will be presented with a selection box (shown in Figure 13.2); be sure to select both Group policies and System Policy Editor. Once installed, the utility will be launched with Start|Programs|Accessories|System Tools|System Policy Editor (see Figure 13.3).

The SPE can also be used to directly edit the Registry by selecting File|Open Registry. Using SPE in this way is the best way to perform Registry edits because you are limited to the elements defined in the policy template. If Remote Administration is enabled, and you have user-level access you can use SPE to edit remote Registries.

Loading The Template

A default template is supplied called ADMIN.ADM, which contains many popular Registry settings that can be used to create system policies. You can use this file as an example to create your own ADM files. The ADMIN.ADM template is automatically loaded when you first launch SPE (see Figure 13.4).

Figure 13.2   The Add/Remove Programs selection box for
\Admin\Aptools\Poledit.

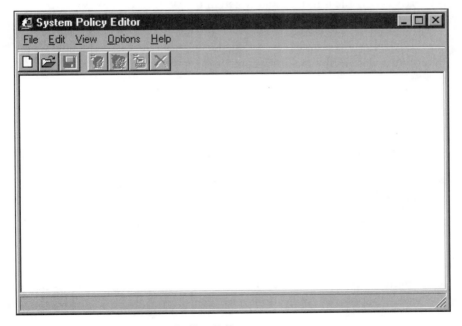

Figure 13.3   The System Policy Editor.

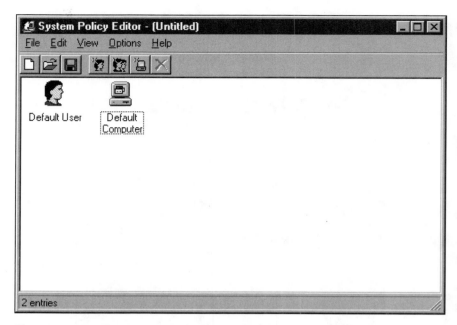

Figure 13.4 The System Policy Editor with the default User and Computer policies of the ADMIN.ADM.

To load a different template, use the Options|Template command. (The ADMIN.ADM file is hidden and stored in the \WINDOWS\INF directory.)

Once a template is loaded, you can view the defaults by selecting File|New. If the ADMIN.ADM template is loaded, the default policies for User and Computer will appear in the main window.

The possible settings in the Default User policy are:

➤ **Control Panel** Restrict access to Display, Network, Passwords, Printers, and System applets

➤ **Desktop** Restrict Desktop options, such as wallpaper and color scheme

➤ **Network** Restrict user ability to change and create shares of printers and/or files

➤ **Shell** Restrict Run command, My Computer, Network Neighborhood, Taskbar, Find, Shutdown, and so on, and force custom constructions of the Start menu or desktop

➤ **System** Disable MS-DOS mode, disable Registry Editor, and restrict access to approved applications

The possible settings in the Default Computer policy are:

➤ **Network** Force user-level security, require validation by network for Windows access, force client used, password restrictions, disable DUN, disable file and print sharing, and so on

➤ **System** Enable profiles, set paths, and automatic launch of application or service on boot

Policies are edited through the Properties interface (Figure 13.5). The hierarchy of settings operates just like Windows Explorer. A policy is modified by altering the checkbox beside each of the listed elements and providing additional information in the Details box when required. Altering the checkbox can take three forms (these are in effect only when you are using SPE in policy file mode, not in Registry mode):

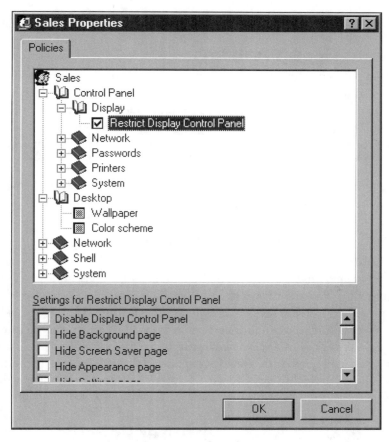

Figure 13.5   The policy-editing interface for a group policy from ADMIN.ADM.

➤ **Gray** This entry is not enabled and does not replace the existing configuration in the Registry for this specific element when this policy is applied.

➤ **Empty** This entry is disabled (not put into use) and does replace the existing configuration in the Registry for this specific element when this policy is applied. Be careful to think about the "double negative" aspect of the entries. For example, when not checked, an entry that states "Restrict access to the Display applet" does *not* restrict access.

➤ **Checked** This entry is enabled (put into use) and replaces the existing configuration in the Registry for this specific element when this policy is applied.

We highly recommend that you take the time to install SPE and review all of the available settings and restrictions of the default user and computer policies. Familiarity with these controls is key to knowing when a system policy can be used to enforce or restrict user and computer access.

Create Group Policies

A group policy is simply a user policy that is applied to a group instead of to an individual user. All of the controls and restrictions of a group policy are the same as those for a user policy. To add a group policy, select Edit|Add Group. You will be prompted for a group name, which must exactly match the name as defined on your network. The new group policy will appear in the main windows of SPE beside the two default policies. (Note: There is no default group policy.)

Once created, you can edit group policies by double-clicking on the policy's icon or by selecting the policy and choosing Edit|Properties.

Set Group Policy Priorities

Because users can belong to multiple groups, it is possible for multiple group policies to apply to them. When multiple policies are in use, it is possible for two or more policies to have conflicting or different settings. Windows 95 uses group policy priorities to determine which settings from which policy will apply. Lower priority group policies are applied first, then each policy up through the highest priority is applied. Each successive application of a policy may overwrite changes made by previously applied policies. Thus, the highest priority policy's settings take precedence. You can set group policy priorities through the Options|Group Priority command (see Figure 13.6).

Create User And Computer Policies

Creating user and computer policies is no different from creating group policies. There are default policies for Users and Computers that apply in the

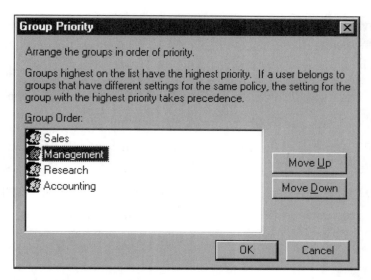

Figure 13.6   The Group Priority dialog box.

absence of a specific policy. When creating new policies (Edit|Add User or Edit|Add Computer) make sure the name of the policy exactly matches the name of the user or computer to which it should apply.

Storing Policies

The SPE creates a single file that contains all defined policies. This file should be named CONFIG.POL. Once a system policy is created, it can be placed in one of three default places:

➤ In the Windows main directory on a share-level computer, a user-level computer, or a computer not attached to a network

➤ In the user's home directory or the NETLOGON directory for user-level computers attached to an NT network

➤ In the user's electronic mail directory or Sys\Public directory for user-level computers attached to a NetWare network

A policy file can be placed in a different location if a .POL file that indicates the alternate storage area is stored in one of these default locations. This is useful for placing shared or centralized policy files in a single shared directory without having to copy the policy file into each and every computer or home directory.

Combined Policies

Windows 95 applies policies in the following manner (see Figure 13.7):

1. System is checked for a user-specific profile. If found, it is applied.

2. If a user-specific profile is not found, the default user policy is applied.

3. If a user-specific profile is present, no group policies are applied.

4. All group polices (for which the user is a member) are located and applied from lowest priority to highest priority.

5. System is checked for a computer-specific profile. If found, it is applied.

6. If a computer-specific profile is not found, the default computer policy is applied.

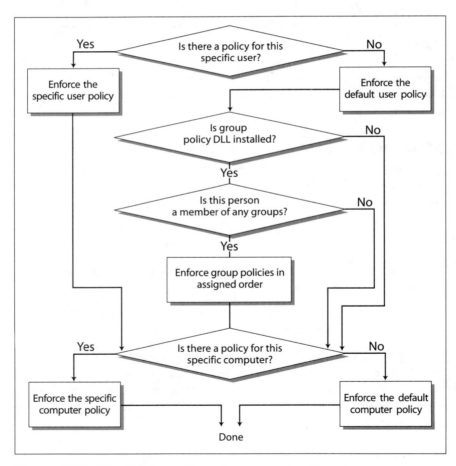

Figure 13.7 The Windows 95 policy processing flowchart.

If no network or server can be located or if no policy can be located, Windows 95 will use the settings currently found in the Registry.

Policy Templates

Policy templates are the .ADM files that define which controls a policy file can contain. Several example templates are available from Microsoft that you can use to create your own policy files. .ADM files can be edited with any text editor, such as Notepad. The *Windows 95 Resource Kit* contains detailed instructions and syntax requirements for creating your own template policy files.

Exam Prep Questions

Question 1

Your organization uses group policies to enforce and restrict computer usage. You have four groups with the following restrictions:

➤ **Admin** No restrictions

➤ **Sales** Restricted access to Network, Display, and Registry Editor

➤ **Accounting** Restricted access to Network and Registry Editor

➤ **Temporary** Same as Sales, but with the additional restriction of approved applications only.

Some users are members of several groups. If no members of Temporary are also members of Admin and your organization is concerned about security related to the transient workers, what is the best priority ordering of these policies? (Assume priority *decreases* from left to right.)

❍ a. Admin, Temporary, Sales, Accounting

❍ b. Temporary, Sales, Accounting, Admin

❍ c. Accounting, Temporary, Admin, Sales

❍ d. Sales, Accounting, Admin, Temporary

The best priority order is Admin, Temporary, Sales, Accounting. Therefore, answer a is correct. Because no member of Temporary is also a member of Admin, Admin can be given the highest priority. This ensures that Sales and Accounting members who are also Admins will be given the correct level of access. In addition, placing Temporary above Sales and Accounting ensures that they have tighter restrictions than the normal Sales and Accounting members. The other three orders do not provide for optimal access. Therefore, answers b, c, and d are incorrect.

Question 2

> You are currently working on two separate Windows 95 clients. Roaming profiles are enabled with all options, and no restrictions are in place. You create a new shortcut on your desktop on Computer 1, then log off. Next, you log off on Computer 2. You return to Computer 1 and log in successfully to the network, but your shortcut is not present. Why?
>
> ○ a. Profiles do not store desktop shortcuts.
>
> ○ b. The shutdown process from Computer 2 overwrote the profile stored by the shutdown on Computer 1.
>
> ○ c. Computer 1 is using a local profile.
>
> ○ d. A cached profile is being used.

The shutdown process from Computer 2 overwrote the profile stored by the shutdown on Computer 1, so the defined shortcut was lost during the overwrite. Therefore, answer b is correct. Profiles do store desktop shortcuts, unless specified otherwise. Therefore, answer a is incorrect. The shortcut would appear if a local profile were being used on Computer 1, but that is not the case, and the question stated that roaming profiles are being used. Therefore, answer c is incorrect. A cached profile cannot be in use because the question stated that a successful network logon was accomplished, and roaming profiles are active. A cached profile is used only when the profile host is unreachable. Therefore, answer d is incorrect.

Question 3

> Profiles use a unique saved copy of which Registry file?
>
> ○ a. SYSTEM.DAT
>
> ○ b. REGLOG.TXT
>
> ○ c. USER.DAT
>
> ○ d. PROFILE.DAT

USER.DAT is the Registry file used by profiles. Therefore, answer c is correct. SYSTEM.DAT is the Registry file that stores system-related configuration details, and it is not used by profiles. Therefore, answer a is incorrect. REGLOG.TXT and PROFILE.DAT are fictional files. Therefore, answers b and d are incorrect.

Question 4

> Which of the following must be true for roaming profiles to function on a Windows NT Server network? [Check all correct answers]
>
> ❑ a. Time synchronized between client and server
> ❑ b. Use of TCP/IP protocol
> ❑ c. Home directory defined for the user
> ❑ d. Microsoft Client for Microsoft Networks installed

Roaming profiles function on an NT network if the time is synchronized, home directories are defined, and the Microsoft Client for Microsoft Networks is installed. Therefore, answers a, c, and d are correct. TCP/IP is not a requirement for roaming profiles, which can operate over any protocol shared by the client and server. Therefore, answer b is incorrect.

Question 5

> Roaming profiles, not local profiles, can be configured so that the Start menu is stored without storing any desktop shortcuts.
>
> ○ a. True
> ○ b. False

All types of profiles can store either Start menu details or Desktop details or both. Therefore, answer b is correct. There is no difference between roaming and local profiles other than that roaming profiles follow users from one client to another. The User Profiles configuration tab of the Passwords applet enables an administrator to control whether Start Menu, Desktop, or both are stored in profiles.

Question 6

> If a checkbox beside an element in a system policy is gray, what does this indicate?
>
> ○ a. It means that this entry is disabled (not put into use) and does replace the existing configuration in the Registry for this specific element when this policy is applied.
>
> ○ b. It means that this entry is enabled (put into use) and does replace the existing configuration in the Registry for this specific element when this policy is applied.
>
> ○ c. It means that this entry is not enabled and does not replace the existing configuration in the Registry for this specific element when this policy is applied.

A gray box means this entry is not enabled and does not replace the existing configuration in the Registry for this specific element when this policy is applied. Therefore, answer c is correct. Answer a is for empty checkboxes, and answer b is for checked checkboxes. Therefore, answers a and b are incorrect.

Question 7

> If profiles fail to operate properly on a specific Windows 95 computer, which of the following are useful and valid troubleshooting techniques? [Check all correct answers]
>
> ❏ a. Check that the appropriate client is installed and set as the primary network logon.
>
> ❏ b. Check that Mail directories exist for each user on NetWare.
>
> ❏ c. Check the time, date, and time zone of each client, and make sure that they are in sync with the network servers.
>
> ❏ d. Check to ensure that profiles are enabled on each Windows 95 computer.

All these actions are useful and valid troubleshooting techniques for profiles. Therefore, answers a, b, c, and d are correct.

Question 8

> What is the name of the default template installed with System Policy Editor that is stored as a hidden file in the \WINDOWS\INF directory?
>
> ○ a. CONFIG.POL
>
> ○ b. USER.DAT
>
> ○ c. TEMPLATE.POL
>
> ○ d. ADMIN.ADM

ADMIN.ADM is the default template file. Therefore, answer d is correct. CONFIG.POL is the name of an actual system policy that is typically stored on a network server in a home directory or a shared common directory. Therefore, answer a is incorrect. USER.DAT is the name of the Registry file used by profiles and is stored in the \WINDOWS\PROFILES\<username> directory. Therefore, answer b is incorrect. TEMPLATE.POL is a fictitious file. Therefore, answer c is incorrect.

Question 9

> If a user has a specific individual policy, which other policies can apply to that user? [Check all correct answers]
>
> ❑ a. Any group policies of groups that user is a member of
>
> ❑ b. Default Computer
>
> ❑ c. Specific computer
>
> ❑ d. Default User

If a user has a defined individual policy, only computer policies can apply. Therefore, answers b and c are correct. However, only one computer policy can apply. If a specific computer policy is defined, it is used rather than the Default Computer. If a user has a defined individual policy, no group polices are used. Therefore, answer a is incorrect. The Default User policy does not apply if a user has a defined individual policy. Therefore, answer d is incorrect.

Question 10

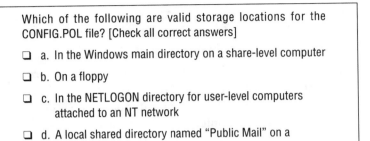

Which of the following are valid storage locations for the CONFIG.POL file? [Check all correct answers]

❑ a. In the Windows main directory on a share-level computer

❑ b. On a floppy

❑ c. In the NETLOGON directory for user-level computers attached to an NT network

❑ d. A local shared directory named "Public Mail" on a NetWare network

The valid storage locations for CONFIG.POL from this list are in the Windows main directory on a share-level computer and in the NETLOGON directory for user-level computers attached to an NT network. Therefore, answers a and c are correct. A floppy is not a valid storage location for CONFIG.POL. Therefore, answer b is incorrect. A shared local directory is not a valid storage location. Therefore, answer d is incorrect. The name "Public Mail" was listed to cause you to think about the proper NetWare storage location of user's mail directories.

Need To Know More?

 Supporting Microsoft Windows 95. Microsoft Press, Redmond, WA, 1995. ISBN 1-55615-931-5. Chapter 9 discusses user profiles. Chapter 19 discusses system policies.

 Mortensen, Lance and Rick Sawtell: *MCSE: Windows 95 Study Guide.* Sybex Network Press, San Francisco, CA, 1996. ISBN: 0-7821-2092-X. Chapter 14 contains information on user profiles. Chapter 15 contains information on system policies.

 Search the TechNet CD (or its online version through www. microsoft.com) and the *Windows 95 Resource Kit* using the keywords "Profiles," "Local profile," "roaming profile," "Mandatory profile," "System Policies," "System Policy Editor," "ADMIN.ADM," and "CONFIG.POL."

Multimedia

Terms you'll need to understand:

√ MIDI (Musical Instrument Digital Interface), .MID

√ .WAV (waveform audio)

√ .AVI (digital video format)

√ AUTORUN.INF

Techniques you'll need to master:

√ Configuring the multimedia-related features of Windows 95

√ Launching and using the multimedia utilities of Windows 95

√ Disabling the AutoPlay feature of Windows 95

Multimedia applications were relatively scarce before the release of Windows 95, partly because of a lack of multimedia driver standards and partly because of a wide, inconsistent range of available hardware. Windows 95 attempted to solve this problem by developing a standard, or universal, set of multimedia drivers to simplify the interface between an application and the hardware. This chapter looks into the multimedia architecture of Windows 95.

The chapter is short mainly for two reasons. The certification exam contains only a few multimedia-related questions, and the multimedia architecture of Windows 95 simplifies what was complex in DOS and Windows 3.x. That is, multimedia in Windows 95 is controlled almost automatically and is usually Plug and Play, requiring little input from users. This chapter touches only on the underlying structure of multimedia. For more detail, consult TechNet or the *Windows 95 Resource Kit*.

Multimedia Architecture

The universal multimedia drivers developed by Microsoft have greatly simplified the work required by application authors. Now, they need only write an interface between their company's software product and the Windows 95 universal multimedia drivers. Likewise, hardware manufacturers either have created hardware that could be driven directly by the Windows 95 universal drivers or have developed their own drivers to interface between the universal driver and hardware.

The following are some of the benefits and features of the Windows 95 multimedia architecture:

➤ Compression services are available for audio, video, and imaging.

➤ Video for Windows Runtime enables digital video.

➤ Enhanced MIDI with 16 channels and multiple instruments has been added.

➤ Sound Recorder enables recording through a microphone or from a MIDI device or CD.

➤ CD Player enables audio CDs to be played.

Drivers And Configuration

Once you have installed the hardware devices and the software applications that require or support multimedia (and installed their drivers through the Add New Hardware or the Add/Remove Programs applet), you can access most of the parameters and configuration options that regulate and control multimedia through two Control Panel applets: Multimedia and Sounds.

The Multimedia applet has five tabs, each with its own configurable parameters:

➤ **Audio** Controls master playback volume, playback and recording device, recording volume, and recording quality (Figure 14.1). The available quality settings are:

➤ **CD-ROM** High-quality stereo

➤ **Radio** Intermediate quality

➤ **Telephone** Lowest quality

➤ **TrueSpeech** High compression for voice-only recordings

➤ **Video** Plays videos in full screen or in a sized window— original size, double, 1/16, 1/4, 1/2, maximized (Figure 14.2).

➤ **MIDI** Sets MIDI output to a single instrument or to a custom setup and adds new instruments (Figure 14.3).

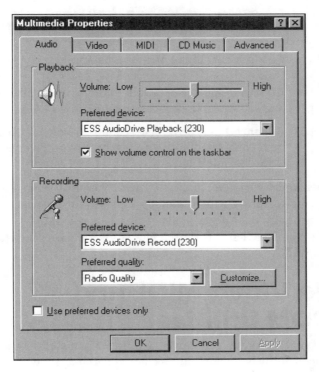

Figure 14.1   The Audio tab of the Multimedia applet.

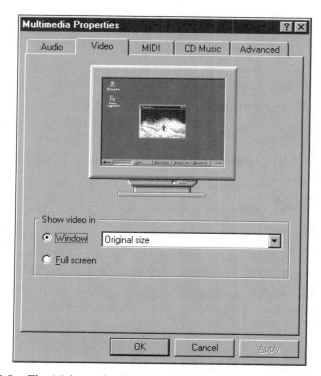

Figure 14.2 The Video tab of the Multimedia applet.

➤ **CD Music** Sets the drive letter from which to play audio CDs and sets headphone jack volume (Figure 14.4).

➤ **Advanced** Sets driver-level configurations. Each installed driver may offer further device- or application-specific controls (Figure 14.5).

The Sounds applet associates audio files with Windows events (see Figure 14.6). You can customize which sounds are played for each event by defining them manually or using a predefined scheme. Windows 95 includes five sound schemes, Microsoft Plus! includes several more, and the Internet provides others.

Audio, Video, MIDI, And CD-ROM Utilities

Windows 95 has a handful of multimedia utilities to support the wide range of available media formats. These utilities allow you to interact with, record, and control multimedia files themselves.

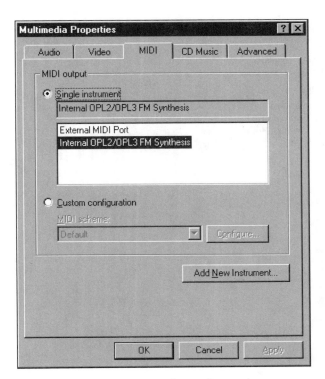

Figure 14.3   The MIDI tab of the Multimedia applet.

The Sound Recorder is used to play .WAV (waveform audio) and .MID (MIDI) files (Figure 14.7). By default, these extensions are associated with Sound Recorder, so double-clicking on a .WAV or a .MID file automatically launches the Sound Recorder and plays the media file. Sound Recorder can also be used to create sound files by recording audio. You can use the Sound Recorder to record an audio source from the microphone or input jack of the sound card, from a MIDI device, or from an audio CD. You can also edit (crop, delete, and insert) audio files, alter their native volume, change their playback speed, add echoes, and reverse their playback direction.

The video playback utility is launched only when an .AVI (digital video format) file is launched. It offers simple controls (pause/play and stop) and a slidebar that shows playback status and can be used to fast-forward and rewind.

The CD Player is used to play audio CDs (Figure 14.8). It offers the basic controls that stereo CD players do: play, pause, stop, skip track forward, skip track reverse, scan forward, scan reverse, and eject. You can define the artist, album name, and song titles. Each time this CD is placed in the CD-ROM

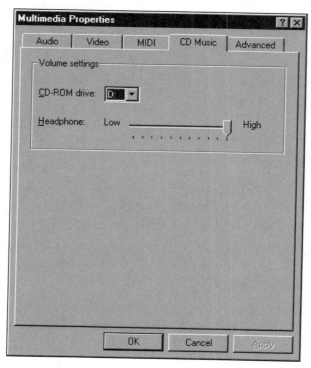

Figure 14.4 The CD Music tab of the Multimedia applet.

drive, Windows 95 will recognize it and restore your entered details from its database.

The Media Player utility combines the playback features of Sound Recorder, the video playback system, and the CD Player (Figure 14.9). Thus, it supports .WAV, .MID, and .AVI files in addition to audio CDs.

The Volume Control utility offers individual level and balance controls for each input and output type (Figure 14.10). This utility should be used to balance the relative volumes of each multimedia type to establish a consistent decibel level. Through the Options menu, you can select which audio types to display and to access Advanced Options if your audio devices offer them.

The AutoPlay feature is a unique function of Windows 95 for both audio and application CD-ROMs. AutoPlay automatically recognizes audio CDs and then launches the CD Player to initiate the playback from the first track. Application CD-ROMs are automatically launched if an AUTORUN.INF file is present. To disable the AutoPlay feature, go to the driver list on the Device

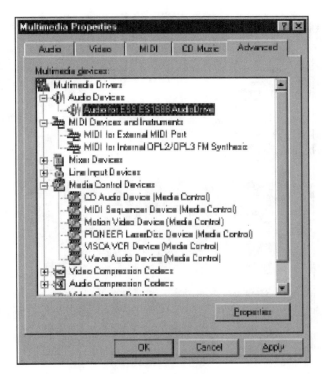

Figure 14.5   The Advanced tab of the Multimedia applet.

Manager tab of the System applet and then to the Settings tab of the Properties dialog box of the CD-ROM drive. Uncheck the Auto insert notification checkbox to disable AutoPlay.

Troubleshooting

Multimedia troubleshooting is usually a simple process in Windows 95. You will likely confront only a handful of problems that the following steps should solve:

➤ Ensure that the latest driver for the multimedia type is installed and that all older, deprecated, or obsolete drivers are removed.

➤ Check that both the physical settings (if applicable) and the software-based Plug and Play settings for the device are correct. This includes DMA, I/I address, IRQ, and so on.

➤ Check that input and output levels are correct within Volume Control; make sure Muting is not enabled.

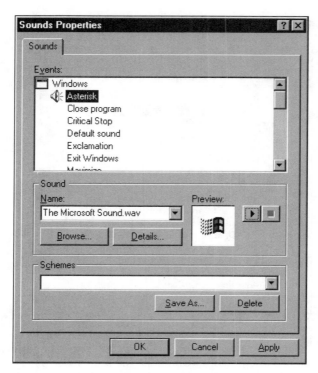

Figure 14.6 The Sounds applet where sound schemes are defined.

➤ Check the application to ensure that it has been properly configured to interact with the correct multimedia device and has been given the proper access settings.

➤ Make sure speakers are operational and properly connected.

If these actions do not resolve the problem, you will need to contact the multimedia device vendor for further troubleshooting tips.

Figure 14.7 The Sound Recorder where audio files are played and/or recorded.

Figure 14.8   The CD Player controls audio CD playing.

Figure 14.9   The Media Player plays all native Windows 95 multimedia types.

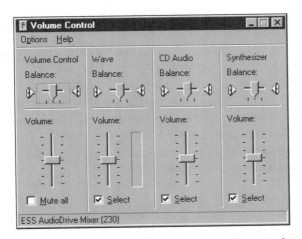

Figure 14.10   The Volume Control, where the relative volumes of audio devices are set.

Exam Prep Questions

Question 1

> TrueSpeech is the best recording quality setting for musical re-
> cordings.
>
> ○ a. True
>
> ○ b. False

TrueSpeech is the best setting for voice-only recordings and does not provide quality recording for nonvocal sounds; therefore, answer b is correct.

Question 2

> Which types of data can be recorded using the Sound Recorder?
> [Check all correct answers]
>
> ❏ a. Music from an audio CD
>
> ❏ b. A radio station through a line-in connection
>
> ❏ c. Voice through a microphone
>
> ❏ d. A tune from a MIDI device

Sound Recorder can record any audio signal sent through the Windows 95 multimedia architecture, so all these media and audio types can be recorded; therefore, answers a, b, c, and d are correct. The trick to this question is that although Windows 95 does not include the hardware or software to receive radio signals, a line-in from a radio to an audio card (just like a microphone) can route audio signals to Sound Recorder.

Question 3

> Where can you disable the AutoPlay feature of Windows 95?
>
> ○ a. Through the CD Player's Options menu
> ○ b. On the Settings tab of the Properties dialog box of the
>   CD-ROM drive driver list on the Device Manager tab of
>   the System applet
> ○ c. In the Multimedia applet
> ○ d. Through the Properties of the CD-ROM drive accessed
>   through Windows Explorer

The AutoPlay feature is disabled on the Settings tab of the Properties dialog box of the CD-ROM drive driver list on the Device Manager tab of the System applet; therefore, answer b is correct. The CD Player's Options menu contains commands for random, continuous, and intro play and for opening the player's interface display properties, but no control for AutoPlay; therefore, answer a is incorrect. The Multimedia applet does not offer a command to disable the AutoPlay feature; therefore, answer c is incorrect. The Properties of the CD-ROM drive itself displays the size of the data stored on the disc and offers control over sharing of the disc, but no control for AutoPlay; therefore, answer d is incorrect.

Question 4

> Which is the best recording level for any type of audio?
>
> ○ a. TrueSpeech
> ○ b. Telephone
> ○ c. Radio
> ○ d. CD-ROM

CD-ROM is the best recording level for any type of audio; therefore, answer d is correct. TrueSpeech is useful only for vocal recordings; therefore, answer a is incorrect. Telephone and Radio are inferior settings to CD-ROM; therefore, answers b and c are incorrect.

Question 5

> Through which Control Panel applet are sounds associated with Windows events?
>
> ○   a. Multimedia
>
> ○   b. Events
>
> ○   c. Sounds
>
> ○   d. System

The Sounds applet is where sounds are associated with Windows events; therefore, answer c is correct. The Multimedia applet is used to set the operational parameters of the universal multimedia drivers; therefore, answer a is incorrect. There is no such applet as Events; therefore, answer b is incorrect. The System applet is used to interact with installed drivers and set system performance and is not used to associate sounds with events; therefore, answer d is incorrect.

Question 6

> Which of the following utilities are able to play both .WAV and .MID files? [Check all correct answers]
>
> ❏   a. CD Player
>
> ❏   b. Sound Recorder
>
> ❏   c. Media Player
>
> ❏   d. Volume Control

Both Sound Recorder and Media Player are able to play .WAV and .MID files; therefore, answers b and c are correct. The CD Player cannot play .WAV or .MID files but can play audio CDs; therefore, answer a is incorrect. Volume Control does not play any file type, but controls the volumes of each media format type; therefore, answer d is incorrect.

Need To Know More?

 Supporting Microsoft Windows 95. Microsoft Press, Redmond, WA, 1995. ISBN 1-55615-931-5. Chapter 26 discusses Windows 95 multimedia.

 Mortensen, Lance and Rick Sawtell; *MCSE: Windows 95 Study Guide*. Sybex Network Press, San Francisco, CA, 1996. ISBN: 0-7821-2092-X. Chapter 22 contains information on the multimedia system in Windows 95.

 Search the TechNet CD (or its online version through www. microsoft.com) and the *Windows 95 Resource Kit* using the keywords "multimedia," "audio," "video," and "MIDI."

Microsoft Exchange Client

15

Terms you'll need to understand:

√ MAPI

√ Exchange client (or messaging client), Inbox

√ Postoffice, Workgroup Postoffice

√ Exchange Client Services

√ Message Profile

√ Personal Address Book/List (.PAB)

√ Personal Folders (.PST)

Techniques you'll need to master:

√ Creating and administering a workgroup postoffice

√ Adding Exchange Client Services

√ Configuring Exchange Client Services and Message Profiles—Microsoft Mail, Microsoft Fax, Personal Address Book, Personal Folders, Internet Mail, and CompuServe Mail

√ Sharing the Fax service

√ Using the Exchange Client

MAPI Introduction

MAPI (Messaging API) is a Microsoft standard that enables communication software and hardware to interface (i.e., communicate and interact). Through the use and support of MAPI, software is device-independent and can operate over many types of hardware. In addition, hardware is software-independent and can support the operation of many types of software. MAPI acts as a mediator between both sides of the communication architecture.

Overview Of Exchange

The Microsoft Exchange messaging client is MAPI-compliant, which means its standard front-end, user-controlled GUI can interact with and support communications over many types of MAPI-compliant hardware and communication systems or services, from email to fax. The MS Exchange client is included with Windows 95 to be a common access point for all of your communications, both internal and external.

The Exchange client is a peer-to-peer communications system that can operate without special server software. This means that members of a workgroup can communicate with electronic messages without installing a server-based support and administration tool. The only requirement for enabling Exchange messaging is to have a "postoffice" to store messages. A postoffice is just a designated directory in which Exchange files are stored.

The Exchange client for Windows 95 is bundled with the workgroup edition of Microsoft Mail Server, which enables workgroup mail communication. Exchange can be configured through the installation of services that enable users to connect to mail gateways, such as an Internet SMTP server or a Microsoft Exchange Server. When Exchange is used to remotely send and receive mail, the DUN (Dial-Up Networking) service must be installed.

The MAPI service provider that ships with Windows 95 can connect to any Microsoft Mail Server postoffices hosted on Windows NT or NetWare servers or to the built-in Windows 95 Microsoft Mail workgroup postoffice. To connect to other postoffices or server types, you must obtain and install the appropriate Exchange client service. Typically, these services are free on the vendor's Web site or are shipped on the distribution CD for the mail or system server. The third-party systems that can be accessed by Exchange client include America Online, Apple, AT&T, Banyan, CompuServe, DEC, Hewlett-Packard, Novell, Octel, RAM Mobile Data, and Skytel.

Postoffice Creation

The first step to using the Microsoft Exchange client is to create a workgroup postoffice. When you create a postoffice, you become the administrator of the postoffice; therefore, make sure you perform this task with the user account through which you want to perform administrative activities. The process for installing a postoffice is as follows:

1. Launch the Microsoft Mail Postoffice applet from the Control Panel.

   Note: If the Microsoft Mail Postoffice applet is not present in the Control Panel, you must install it from the Windows Setup tab of the Add/ Remove Programs applet. Select Microsoft Exchange and verify that both Exchange and Mail Services are checked.

2. Select Create a new Workgroup Postoffice, then click Next (Figure 15.1).

3. Define a location for the postoffice (Figure 15.2). This can be a local or a network drive; be sure this drive is always accessible to other clients. Click Next.

4. You'll be told the postoffice will be created; click Next again.

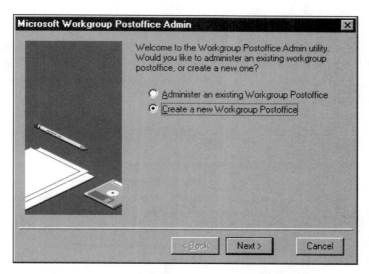

Figure 15.1   The Microsoft Workgroup Postoffice Admin wizard: Select Create a new Workgroup Postoffice.

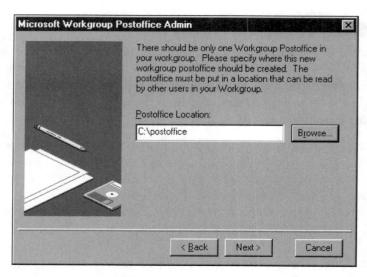

Figure 15.2   The Microsoft Workgroup Postoffice Admin Wizard:
Define Postoffice Location.

5. Fill in the details on the Administrator Account Details dialog box
(Figure 15.3), then click OK. Take note of the mailbox name and
the password. You will need these to regain access to administer
this postoffice.

Once the postoffice has been created, you need to share the WGPO directory
to the network with full access. If you do not share the postoffice directory,
other clients will not be able to interact with the workgroup postoffice you've
just created.

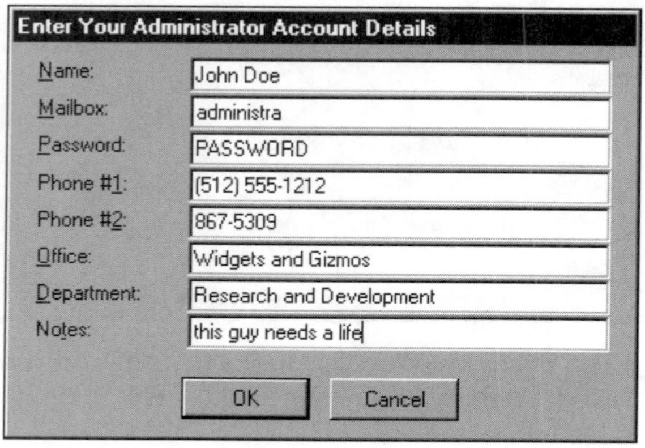

Figure 15.3   The Enter Your Administrator Account Details
dialog box.

Postoffice Administration

To administer the postoffice, return to the Microsoft Mail Postoffice applet. This time, select Administer an existing Workgroup Postoffice (Figure 15.4), verify the path, and provide your administrative name and password. The Postoffice Manager appears (Figure 15.5). This utility is used to add and remove postoffice users, modify a user's details, and get a statistics list from the messaging system. As you can see, there is very little to do in the way of postoffice

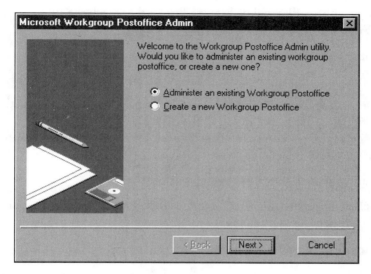

Figure 15.4 The Microsoft Workgroup Postoffice Admin wizard: Select Administer an existing Workgroup Postoffice.

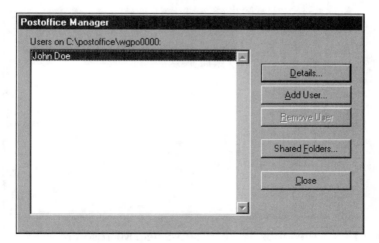

Figure 15.5 The Postoffice Manager.

administration. When a user is deleted, the mailbox for that user is deleted; however, any Personal Folders on the user's local machine are retained.

Adding Exchange Client Services

Once a postoffice is established, you can install the Exchange client in the Inbox Setup Wizard, which you can access in one of two places:

➤ **Mail and Fax applet** The first time you launch this Control Panel applet, no profiles will be listed. Click Add to reach the Inbox Setup Wizard.

➤ **Inbox icon** Double-click to reach the Inbox Setup Wizard.

Once you are in the Inbox Setup Wizard, perform the following steps:

1. Depending on which options you select during the initial installation, different services will appear in the dialog box: Microsoft Mail, Microsoft Fax, Internet mail, and so on. Deselect all but Microsoft Mail (Figure 15.6), then click Next.

2. Verify the path to the workgroup postoffice.

3. Select the user mailbox (this requires that the administrator has already established the user mailbox).

4. Provide your access password.

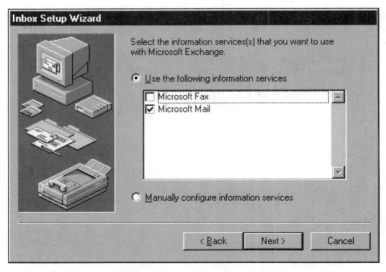

Figure 15.6 The Inbox Setup Wizard: Select Microsoft Mail.

5. Select a destination for your Personal Address Book.

6. Select a destination for your Personal Folders (where your downloaded mail will be stored locally).

7. Indicate whether to add the Inbox to the StartUp group. By enabling this feature, your mail will be downloaded automatically each time you boot your system.

Now, your Exchange client is installed. You can launch the Inbox from the desktop to pick up your email.

Configuring Exchange

Microsoft Exchange uses message profiles (not the same as user profiles discussed in Chapter 13) to define how data is handled and transmitted. Message profiles are managed through the Mail and Fax applet. When you launch this applet from the Control Panel, you will see the MS Exchange Settings Properties dialog box (Figure 15.7). This dialog box is named <MESSAGE PROFILE> Properties. However, because MS Exchange Settings is the only message profile currently present on this system and it is set as the default profile, the Mail and Fax applet loads its properties. To edit, copy, or add message profiles, click on the drop-down button called "When starting Microsoft

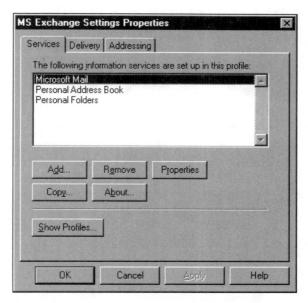

Figure 15.7   The MS Exchange Settings Properties dialog box.

Exchange, use this profile:" (Figure 15.8). From this point, you can add and remove profiles or select one to manage by clicking Properties. Doing this will bring up a <MESSAGE PROFILE> Properties dialog box that does not have a Show Profiles button.

The <MESSAGE PROFILE> Properties dialog box has three tabs: Services, Delivery, and Addressing. The Services tab installs, removes, and manages Exchange-related information services (Figure 15.9). The Delivery tab defines the primary and secondary delivery locations and the processing order for messaging services (Figure 15.10). The Addressing tab defines the configuration for where and how addresses are stored (Figure 15.11).

On the Services tab, you can open configuration Properties dialog boxes for each of the information services installed and in use through this message profile. The three default services that should appear here are Microsoft Mail, Personal Address Book, and Personal Folders.

Microsoft Mail contains the following configuration tabs and the properties you can assign:

➤ **Connection** Set the postoffice path and how the service should connect at startup

➤ **Logon** Set the postoffice name, automatically apply password, and change password

Figure 15.8 The Microsoft Exchange Profiles dialog box.

Figure 15.9   The MS Exchange Settings Properties dialog box Services
tab (accessed through Microsoft Exchange Profiles).

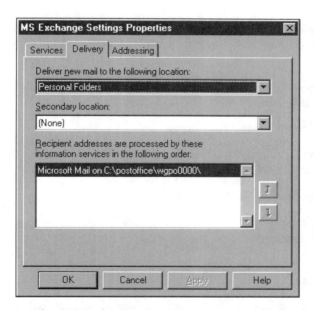

Figure 15.10   The MS Exchange Settings Properties dialog box
Delivery tab.

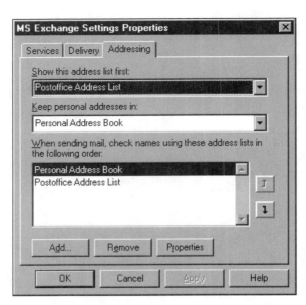

Figure 15.11 The MS Exchange Settings Properties dialog box Addressing tab.

➤ **Delivery** Set inbound or outbound mail delivery, set delivery address type, check new mail interval, alert on new mail, and display only Global Address list

➤ **LAN Configuration** Use Remote Mail, local copy, or external delivery agent (LAN only)

➤ **Log** Record log and path of log file

➤ **Remote Configuration** Use Remote Mail, local copy, or external delivery agent (DUN only)

➤ **Remote Session** Automate DUN activity

➤ **Dial-Up Networking** Define which DUN connection to use, retries, and confirmations

Personal Address Book contains the following configuration tabs and the properties you can assign:

➤ **Personal Address Book** Name the address book, set path, and FNF or LNF

➤ **Notes** Comment on address book

Personal Folders contains one configuration tab:

➤ **General** Define name, change password, compact, and provide a comment

Adding Services—Fax

You can install additional Exchange information services; Microsoft Fax is one that is included with Windows 95. This (and any other) service is installed following this procedure:

1. Open the <MESSAGE PROFILE> Properties dialog box through the Mail and Fax applet.

2. On the Services tab, click Add.

3. Select the service to install (e.g., Microsoft Fax).

Next, a service-specific configuration dialog box, usually with multiple tabs, will appear. This is the same dialog box that appears when you change the configuration from the Services tab when you click Properties. Provide the information required by the service.

Microsoft Fax contains the following configuration tabs and the properties you can assign:

➤ **User** Define user name, country, fax number, mailbox, and general company information

➤ **Modem** Select or install a modem (incoming call answering, speaker, and dial-tone preferences are set through the top Properties button) and share this fax with the network (share name and password/user/group access is defined through the bottom Properties button); a shared fax is accessed just like any shared printer (Figure 15.12)

➤ **Dialing** Select which Dialing Properties to use (see Chapter 11), define toll prefixes, and set retries

➤ **Message** Set send time parameters, message format, and cover page

Once you fill in the appropriate details for Microsoft Fax, you can send faxes from any application by printing to the MS Fax printer. All incoming faxes (if enabled) are deposited into your Inbox.

When Microsoft Fax is set to await incoming calls, Windows 32-bit applications can access the modem's COM port, but Windows 16-bit and DOS applications may not be able to.

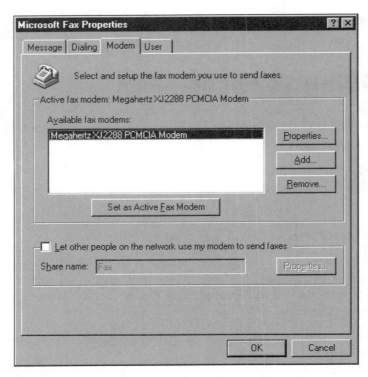

Figure 15.12 The Microsoft Fax Properties Modem tab.

Adding Services—Internet Mail

The Internet Mail drivers are available with Microsoft Plus! (installed as part of the Internet Jumpstart Kit) and can be downloaded from the Microsoft Windows 95 Web area (www.microsoft.com/windows95/info/inetmail.htm). Once the Internet Mail drivers are on your system, they are installed into Exchange in the same manner as the Fax service.

When you select the Internet Mail service to install, a two-tabbed configuration dialog box appears. Fill in the appropriate details on each tab:

➤ **General** Set name, email address, mail server, account name, password, message format, and alternate outbound SMTP server

➤ **Connection** Set connection type to LAN or modem, DUN connection, offline operation, scheduling, and logging

Now your Exchange client can send and receive email from Internet email servers.

Adding Services— CompuServe Mail

To add support for CompuServe Mail to the Microsoft Exchange client, you need to have the following information available:

➤ CompuServe directory (used to share scripts and the address book)

➤ User name

➤ CompuServe user ID

➤ Password

➤ Access phone number

Then follow these steps:

1. Execute the SETUP.EXE program from the Windows 95 CD located in the Drivers\Other\Exchange\Compusrv Directory.

2. When prompted, supply your CompuServe connection information.

3. Add the CompuServe Mail service to your Exchange profile through the Mail and Fax applet.

Once completed, the Exchange client will send and receive email from CompuServe.

Using The Client

Using the Exchange client is quite simple and intuitive. Launch the Exchange client by double-clicking on the Inbox on the Desktop, then select View|Folders from the menu bar to add the folder list to the display area (Figure 15.13). From this interface, you can view any received messages, create and send new messages, or file and organize your Personal Folders. If you have more than one service type installed for the active Message Profile, all possible information services will be polled for new messages on startup and at each retrieve-mail interval. When you create new messages, the address type selected will determine which information service will be used to send the message.

The address book can be accessed through the Tools|Address Book command, which allows you to edit, add, or delete addresses stored in your Personal Address List or any other address list to which you have access. To create new addresses, select the File|New Entry command. The New Entry dialog box (Figure 15.14) prompts you for the email address type to create. Then, a

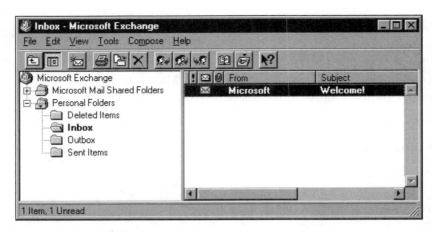

Figure 15.13 The Exchange client with folders visible.

multitabbed address book property dialog box appears in which you can define numerous details about the new entry. A Personal Distribution list can be created by selecting Personal Distribution List from the New Entry dialog box. The address book is stored in a .PAB file in your local Exchange directory. Existing .PAB files can be imported using the File|Import command.

Personal Folders is a customizable storage bin for messages that is stored as a single .PST file in your local Exchange directory. You can create new subfolders beneath any selected folder using the File|New Folder command. Additional top-level Personal Folders can be created through the Message Profile Properties dialog box accessed through the Mail and Fax applet.

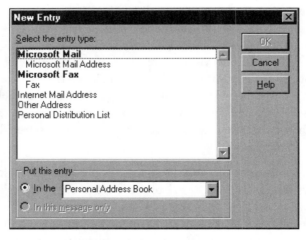

Figure 15.14 The New Entry dialog box.

In addition to all the configuration options for Exchange client services, there is yet another set of configuration screens for the client itself. These are accessed through Tools|Options:

➤ **General** Set new mail notification, deletion control, and startup profile

➤ **Read** Set action after move or delete and handle reply and forward

➤ **Send** Set font, receipt, sensitivity, importance, and save copy in Sent Items

➤ **Services, Delivery, and Addressing** Same as that offered through <MESSAGE PROFILE> Properties

Exam Prep Questions

Question 1

> Where is Microsoft Mail configured to access information services over dial-up connections?
>
> ○ a. Through the Microsoft Mail Postoffice applet
>
> ○ b. Through the Tools|Microsoft Mail Tools menu within the Exchange client
>
> ○ c. Through the Mail and Fax applet
>
> ○ d. Through the Internet applet

Microsoft Mail is configured to access information services over dial-up connections through the Mail and Fax applet; therefore, answer c is correct. The Microsoft Mail Postoffice applet is used to create and administer workgroup postoffices, not DUN-accessed messaging services; therefore, answer a is incorrect. The Tools|Microsoft Mail Tools menu within the Exchange client does not offer access to modify the Microsoft Mail service DUN settings; therefore, answer b is incorrect. The Internet applet is used to set autodial and proxy settings for Internet access, not to set the Microsoft Mail DUN parameters; therefore, answer d is incorrect.

Question 2

> Which of the following are required to enable the Exchange client to send and receive mail to remote systems?
>
> ○ a. Microsoft Fax
>
> ○ b. Internet Mail
>
> ○ c. TCP/IP
>
> ○ d. Dial-Up Networking

Dial-Up Networking is the only component that needs to be installed to enable the Exchange client to send and receive mail remotely; therefore, answer d is correct. Microsoft Fax is not required and is used to send faxes, not mail; therefore, answer a is incorrect. Internet Mail is required only when the remote mail server is an Internet-hosted system; therefore, answer b is incorrect. TCP/IP need be present only if the information service used requires it or the connection to the remote system requires it; therefore, answer c is incorrect.

Question 3

Three different people are using the same Windows 95 computer, each on a different eight-hour shift. You need to create three individual message profiles so they can send and retrieve email separately and securely. Where is this activity performed?

○ a. The Passwords applet

○ b. Through the Inbox's Tools|Options command

○ c. The Mail and Fax applet

○ d. The Profiles applet

Multiple message profiles are created through the Mail and Fax applet; therefore, answer c is correct. The Passwords applet is used to change passwords and enable user profiles, not to create messaging profiles; therefore, answer a is incorrect. The Options command in the Inbox cannot be used to create message profiles because any instance of the Exchange client can modify only the settings within the profile it used to launch itself; therefore, answer b is incorrect. There is no Profiles applet; therefore, answer d is incorrect.

Question 4

Which of the following are valid methods of installing the Exchange client? [Check all correct answers]

❑ a. By double-clicking on the Inbox icon on the Desktop

❑ b. During the initial installation of Windows 95

❑ c. Through the Internet applet

❑ d. Through the Add/Remove Programs applet

The Exchange client can be installed by double-clicking on the Inbox icon on the Desktop, during the initial installation of Windows 95, and through the Add/Remove Programs applet; therefore, answers a, b, and d are correct. The Internet applet cannot be used to install the Exchange client; therefore, answer c is incorrect.

Question 5

A single Windows 95 computer in your workgroup has a fax/modem and is being used as an Exchange-based fax server. Which mechanism within Exchange automatically forwards inbound faxes to the intended recipient?

○ a. MAPI

○ b. The name of the mailbox included in the fax header

○ c. Microsoft Fax

○ d. Inbound faxes are not forwarded to user mailboxes automatically by Exchange

Inbound faxes are not forwarded to user mailboxes automatically by Exchange; rather, they must be manually forwarded by an administrator; therefore, answer d is correct. MAPI is a communication interface independent of the features and functions of the applications that support it and has no control over how data is received or handled; therefore, answer a is incorrect. The ability to specify recipients in a fax header or by other means is not a feature in the fax service included with Windows 95 (although this type of feature may be available in other commercial fax products); therefore, answer b is incorrect. Microsoft Fax has no configurable settings that would enable a fax-forwarding feature; therefore, answer c is incorrect.

Question 6

How do you administer a workgroup postoffice?

○ a. Through the Mail and Fax applet's configuration tab

○ b. By launching the Microsoft Mail Postoffice applet and selecting the Administer An Existing Workgroup Postoffice radio button

○ c. Through the Start|Programs|Administration|Workgroup Postoffice application

○ d. Open the Microsoft Mail Postoffice applet and select the Administration tab

A workgroup postoffice can be administered only by launching the Microsoft Mail Postoffice applet and selecting the Administer An Existing Workgroup Postoffice radio button; therefore, answer b is correct. The Mail and Fax applet does not have a Configuration tab and is not used to administer workgroup postoffices; therefore, answer a is incorrect. There is no Workgroup Postoffice application in the Start menu; therefore, answer c is incorrect. The Microsoft Mail Postoffice applet does not have an Administration tab; rather, it has a radio button to select create or admin; therefore, answer d is incorrect.

Question 7

Which information services can Exchange be configured to use? [Check all correct answers]

❑   a. Microsoft Mail Server

❑   b. Internet email

❑   c. CompuServe Mail

❑   d. Fax systems

The Exchange client can be configured to use all of these (and many more) information services simply by installing the service (drivers) through the Mail and Fax applet; therefore, answers a, b, c, and d are correct.

Question 8

All installed messaging information services must be individually checked for new messages.

○   a. True

○   b. False

All installed messaging information services are checked automatically when the Exchange client (Inbox) launches and at each check messages interval; therefore, answer b is correct.

Question 9

> Which of the following can be assigned passwords? [Check all correct answers]
>
> ❏ a. Personal Address Book
>
> ❏ b. User's mailbox
>
> ❏ c. Personal Folders
>
> ❏ d. Dialing Properties

The Exchange components that can have passwords assigned to them are the Personal Address Book, User's mailbox, and Personal Folders; therefore, answers a, b, and c are correct. Dialing Properties are not password protected; therefore, answer d is incorrect.

Question 10

> If more than one messaging profile is created on a single Windows 95 computer, how does the Exchange client determine which profile to use when it is launched? [Select all correct answers]
>
> ❏ a. You are prompted with a selection dialog box when Inbox is opened.
>
> ❏ b. It is defined through the Mail and Fax applet; the setting is used when Inbox is opened.
>
> ❏ c. The Address Book with the highest priority is used to open the Inbox.
>
> ❏ d. The General tab of Tools|Options within Inbox sets the profile to use next time the Inbox is opened.

The messaging profile to be used by Inbox is determined through the Mail and Fax applet and the General tab of Tools|Options within Inbox; therefore, answers b and d are correct. Inbox shows a logon dialog box to request a name and password rather than displaying a selection dialog box for messaging profiles when it is opened; therefore, answer a is incorrect. The ordering of the Address Books/Lists does not have any effect on what messaging profile is used by Inbox; therefore, answer c is incorrect.

Need To Know More?

 Supporting Microsoft Windows 95. Microsoft Press, Redmond, WA, 1995. ISBN 1-55615-931-5. Chapter 22 discusses the Microsoft Exchange Client, including installation, configuration, and use.

 Mortensen, Lance and Rick Sawtell: *MCSE: Windows 95 Study Guide*. Sybex Network Press, San Francisco, CA, 1996. ISBN: 0-7821-2092-X. Chapter 19 contains information on the Microsoft Exchange Client and its use.

 Search the TechNet CD (or its online version through www. microsoft.com) and the *Windows 95 Resource Kit* using the keywords "MAPI," "Exchange client," "Inbox," "Postoffice," "Exchange Client Services," "Message Profile," "Personal Address Book/List (.PAB)," and "Personal Folders (.PST)."

Plug And Play

Terms you'll need to understand:

- √ Plug and Play
- √ Bus Enumerators
- √ Configuration Manager
- √ Resource Arbitrator
- √ Docking

Techniques you'll need to master:

- √ Understanding the requirements for Plug and Play systems
- √ Understanding the components of the Windows 95 Plug and Play architecture
- √ Knowing the Plug and Play process that operates at bootup
- √ Troubleshooting Plug and Play

Plug and Play is one of the most significant improvements in Windows 95 over Windows 3.x. Basically, Plug and Play is the ability of the operating system to locate, recognize, and configure hardware devices on the fly. This chapter discusses Plug and Play as it appears on the certification exam.

Plug And Play Introduction

Plug and Play is an industry-standard design philosophy and a set of computer hardware specifications. The main goal of Plug and Play is to manage system changes by recognizing new hardware, installing drivers, and enabling the new device's operation without user input or rebooting the system. For Plug and Play to function, the BIOS, the operating system, and the hardware must interact and cooperate. The requirements for such a system are:

BIOS support:

➤ The configuration of expansion devices is BIOS based.

➤ Configuration information needs to be known by the BIOS and communicated to the operating system.

➤ Must notify the operating system when a change occurs.

Operating system support:

➤ Must handle notification events and communication with BIOS.

➤ Must load and unload drivers as needed.

➤ Must simultaneously host Plug and Play and legacy devices.

Hardware support:

➤ Identifies and enumerates resource needs.

➤ Provides support for live configuration alteration.

Windows 95 Plug And Play

The Windows 95 operating system supports Plug and Play through multilevel architecture, the major components of which are the Registry, Bus Enumerators, Configuration Manager, and Resource Arbitrator.

The Registry maintains a detailed list of configuration settings for the computer. The base (or default) settings are read from the HKEY_LOCAL_ MACHINE key and the devices themselves; this information is stored in the HKEY_DYN_DATA for Plug and Play devices.

Bus Enumerators are device drivers for the various bus types. Most systems have a motherboard bus, an ISA bus, a PCI bus, a keyboard controller bus, and a display controller bus. If you have SCSI devices or a PCMCIA card slot, you have a SCSI bus and/or a PCMCIA bus. A bus is any device in your computer to which other devices can be attached. A Bus Enumerator gives each bus a unique identifier number, gathers configuration information from the Registry, and mediates with the Resource Arbitrator to assign resources to the buses and devices.

The Configuration Manager is responsible for the task of managing the flow of information during the initialization and configuration process. It instructs components and devices when to take actions such as assigning IRQs or reserving memory blocks.

The Resource Arbitrator assigns resources to devices. Resources are IRQs, DMA channels, I/O addresses, and memory. Because some devices are limited to a few restricted resource settings and others can accept almost any setting, the Resource Arbitrator has the daunting task of assigning resources so that each device is able to operate. For example, assume the following devices are present in a computer and can accept the following IRQ settings:

➤ Modem (7, 9, 11, 15)

➤ Legacy Printer Port (11)

➤ Audio card (7, 15)

➤ Network card (9, 11, 15)

The Resource Arbitrator would attempt to assign a legal value to each device without isolating any other device (if possible). A solution to the above example would be:

➤ Modem (7)

➤ Legacy Printer Port (11)

➤ Audio card (15)

➤ Network card (9)

One of the tools or techniques used to assign resources is to give legacy or non-Plug and Play devices their requested resources first and then attempt to assign remaining legal resources to all other devices.

Plug And Play Process

Windows 95 Plug and Play uses the following step-by-step process for device configuration:

1. All devices are placed into configuration mode by their appropriate Bus Enumerator, as instructed by the Configuration Manager.

2. Device information, such as resource requirements, is retrieved from the Registry and from the devices themselves by the Bus Enumerators, which communicate it to the Configuration Manager.

3. Device information is passed from the Configuration Manager to the Resource Arbitrator.

4. The Resource Arbitrator decides which resources to assign to which devices, then passes this information back to the Bus Enumerators through the Communication Manager.

5. The Bus Enumerators set, define, or inform each device of its assigned resources.

6. The Configuration Manager informs the system that bootup can continue.

7. The Bus Enumerators activate all devices with the new settings.

Plug And Play In Action

For the most part, Plug and Play takes place behind the scenes in Windows 95, so you notice it only when it doesn't work correctly. You should be aware of several situations that will appear on the certification exam:

➤ Docking station

➤ Infrared devices

➤ Eject methods

A docking station is a special device used with notebook and portable computers. It is a stationary component into which a notebook is "plugged" to add hardware, storage, printing, or display capabilities. There are three types of docking:

➤ **Hot docking** The notebook is attached to a docking station while fully powered and operational.

> **Warm docking** The notebook is attached to a docking station while in standby, suspend, or sleep mode.

> **Cold docking** The notebook is attached to a docking station while completely powered down.

Infrared devices offer special functionality. If an infrared-capable notebook enters a room with an active infrared peripheral (such as a printer), that device will be automatically recognized. Drivers will be loaded and made available for the user. Once the peripheral is out of range, it will be removed from the available resources and its drivers unloaded.

Plug and Play can handle removable media and devices by means of both auto and manual ejection. Auto-eject is controlled by the system; devices or media are ejected when the system has saved files, shut down access, and closed processes that depend on the resource. Manual ejection occurs when a user removes a device or media by hand without any automated software mechanisms. The system must recover from the removed resource once it is discovered as missing. This is sometimes called "surprise ejection."

Troubleshooting

Plug and Play often simplifies the configuration process, especially for newly installed hardware. However, Plug and Play might not always offer satisfactory or operational results. In such cases, you may need to intervene.

Plug and Play troubleshooting techniques:

> Manually alter the jumper/dip switch configuration settings on legacy or non-Plug and Play cards to more optimum configurations.

> Move legacy or non-Plug and Play cards to the lower slots on the bus (usually located toward the connection point for the power supply).

> Use the Device Manager tab of the System applet to manually force a configuration setting and prevent Windows 95 from automatically changing or altering it (deselect Use automatic settings).

> View the resource assignments by selecting Computer and clicking the Properties button on the Device Manager tab of the System applet.

> Remove unnecessary cards and devices, especially legacy or non-Plug and Play devices.

> Upgrade to Plug and Play devices.

Exam Prep Questions

Question 1

> Which components must be present on your computer system to use Plug and Play? [Check all correct answers]
>
> ❑ a. Windows 95 or another Plug and Play operating system
>
> ❑ b. An Intel CPU
>
> ❑ c. BIOS that supports Plug and Play
>
> ❑ d. Devices that are compliant with Plug and Play

Plug and Play requires a supported operating system, BIOS, and devices; therefore, answers a, c, and d are correct. An Intel CPU is required for Windows 95, but not all Plug and Play systems are Intel-based (in fact, Plug and Play originated on the Macintosh); therefore, answer b is incorrect.

Question 2

> Which component of Windows 95 is responsible for supplying configuration and resource requirement information when a notebook computer is hot docked?
>
> ○ a. User profile
>
> ○ b. Resource Arbitrator
>
> ○ c. Bus Enumerators
>
> ○ d. HKEY_LOCAL_MACHINE

Bus Enumerators are responsible for supplying configuration and resource requirement information when a notebook computer is hot docked; therefore, answer c is correct. A user profile defines the look and feel of the operational environment but does not manage or handle docking or device mechanisms; therefore, answer a is incorrect. The Resource Arbitrator assigns resources to devices and does not obtain the configuration requirements when new devices are located; therefore, answer b is incorrect. HKEY_LOCAL _MACHINE is the Registry key where the last used hardware configuration is stored and does not interact with new devices; therefore, answer d is incorrect.

Question 3

> Which of the following actions are possible through the Device Manager? [Check all correct answers]
>
> ❏ a. Editing the Registry directly
> ❏ b. Disabling Plug and Play automated resource assignment
> ❏ c. Removing conflicting drivers
> ❏ d. Identifying unallocated resources

The Device Manager can be used to disable automatic resource assignment, remove conflicting drivers, and identify available resources; therefore, answers b, c, and d are correct. The Device Manager cannot be used to edit the Registry directly; therefore, answer a is incorrect.

Question 4

> A new network interface card has been added to your Windows 95 computer system. It is a Plug and Play device that can accept the IRQ settings of 7, 9, or 11. You already have a Plug and Play modem card that usually uses IRQ 5 and a legacy sound card that is set by dip switches to use IRQ 9. During the boot process of Windows 95, which IRQ is assigned first?
>
> ○ a. IRQ 5
> ○ b. IRQ 7
> ○ c. IRQ 9
> ○ d. IRQ 11

IRQ 9 is assigned first because it is the only legacy card in the system and its required resource must be assigned before Plug and Play devices with variable assignments are configured; therefore, answer c is correct. IRQs 5, 7, and 11 may be assigned in any order, but because the Plug and Play process is dynamic, the actual order is not definitely known, and these IRQs are always secondary to the assignments of any resource allocations required by legacy cards; therefore, answers a, b, and d are incorrect.

Question 5

> Which type of docking requires the notebook computer to be in sleep mode?
>
> ○ a. Hot
> ○ b. Warm
> ○ c. Cold

Warm docking requires the notebook to be in sleep, standby, or suspend mode; therefore, answer b is correct. Hot docking allows fully powered notebooks to connect, whereas cold docking requires the computer to be powered off; therefore, answers a and c are incorrect.

Question 6

> Which of the following are components of the Windows 95 Plug and Play architecture? [Check all correct answers]
>
> ❑ a. Resource Arbitrator
> ❑ b. Response Director
> ❑ c. Bus Enumerators
> ❑ d. Registry

The Resource Arbitrator, Bus Enumerators, and Registry are all part of the Plug and Play architecture of Windows 95 (Configuration Manager is not listed); therefore, answers a, c, and d are correct. Response Director is a fictional component; therefore, answer b is incorrect.

Question 7

> Which resources are configured and assigned by the Resource Arbitrator? [Check all correct answers]
>
> ❑ a. IRQs
> ❑ b. DMA
> ❑ c. I/O addresses
> ❑ d. Memory

The Resource Arbitrator assigns IRQs, DMA channels, I/O address, and memory; therefore, answers a, b, c, and d are correct.

Question 8

Assume your computer has the following devices with the possible IRQ assignments:

- Legacy Printer Port (11)

- Legacy Video card (7)

- NIC (5, 7, 9, 11)

- Modem (3, 7, 9)

- Sound card (5, 7, 11)

Which of the following are possible settings of each device after Plug and Play assigns resources?

- ○ a. Legacy Printer Port (11), Legacy Video card (7), NIC (5), Modem (9), Sound card (9)

- ○ b. Legacy Printer Port (11), Legacy Video card (7), NIC (9), Modem (3), Sound card (5)

- ○ c. Legacy Printer Port (11), Legacy Video card (5), NIC (9), Modem (7), Sound card (11)

- ○ d. Legacy Printer Port (7), Legacy Video card (6), NIC (9, 11), Modem (3), Sound card (5)

Legacy Printer Port (11), Legacy Video card (7), NIC (9), Modem (3), Sound card (5) is the only possible setting for these devices; therefore, answer b is correct. The other three options either assign the same resource to multiple devices or assign an invalid IRQ to a device; therefore, answers a, c, and d are incorrect.

Need To Know More?

 Supporting Microsoft Windows 95. Microsoft Press, Redmond, WA, 1995. ISBN 1-55615-931-5. Chapter 6 discusses Windows 95 and Plug and Play.

 Mortensen, Lance and Rick Sawtell: *MCSE: Windows 95 Study Guide*. Sybex Network Press, San Francisco, CA, 1996. ISBN: 0-7821-2092-X. Chapter 20 contains information about the Plug and Play architecture of Windows 95.

 Search the TechNet CD (or its online version through www.microsoft.com) and the *Windows 95 Resource Kit* using the keywords "Plug and Play," "Bus Enumerators," "Configuration Manager," "Resource Arbitrator," and "docking."

Troubleshooting

Terms you'll need to understand:

√ Device Manager

√ Control Panel

√ System Configuration Editor

√ System Monitor

√ Net Watcher

√ Auditing

√ Safe Mode

Techniques you'll need to master:

√ Diagnosing Windows 95 faults

√ Using the Device Manager, Control Panel, System Configuration Editor, System Monitor, and Net Watcher for troubleshooting purposes

√ Using the log file to audit system activity

√ Improving common issues: memory, swap file, and hung applications

√ Booting with the Startup menu to Safe Mode

Unfortunately, Windows 95 will experience system failures and operational faults from time to time. You are responsible for knowing your system and Windows 95 thoroughly enough to diagnose, isolate, and resolve any problems that might occur. This chapter discusses some of the troubleshooting techniques and tools to help you in this process.

Diagnosis

The first step in troubleshooting is to attempt to diagnose or isolate the fault. This process is more an art than a science, so an exact course of action can't be outlined here. However, several questions can guide you in this task:

➤ Which hardware and software components are involved?

➤ Has the current configuration ever worked before? If so, what changed?

➤ Does the problem occur only with a single program?

➤ Can you reproduce the fault?

➤ Does it occur when you boot into Safe Mode?

➤ Are any Real Mode drivers or TSRs in use or involved with the fault?

➤ What was the most recent change to the system?

Once you've determined the problem or its most likely cause, you should check the documentation and troubleshooting resources to see whether others have encountered the problem. If they have, you might find a solution already spelled out for you.

Built-In Tools

You can use several tools that are built in to Windows 95 to help troubleshoot system faults: Device Manager, Control Panel, System Configuration Editor, System Monitor, and Net Watcher.

Device Manager

 The Device Manager offers a graphical interface to all the drivers installed under Windows 95. The Device Manager is one of the tabs of the System applet (Figure 17.1). By default, only the top-level driver categories are displayed. A conflict or a problem with one or more drivers will expand those categories to reveal the driver names, and a red exclamation point will appear on top of the driver's icon. If duplicate drivers are present, a yellow exclamation point will appear on the driver's icon.

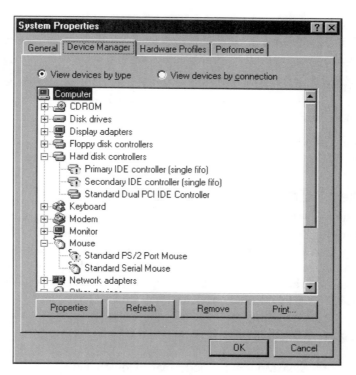

Figure 17.1   The Device Manager tab of the System applet.

 By selecting any listed driver, you can open its properties and alter any settings in an attempt to resolve the conflict; reboot to guarantee that your changes are put into effect. You can also select a duplicate driver and use the Remove button to clear it from the system. However, be sure to remove the driver you do not need.

By default, the Device Manager displays drivers by type. Using the radio selection button above the main display area, you can select to show drivers by their connections (i.e., the physical construction of the devices).

Control Panel

The applets in the Control Panel can also help in troubleshooting situations. The most useful applets for this purpose are:

➤ **Add New Hardware** Use this applet to add new drivers for hardware when a device fails to function because of a missing driver.

➤ **Add/Remove Programs** Use this applet to add or remove both native Windows 95 software and 32-bit applications and to create a new startup disk.

➤ **Display** Use this applet to change the display settings, such as resolution and color depth. It can be accessed by right-clicking over the desktop and selecting Properties from the context menu.

➤ **Modems** Use this applet to add or remove modems and to diagnose a COM port and/or modem.

System Configuration Editor

The System Configuration Editor is a text-editing tool that simplifies the process of editing the most common .INI and configuration files of Windows 95. It is launched from the Start|Run command or from a command prompt using "sysedit" or "sysedit.com" (see Figure 17.2). It loads six files by default (if they are present on the system): AUTOEXEC.BAT, CONFIG.SYS, WIN.INI, SYSTEM.INI, PROTOCOL.INI, and MSMAIL.INI.

System Monitor

 System Monitor is a performance tool that can be used to view several aspects of the Windows 95 operating environment in realtime. Using the System Monitor, you can establish a baseline for normal operation so you will know when the system is performing outside its standard parameters. System Monitor takes measurements from various objects in the Windows 95 system and gives you some understanding about how the system is performing (Figure 17.3). The types of objects available to measure vary, depending on which services and tools are installed on the system. Generally, the System Monitor can track details from the following categories: file system, IPX/SPX, kernel, memory, Client for NetWare Networks, and Client for Microsoft Networks.

Net Watcher

The Net Watcher tool is essentially a remote administration tool that can be used to manage resources located on Windows 95 servers elsewhere on your network (see Figure 17.4). There are many cases in which altering the actions of a remote system will help troubleshoot a local problem, especially if the problem is related to accessing files through a network share hosted on a remote system. Net Watcher gives you the ability to see which users are currently

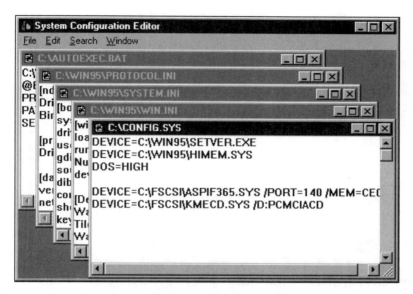

Figure 17.2   The System Configuration Editor.

online and allows you to disconnect those users from the network. Net Watcher also lets you view shared resources and see which files are currently in use. You can close an open file, change the properties of a shared folder, or create new shares using Net Watcher.

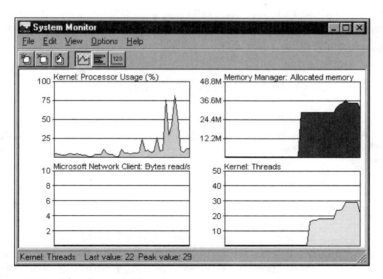

Figure 17.3   The System Monitor.

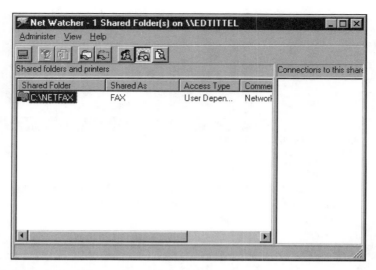

Figure 17.4 The Net Watcher.

SNMP

Windows 95 includes an SNMP (Simple Network Management Protocol) agent that enables network managers to remotely monitor the system using standard SNMP management consoles. As part of the SNMP support, an extensible MIB handler interface and MIB-II support via TCP/IP are also included. SNMP is installed as a service via the Network applet. Windows 95 support for SNMP allows for remote monitoring; however, support for remote changes to the system or Registry via SNMP is not currently available.

Auditing And Log Files

Windows 95 does not have a true auditing system as Windows NT does. However, some details about the operation and failure of Windows 95 are recorded in log files that can provide information similar to what an audit system would. The log files of Windows 95 include:

➤ **BOOTLOG.TXT** Located in the root of the boot drive, this log file is recorded during the first boot sequence following a successful installation. This file is written to only after this first instance by selecting the Logged option from the Startup menu (pressing F8 when "Starting Windows 95" is displayed on bootup). This file records all devices and drivers loaded by the system.

> **DETLOG.TXT** Located in the root of the boot drive, this log file records whether a device was detected and, if so, which parameters were read from it. This file is created during installation and is amended each time the Add New Hardware Wizard is used.

> **SETUPLOG.TXT** Located in the root of the boot drive, this log file records all the successes and failures encountered during the installation process.

> **NETLOG.TXT** Located in the root of the boot drive and similar to SETUPLOG and DETLOG, this file records successes and failures associated with network device detection and installation.

By using a text editor such as Notepad to view these files, you might discover problem areas in your system or determine whether a driver was loaded properly.

Common Issues

Windows 95 users have consistently had to deal with certain problem areas or areas in which improvement over the default settings is desirable. The next three sections cover these areas: memory, the swap file, and hung applications.

Memory

The memory architecture of Windows 95 is a great improvement over the architecture Windows 3.x uses. In fact, no additional (third-party) memory managers are required if sufficient physical RAM is installed. However, the performance and use of available memory may not be optimal. The following guidelines can improve the memory performance of a system:

> **Open only necessary applications** Limit yourself to having one or two applications open at a time. Close any large applications before attempting to launch others. The more applications that are active, the more Windows 95 must page memory to maintain a functioning environment.

> **Reduce network services** Network services, even when not in use, remain in memory at all times. Remove all nonessential services to increase the available memory and to streamline network connections.

> **Run DOS applications in full screen instead of windowed** A windowed DOS application uses more system resources than one with full control of the display screen.

> **Keep the Clipboard empty** Although you never see it, the Clipboard can hold a significant amount of data, especially if OLE or graphics are

involved. Simply copy something small, such as a single character, to reduce the memory footprint of the Clipboard.

➤ **Reboot often** Many applications and even Windows 95 itself can lose control of resources and memory. Rebooting at least once a day will restore the system to its best possible state.

Swap File

The swap file is used by the Windows 95 Virtual Memory Manager to provide the system with more memory resources than are actually present in RAM. By default, the swap file is managed by Windows 95. If memory performance is not as good as you expected, you can change the settings of the swap file manually. You access the Virtual Memory controls by clicking the Virtual Memory button on the Performance tab of the System applet. Here you can specify which drive to host the swap file, and the minimum and maximum size of the swap file. The following are additional ways to improve swap file performance:

➤ Host the swap file on the fastest drive.

➤ Host the swap file on a drive with sufficient free space.

➤ Use the System Monitor to track the size of the swap file.

➤ Defragment the drive hosting the swap file regularly.

➤ Avoid placing the swap file on a compressed drive.

➤ Do not use a network drive to host the swap file.

Hung Applications

Windows 16- and 32-bit applications can fail no matter how much Microsoft claims 32-bit applications are impregnable. When failure occurs, the rest of the system might operate normally, or it might be slowed down while the system attempts to deal with the failed or failing process. You can shortcut the sludge by terminating hung applications using the Task Manager, which is accessed by pressing the attention keystroke (CTRL+ALT+DEL) one time. The Task Manager dialog box should appear, listing all applications currently in memory. You can select one of the applications and click End Task to terminate it. You can also click Shut Down to abort the current computing session. Note that any unsaved information will be lost when you shut down the system.

Safe Mode

If Windows 95 fails because of a corrupted driver or a botched installation or configuration action, you can attempt to return the system to normal working order by booting into Safe Mode, which you can access in the Startup menu (pressing F8 when "Starting Windows 95" is displayed on bootup). Among the possible selections are:

➤ **Normal** Launches Windows normally and loads all startup files and Registry values

➤ **Logged (BOOTLOG.TXT)** Launches Windows and records a startup log file

➤ **Safe Mode** Launches Windows, bypasses all startup files, and uses only basic system drivers

➤ **Safe Mode with Network Support** Launches Windows, bypasses startup files, and uses only basic system drivers and basic networking support

➤ **Step-By-Step Confirmation** Launches Windows and requests user confirmation for each line of each startup file

➤ **Command Prompt Only** Launches the DOS 7.0 command prompt and uses the normal startup files

➤ **Safe Mode Command Prompt Only** Launches the DOS 7.0 command prompt and bypasses all startup files

➤ **Previous version of MS-DOS** Launches the previous version of DOS installed on this computer

Rebuilding Groups

If your Start menu becomes corrupted or you wish to restore the default groups within the menu, the grpconv /r command will rebuild the Start menu default groups. All new groups and shortcuts are unaffected by this action. The command can be issued from the Start|Run command or from a command prompt.

WIN.COM Switches

By booting to a command prompt through the Startup menu, you can launch Windows 95 using WIN.COM. By launching Windows in this method, you can use command line switches to alter how functions help isolate or detect system errors. The command line options for WIN.COM are:

```
win [/d:[f] [m] [n] [s] [v] [x]]
```

The /d: switch is used to initiate one of the following troubleshooting boot parameters:

➤ **f** Turns off 32-bit disk access; equivalent to 32BitDiskAccess=FALSE in SYSTEM.INI.

➤ **m** Launches Windows 95 in Safe Mode.

➤ **n** Launches Windows 95 in Safe Mode with Networking.

➤ **s** Instructs Windows 95 not to use ROM address space between F000:0000 and 1 MB for a break point; equivalent to SystemROMBreakPoint=FALSE in SYSTEM.INI.

➤ **v** Forces the ROM routine to handle interrupts from the hard disk controller; equivalent to VirtualHDIRQ=FALSE in SYSTEM.INI.

➤ **x** Excludes all expansion card memory addresses from Windows 95's scan to find unused space; equivalent to EMMExclude=A000-FFFF in SYSTEM.INI.

Startup Disk

A Startup disk for Windows 95 is little more than a floppy that can be used to boot the system to a command prompt. A handful of DOS-based tools, such as ATTRIB, FORMAT, CHKDISK, SCANDISK, EDIT, FDISK, and REGEDIT, can help troubleshoot a failing system.

Resources

Several useful resources for operating, maintaining, and troubleshooting Windows 95 include:

➤ **Microsoft TechNet** Microsoft distributes this monthly CD that contains technical documentation, white papers, and knowledge-based articles for all Microsoft products.

➤ **Microsoft's Web site** The most concentrated collection of Windows 95 documentation anywhere can be found at www.microsoft.com/windows95/.

➤ **Windows 95 Resource Kit** An invaluable tool for administrators and power users. It contains extended documentation and several tools and utilities not shipped with the original product.

Exam Prep Questions

Question 1

> If Safe Mode is used to boot Windows 95, which of the following files are bypassed? [Check all correct answers]
>
> ❏ a. AUTOEXEC.BAT
>
> ❏ b. WIN.INI
>
> ❏ c. CONFIG.SYS
>
> ❏ d. The Registry

The files or data components that Safe Mode skips include AUTOEXEC. BAT, CONFIG.SYS, and the Registry. Therefore, answers a, c, and d are correct. WIN.INI cannot be bypassed because it contains base operational parameters for Windows 95. Therefore, answer b is incorrect.

Question 2

> Which ASCII files can be edited through the System Configura-tion Editor? [Check all correct answers]
>
> ❏ a. AUTOEXEC.BAT
>
> ❏ b. WIN.INI
>
> ❏ c. BOOTLOG.TXT
>
> ❏ d. PROTOCOL.INI

AUTOEXEC.BAT, WIN.INI, and PROTOCOL.INI (not to mention CONFIG.SYS, SYSTEM.INI, and MSMAIL.INI) are all ASCII files edited through the System Configuration Editor. Therefore, answers a, b, and d are correct. The System Configuration Editor cannot load files other than the six default files, so BOOTLOG.TXT cannot be edited or viewed using the SCE. Therefore, answer c is incorrect.

Question 3

> Which troubleshooting tool is used to monitor the activity and performance of several system components and resources?
>
> ○ a. Task Manager
>
> ○ b. Net Watcher
>
> ○ c. System Monitor
>
> ○ d. Control Panel

The System Monitor is used to monitor the activity and performance of several system components and resources. Therefore, answer c is correct. The Task Manager can be used to terminate an application or abort the current computing session. Therefore, answer a is incorrect. The Net Watcher is used to manage remote resources and does not measure performance. Therefore, answer b is incorrect. The Control Panel has several applets that control and manage various aspects of Windows 95, but none is used to measure performance. Therefore, answer d is incorrect.

Question 4

> Which file is created during the first bootup of Windows 95 and when specifically instructed by users from the Startup menu?
>
> ○ a. BOOTLOG.TXT
>
> ○ b. DETLOG.TXT
>
> ○ c. SETUPLOG.TXT
>
> ○ d. NETLOG.TXT

BOOTLOG.TXT is recorded during the first boot after installation and when instructed through the Startup menu. Therefore, answer a is correct. DETLOG.TXT is recorded during installation and when the Add New Hardware Wizard is used. Therefore, answer b is incorrect. SETUPLOG.TXT is recorded during installation only. Therefore, answer c is incorrect. NETLOG.TXT is recorded only during the installation of network components. Therefore, answer d is incorrect.

Question 5

> Which of the following may improve system performance? [Check
> all correct answers]
>
> ❑ a. Adding physical RAM
>
> ❑ b. Reducing swap file size
>
> ❑ c. Reducing the number of simultaneous running
>   applications
>
> ❑ d. Installing all networking services

Performance may be improved by adding physical RAM and reducing applications. Therefore, answers a and c are correct. Reducing the swap file size and
installing all networking services will most likely degrade system performance.
Therefore, answers b and d are incorrect.

Question 6

> Which of the following is the most significant problem on a Win-
> dows 95 system?
>
> ○ a. Sharing a printer with the network
>
> ○ b. Hosting four internal SCSI hard drives
>
> ○ c. Disabling the swap file
>
> ○ d. Holding large OLE objects in the clipboard

Disabling the swap file is the most significant problem on a Windows 95 system. Therefore, answer c is correct. Sharing a printer with the network will
increase system load, but not significantly. Therefore, answer a is incorrect.
Hosting multiple hard drives most often will improve rather than hinder a
system. Therefore, answer b is incorrect. Holding large amounts of data in the
Clipboard can slow performance, but not as significantly as not having a swap
file. Therefore, answer d is incorrect.

Question 7

A single activation of the attention keystroke (CTRL+ALT+DEL) will cause what to happen in Windows 95?

○ a. System reboot

○ b. Nothing—that keystroke is ignored

○ c. Launches the Task Manager

○ d. Terminates the current foreground application

The attention keystroke (CTRL+ALT+DEL) launches the Task Manager. Therefore, answer c is correct. This keystroke would reboot the system in DOS, but when Windows 95 is active, even in the background, it is intercepted as a call for the Task Manager. If the attention keystroke is pressed a second time while the Task Manager is active, the system will reboot. Therefore, answer a is incorrect. The keystroke is not ignored. That is why it is called the *attention* keystroke. Therefore, answer b is incorrect. The attention keystroke does not automatically terminate any applications. Rather, the Task Manager can be used to terminate an application. Therefore, answer d is incorrect.

Question 8

If you manually alter the settings on a device, where can you go in Windows 95 to manually set or define these new settings for the driver controlling that device?

○ a. Device Manager tab of the System applet

○ b. Add/Remove Programs applet

○ c. Sounds applet

○ d. Add New Hardware applet

The Device Manager tab of the System applet is where changes to the physical settings of a device can be defined for the driver (if they are not automatically detected). Therefore, answer a is correct. The Add/Remove Programs applet is used to add or remove Windows components and 32-bit software and to create a startup disk. Therefore, answer b is incorrect. The Sounds applet is used to associate sounds with system events. Therefore, answer c is incorrect. The Add New Hardware applet is used to install new drivers for hardware, which would occur only if the previous driver for the device were deleted. Therefore, answer d is incorrect.

Need To Know More?

 Supporting Microsoft Windows 95. Microsoft Press, Redmond, WA, 1995. ISBN 1-55615-931-5. Chapter 27 discusses Windows 95 troubleshooting.

 Mortensen, Lance and Rick Sawtell; *MCSE: Windows 95 Study Guide.* Sybex Network Press, San Francisco, CA, 1996. ISBN: 0-7821-2092-X. Chapter 23 contains information about troubleshooting Windows 95.

 Search the TechNet CD (or its online version through www. microsoft.com) and the *Windows 95 Resource Kit* using the keywords "troubleshooting," "Device Manager," "Control Panel," "System Configuration Editor," "System Monitor," "Net Watcher," and "Startup menu."

Sample Test

In this chapter, we provide a number of pointers for developing a successful test-taking strategy, including how to choose proper answers, how to decode ambiguity, how to work within the Microsoft framework, how to decide what to memorize, and how to prepare for the test. At the end, we provide a number of questions that cover subject matter that is pertinent to the Implementing and Supporting Microsoft Windows 95 exam. Good luck!

Questions, Questions, Questions

There should be no doubt in your mind that you are facing an exam full of questions. The exam comprises 49 questions, and you are allotted 90 minutes to complete it. Remember, questions are of four basic types:

➤ Multiple choice with a single answer

➤ Multiple choice with multiple answers

➤ Multipart with a single answer

➤ Picking the spot on the graphic

Always take the time to read a question twice before selecting an answer, and be sure to look for an Exhibit button. The Exhibit button brings up graphics and charts to help explain the question, provide additional data, or illustrate layout. You'll find it difficult to answer these questions without looking at the exhibits.

Not every question has a single answer, and many of the questions require more than one answer. In fact, some questions require that *all* the answers be marked. Read the question carefully so you know how many answers are required and look for additional instructions for marking your answers. These instructions are usually in brackets.

Picking Proper Answers

Obviously, the only way to pass any exam is by selecting the correct answers, but the Microsoft exams are not standardized like the SAT and GRE exams; rather, they are more convoluted. Some questions are so poorly worded that deciphering them is nearly impossible, in which case you may need to rely on answer elimination skills. Usually, at least one answer out of the possible choices can be immediately eliminated because:

➤ The answer doesn't apply to the situation.

➤ The answer describes a nonexistent issue.

➤ The answer is already eliminated by the question text.

Once you eliminate obviously wrong answers, you must rely on your retained knowledge to eliminate further answers. Look for items that sound correct but that refer to actions, commands, or features not present or not available in the described situation.

If, after these phases of elimination, you still face a blind guess between two or more answers, reread the question. Try to picture in your mind's eye the situation and how each of the possible remaining answers would affect the situation.

If you have exhausted your ability to eliminate answers and are still unclear about which of the remaining possible answers is the correct one—guess. You get no points for an unanswered question, but guessing gives you a chance of getting a question right. However, don't be too hasty in making a blind guess. Wait until your last round of reviewing marked questions before you start to guess, and do it as a last resort.

Decoding Ambiguity

Microsoft exams have a reputation for including questions that are sometimes difficult to interpret, whether they be confusing or ambiguous. We consider this reputation to be completely justified. The Microsoft exams are difficult. They are designed specifically to limit the number of passing grades to about 30 percent of all who take the exam; in other words, Microsoft seems to want 70 percent of the exam takers to fail.

The only way to beat Microsoft at its own game is to be prepared. You'll discover that many exam questions test your knowledge of things that are not directly related to the issue the question raises. This means that the answers offered to you, even the incorrect ones, are just as much a part of the skill assessment as the question itself. If you don't know about all aspects of Windows 95 cold, you may not be able to eliminate obviously wrong answers because they relate to a different area of 95 than the one being addressed by the question.

Questions often give away the answers, but you have to be better than Sherlock Holmes to see the clues. Often, subtle hints are included in the text in such a way that they seem like irrelevant information. You must realize that each question is a test in and of itself, and you need to inspect and successfully navigate each question to pass the exam. Look for small clues, such as the mention of times, group names, configuration settings, and even local or remote-access methods, that can point out the right answer. However, if you miss them, you can be left facing a blind guess.

Another common difficulty is that of vocabulary. Microsoft has an uncanny knack for naming utilities and features very obviously on some occasions and completely inanely in others. This is especially true in the area of printing and remote access, so be sure to brush up on the terms presented in those chapters. You may also want to review the Glossary before approaching the test.

Working Within The Framework

The exam questions are presented to you in a random order, and many of the elements or issues are repeated in multiple questions. It is not uncommon to find that any one answer is correct in one question and wrong in another. Take the time to read each answer, even if you know the correct one immediately. The incorrect answers might spark a memory that helps you on another question.

You can revisit any question as many times as you like. If you are uncertain of the answer to a question, mark the box provided and come back to it later. You should also mark questions you think might offer data that you can use to solve other questions. We've marked 25 percent to 50 percent of the questions on exams we've taken. The testing software is designed to help you mark an answer for every question, so use its framework to your advantage. You should mark everything you want to see again; the testing software will help you return to those items.

Deciding What To Memorize

The amount of memorization you must do for the exam depends on how well you remember what you've read. If you are a visual learner and can see the pull-down menus and dialog boxes in your head, you won't need to memorize as much as someone who is less visually oriented. The exam will stretch your recollection of commands and the locations of features of the utilities.

The important types of information to memorize are:

➤ The order of steps in setup or configuration

➤ Features or commands found in pull-down menus and configuration dialog boxes

➤ Applications found by default in the Start menu

➤ Applets in the Control Panel

➤ Names and functions of the five main Registry keys

If you worked your way through this book while sitting at a Windows 95 computer, you should have little or no problem interacting with most of these important items.

Preparing For The Exam

The best way to prepare for the exam—after you've studied—is to take at least one practice exam. We've included a practice exam in this chapter. Give yourself 90 minutes to take the exam. Keep yourself on the honor system, and don't cheat by looking back at the text. Once your time is up or you finish, you can check your answers in the next chapter.

If you want additional practice exams, visit the Microsoft Training and Certification site (www.microsoft.com/train_cert/) and download the Self-Assessment Practice Exam utility.

Taking The Exam

Relax. Once you are sitting in front of the testing computer, there is nothing more you can do to increase your knowledge or preparation. Take a deep breath, stretch, and attack the first question.

Don't rush; there is plenty of time to complete each question and to return to skipped questions. If you read a question twice and are clueless, mark it and move on. Both easy and difficult questions are dispersed throughout the test randomly. Don't cheat yourself by spending so much time on a difficult question in the beginning that it prevents you from answering numerous easy questions positioned near the end. Move through the entire test, and before you return to the skipped questions, evaluate your time in light of the number of skipped questions. As you answer questions, remove the marks. Continue to review the remaining marked questions until your time expires or you complete the exam.

That's it for pointers. Here are some questions for you to practice.

Sample Exam

Question 1

Your boss has requested that you implement a fax system on your Windows 95 workgroup and has insisted that you do so with no additional costs. Because you are being restricted to the Exchange system that ships as a component of Windows 95, you set up one of the computers as an Exchange-based fax server. What mechanism within Exchange automatically forwards inbound faxes to the intended recipient?

- ○ a. MAPI
- ○ b. The name of the mailbox included in the fax header
- ○ c. Microsoft Fax
- ○ d. Inbound faxes are not forwarded to user mailboxes automatically by Exchange.

Question 2

You are running two 32-bit applications and a DOS application. What occurs when you press the attention keystroke (CTRL+ ALT+DEL)?

- ○ a. The system reboots.
- ○ b. Nothing. That keystroke is ignored.
- ○ c. The Task Manager is launched.
- ○ d. The current foreground application is terminated.

Question 3

You use a custom DOS application written by your organization's programming staff. Because of the limited RAM resources on your computer, you must carefully manage how system resources are used. Usually, you can use the DOS application without restriction. However, when your accounting program is active, you must limit the memory resources used by the DOS application (even though this makes it run very slowly); otherwise, the accounting program fails. What is the best way to set up your system so that you can launch the DOS application with two different memory settings?

○ a. Edit the DOS application's PIF to match the needed settings each time you launch the application.

○ b. Use the PIF Editor to create a menu to select the launch type each time you access the DOS application.

○ c. Create a PIF for the DOS application, make a copy of the PIF, and change the settings of the second PIF to reflect the memory limitations.

○ d. Windows 95 does not allow this type of configuration.

Question 4

Your Windows 95 computer hosts a data drive for your workgroup. This data drive stores individual data files,which are 4, 8, 12, and 16 KB in size. What size partition would offer the most efficient use of space for this drive?

○ a. 250 MB

○ b. 500 MB

○ c. 750 MB

○ d. 2,000 MB

Question 5

After moving your network to a new office, users discover that their desktop settings are no longer present. You suspect that the roaming profiles are not operating correctly. You performed several setup and configuration tasks on most of the computers during the move. What steps can you take to locate and resolve the problem with roaming profiles? [Check all correct answers]

❑ a. Check that the appropriate client is installed and set as the primary network logon.

❑ b. Check that Mail directories exist for each user on NetWare.

❑ c. Check the time, date, and time zone of each client; make sure they are in sync with the network servers.

❑ d. Check to ensure that profiles are enabled on each Windows 95 computer.

Question 6

After installing new device drivers, your Windows 95 system fails to operate properly. You think booting into Safe Mode will enable you to remove the drivers, but this will occur only if they are not loaded. Which files are bypassed when booting into Safe Mode? [Check all correct answers]

❑ a. AUTOEXEC.BAT

❑ b. WIN.INI

❑ c. CONFIG.SYS

❑ d. The Registry

Question 7

You attach a new Windows 95 computer to your network. Your primary protocol is TCP/IP. You test the new setup by using the PING utility against a remote host located in a different subnet. The first host you PING returns the packets quickly. However, when you attempt to PING another host a few minutes later within the same remote subnet, you get a timeout. What can you deduce from this? [Check all correct answers]

- ❑ a. The host is offline or not responsive.
- ❑ b. Your local TCP/IP settings are wrong.
- ❑ c. The traffic on the network or Internet is preventing timely delivery of packets.
- ❑ d. You used the wrong IP address for the remote host.

Question 8

Because of a bad sector on your hard drive, the SYSTEM.DAT file has been destroyed. How can you restore the Registry and the system to working order? [Check all correct answers]

- ❑ a. Boot into Safe Mode.
- ❑ b. Copy the .DA0 files over the .DAT files.
- ❑ c. Use the Startup disk to boot.
- ❑ d. Reinstall Windows 95.

Question 9

Your organization requires that system policies be used to enforce or restrict users' computing environment. If you create a policy for a specific individual's user account, which other policies can apply to that user? [Check all correct answers]

- ❑ a. Any group policies of groups of which that user is a member
- ❑ b. Default Computer
- ❑ c. Specific computer
- ❑ d. Default User

Question 10

While you are using a new DOS application, it locks up and stops responding. You launched the DOS application from Windows 95. Because it was a new application and not listed in the APPS.INF file, DEFAULT.PIF was used to configure its operational param- eters. What will happen if you pressed CTRL+ALT+DEL in this situation?

○ a. The computer will reboot.

○ b. The DOS application will terminate.

○ c. The Close Program dialog box will appear.

○ d. Nothing.

Question 11

After installing and configuring Windows 95, you realize it is not performing properly. You decide to alter the method of booting used by Windows 95 in an attempt to isolate or locate the prob- lem. What options do you have in modifying how Windows 95 boots? [Check all correct answers]

❑ a. Editing MSDOS.SYS

❑ b. Editing the MBR

❑ c. Using the Startup menu

❑ d. Editing BOOT.INI

Question 12

Your network comprises both Windows NT and NetWare servers. A new printer is attached to your Windows 95 workstation. Which components need to be installed on Windows 95 so that this printer can receive print jobs from NetWare-hosted print queues? [Check all correct answers]

❑ a. File and Printer Sharing for NetWare Networks

❑ b. Microsoft Print Server for NetWare

❑ c. IPX/SPX

❑ d. Microsoft Client for NetWare Networks

Question 13

You enable profiles on your Windows 95 workstations. Because several users are inexperienced and may not remain with the organization long, you want to implement mandatory profiles. Which Registry file must you rename to have a .MAN extension so profiles are enforced?

○ a. SYSTEM.DAT

○ b. REGLOG.TXT

○ c. USER.DAT

○ d. PROFILE.DAT

Question 14

The network in your office is a five-machine Windows 95 workgroup. Two new employees are hired, but they will be telecommuting from home. To accommodate them, you need to enable the office network to accept inbound connections by installing Dial-Up Server from the Windows 95 Plus! pack. Once this is complete, which types of clients can the new telecommuting employees use to connect to the office workgroup? [Check all correct answers]

❑ a. PPP

❑ b. IPX

❑ c. SLIP

❑ d. Windows NT

Question 15

Three different people are using the same Windows 95 computer, each on a different eight-hour shift. You need to create three individual message profiles so they can send and retrieve email separately and securely. Where is this activity performed?

○ a. Through the Passwords applet

○ b. Through the Inbox's Tools|Options command

○ c. Through the Mail and Fax applet

○ d. Through the Profiles applet

Question 16

After installing a new Adaptec SCSI controller card and a Hewlett-Packard SCSI DAT tape backup drive on your Windows 95 computer, you launch Microsoft Backup. Backup claims that no tape devices are present. Why?

○ a. You forgot to install the SCSI controller card's drivers.

○ b. You forgot to install the DAT device's drivers.

○ c. You forgot to configure the tape device from Backup's Tools menu.

○ d. Windows 95 Microsoft Backup does not support SCSI tape devices.

Question 17

The memory architecture of Windows 95 is a significant improvement over that of Windows 3.x. However, one item that both versions of Windows have in common is combining _____ with _____ to offer applications more memory than would otherwise be available. [Check two answers to fill in the blanks]

❑ a. Time slices

❑ b. Physical RAM

❑ c. Expanded Memory Manager (EMS)

❑ d. Hard drive storage space

Question 18

Your NT Server-based network is growing quickly. You will soon be unable to keep track of the names and addresses of all the devices manually. To improve and streamline name resolution, your administrator installs WINS and helps you configure your Windows 95 workstation to use WINS. Which functions does WINS perform? [Check all correct answers]

❑ a. Enables internetwork browsing

❑ b. Maps FQDNs to IP addresses

❑ c. Maps NetBIOS names to IP addresses

❑ d. Maps NetBIOS names to MAC addresses

❑ e. Assigns clients IP addresses

Question 19

A traveling salesman has an AT&T WorldNet account that allows him to connect to the Internet from all of the cities he frequents using a Windows 95 notebook computer. This is convenient because it allows him to remain in contact by email. The home office has a network that stores all of the product inventory and cost statistics. The salesman currently connects with the network via a long-distance telephone call to retrieve the product details on a daily basis. What can be done with this notebook computer to reduce the cost and headache of communicating with the network?

   ○ a. Have a secretary email the product detail files each day.

   ○ b. Fax the product information to the salesman's hotel.

   ○ c. Use PPTP to create a VPN connection over the Internet.

   ○ d. This is already the best solution.

Question 20

Assume your computer has the following devices with these possible IRQ assignments:

➤ Legacy Printer Port (11)

➤ Legacy Video card (7)

➤ NIC (5, 7, 9, 11)

➤ Modem (3, 7, 9)

➤ Sound card (5, 7, 11)

Which of the following are possible settings of each device after Plug and Play assigns resources?

   ○ a. Legacy Printer Port (11), Legacy Video card (7), NIC (5), Modem (9), Sound card (9)

   ○ b. Legacy Printer Port (11), Legacy Video card (7), NIC (9), Modem (3), Sound card (5)

   ○ c. Legacy Printer Port (11), Legacy Video card (5), NIC (9), Modem (7), Sound card (11)

   ○ d. Legacy Printer Port (7), Legacy Video card (6), NIC (9, 11), Modem (3), Sound card (5)

Question 21

Your boss has requested that you implement all information services supported by Exchange on his Windows 95 computer. You search the Windows 95 CD-ROM, Windows 95 Plus!, and the Windows Web site to discover the following list of services. Which ones can be installed into Exchange? [Check all correct answers]

❑ a. Microsoft Mail Server

❑ b. Internet email

❑ c. CompuServe Mail

❑ d. Fax systems

Question 22

What is the last segment of the Windows 95 boot process?

○ a. BIOS Bootstrap

○ b. MBR and boot sector

○ c. Real Mode boot

○ d. Protected Mode boot

Question 23

When you installed Windows 95, you selected an alternate installation directory instead of upgrading your previous Windows 3.x system. As a result of this, none of your custom groups from the old operating system is present in Windows 95. Which utility can you use to convert your old group files into Windows 95 Start menu items?

○ a. SETUP

○ b. CONVERT

○ c. GRPCONV

○ d. NETSETUP

Question 24

When does a Browser election occur? [Check all correct answers]

❑ a. When a Backup Browser is unable to contact the Master Browser

❑ b. When the Master Browser goes offline

❑ c. When a computer boots into the network that is set to become a Master Browser

❑ d. When an administrator forces it

Question 25

When should the Disk Defragmenter utility be used? [Check all correct answers]

❑ a. If the drive is over 10 percent fragmented

❑ b. After deleting large or numerous files

❑ c. If the system is performing sluggishly

❑ d. When disk activity is high (not associated with demand paging)

Question 26

Your Windows 95 computer is equipped with multimedia capabilities and a CD-ROM drive. You are performing research that requires switching CDs frequently. However, each time you put in a new disk, the install utility launches and an attention sound is played. This has become extremely annoying. Where can you disable the AutoPlay feature of Windows 95?

○ a. Through the CD Player's Options menu

○ b. On the Settings tab of the Properties dialog box of the CD-ROM drive driver list on the Device Manager tab of the System applet

○ c. In the Multimedia applet

○ d. Through the Properties of the CD-ROM drive accessed through Windows Explorer

Question 27

You are a traveling sales representative and you carry a Windows 95 notebook with you. Your office has recently deployed an email system, and you need to use your notebook to retrieve your messages while on the road. Where is your Exchange client configured to access information services over dial-up connections?

○ a. Through the Microsoft Mail Postoffice applet

○ b. Through the Tools|Microsoft Mail Tools menu within the Exchange client

○ c. Through the Mail and Fax applet

○ d. Through the Internet applet

Question 28

Support for a wide variety of application types is an important consideration when selecting a new operating system. Which application types does Windows 95 support? [Check all correct answers]

❑ a. DOS

❑ b. Win16

❑ c. OS/2

❑ d. Win32

❑ e. POSIX

Question 29

After you have attempted several times to configure a DOS application's PIF, a new and important utility simply will not function within a Windows 95 VM. What enables you to maintain Windows 95 on your computer and still be able to use the DOS utility?

○ a. Virtual Memory

○ b. DOS Mode

○ c. Ring 0 Protected Mode

○ d. Message queues

Question 30

Your modem is no longer establishing reliable connections with your Internet service provider. To start your troubleshooting, you want to inspect the communication-related log files. When you look in the Windows main directory, which log files will you find that can provide you with useful information? [Check all correct answers]

❑   a. DUN.LOG

❑   b. MODEMLOG.TXT

❑   c. PPPLOG.TXT

❑   d. USERS.DAT

Question 31

You run a small business from a desktop computer and a notebook that you take with you on sales calls. Recently, your data files have become so large they no longer fit onto a floppy. What is the simplest option for transferring files between your two Windows 95 computers? Remember that you need to exchange files only when you are back at the office, and you don't have a lot of money to spend.

○   a. Install NICs and create a network

○   b. Use a Direct Cable Connection

○   c. Install modems, dial into an Internet server, and use FTP

○   d. Use a backup tape device

Question 32

The hardware configuration details of the currently active session are stored in which key of the Registry?

○   a. HKEY_LOCAL_MACHINE

○   b. HKEY_DYN_DATA

○   c. HKEY_CURRENT_CONFIG

○   d. HKEY_CURRENT_USER

Question 33

Most of the configuration changes to devices are performed through the Device Manager tab of the System applet. Which functions or actions can be performed through the Device Manager? [Check all correct answers]

❑ a. Edit the Registry directly

❑ b. Disable Plug and Play automated resource assignment

❑ c. Remove conflicting drivers

❑ d. Identify unallocated resources

Question 34

The process of booting Windows 95 is a multistep one. Fortunately, most or all of the required activities are performed automatically each time the system is started. Which activities occur during the portion of setup labeled Real Mode Setup? [Check all correct answers]

❑ a. File system integrity check

❑ b. Windows 95 startup disk creation

❑ c. Hardware detection and identification

❑ d. TSR management

❑ e. Help system built

Question 35

Protected Mode drivers are the pieces of code used by the Windows 95 system to operate devices in high-performance Virtual Mode. Which of the following are not extensions associated with Protected Mode drivers? [Check all correct answers]

❑ a. SYS

❑ b. DRV

❑ c. VXD

❑ d. 386

Question 36

Passwords are the most common form of security within the Windows 95 operating system. Which of the following can be protected by being assigned a password? [Check all correct answers]

❑ a. Personal Address Book

❑ b. User's mailbox

❑ c. Personal Folders

❑ d. Dialing Properties

Question 37

You create several shortcuts on your desktop to simplify access to your most frequently used applications and documents. Once the shortcut is created, which additional configuration options are available to you to control how each shortcut operates? [Check all correct answers]

❑ a. Command-line parameters

❑ b. Window launch size

❑ c. Memory usage

❑ d. Quick-launch keystroke

Question 38

You are a bit disappointed with the performance of your computer system once you finish the initial installation of Windows 95. Which options are available to you to improve system performance? [Check all correct answers]

❑ a. Add physical RAM

❑ b. Reduce swap file size

❑ c. Reduce the number of simultaneous running applications

❑ d. Install all networking services

Question 39

Which of the following statements about the VFAT file system of Windows 95 is true?

- ○ a. 512 LFN directory entries can be placed in the root directory, even if each file name is 50 characters long.
- ○ b. All backup utilities, including those built for DOS, preserve LFNs.
- ○ c. Windows 95 LFN-supporting utilities can reference files and paths using the 8.3 equivalents.
- ○ d. A complete LFN path and file name have no length restriction.

Question 40

Windows 95 supports both 32- and 16-bit applications and core components; 32-bit code can be used by several processes simultaneously without causing problems, but this is not the case with 16-bit code. Which element of Windows 95 prevents one process from trying to use 16-bit code when it is already in use by another process?

- ○ a. Thunking
- ○ b. Memory swapping
- ○ c. Setting the Win16Mutex flag
- ○ d. Ring 0 protection

Question 41

When networking is enabled or installed during the initial setup of Windows 95, which protocols are installed automatically? [Check all correct answers]

- ❑ a. TCP/IP
- ❑ b. IPX/SPX
- ❑ c. NetBEUI
- ❑ d. DLC
- ❑ e. NetBIOS

Question 42

Dial-Up Networking is the component or service of Windows 95 that enables you to connect to other computer systems over modems and similar communication devices. DUN allows network and other communication to occur over long-distance connections. Which protocols can be used over a Dial-Up Networking connection? [Check all correct answers]

❑ a. PPP

❑ b. TCP/IP

❑ c. IPX/SPX

❑ d. NetBEUI

Question 43

Windows 95 is able to address or use up to 4 GB of memory. Most computers are not able to provide hardware support for this much physical RAM, but Windows 95 is able to manage that address space size using page swapping. However, not all 4 GB of address space is made available for all processes. Which section of the possible 4 GB address space can be used by both Win32 and Win16 applications?

○ a. 0 through 1 MB

○ b. 1 through 4 MB

○ c. 4 MB through 2 GB

○ d. 2 through 3 GB

○ e. 3 through 4 GB

Question 44

You need to monitor the overall performance of your Windows 95 computers periodically to determine whether they are sustaining adequate computing power or are slowly degrading in responsiveness. Which native Windows 95 tool can you use to establish a performance baseline and take measurements to compare against the baseline?

❍ a. Task Manager

❍ b. Net Watcher

❍ c. System Monitor

❍ d. Control Panel

Question 45

Windows 95 supports several application types to provide a robust operating system with useful backward compatibility for older or legacy applications. Which types of applications are executed within the System VM? [Check all correct answers]

❑ a. Kernel

❑ b. Win16

❑ c. Win32

❑ d. DOS

Question 46

You have an HP LaserJet attached to your Windows 95 computer that is acting as the print server for 20 other Windows 95 computers on your network. Hewlett-Packard has just released an updated printer driver. What must you do to distribute the updated driver to all the computers that print to this print server?

○ a. Install the updated driver on all client computers; there is no need to update the server.

○ b. Install the updated driver on the print server and do nothing more.

○ c. Install the updated driver on the print server and on all client computers.

○ d. Create a separate logical printer with the updated driver on the print server and tell all your users to print to the new printer.

Question 47

You have just installed a new printer on your Windows 95 print server. You send a print job to the printer, but it comes out as pages of nonsense. What is the most likely cause of the problem?

○ a. The NetBEUI protocol is not installed.

○ b. The print spooler is corrupt.

○ c. An incorrect printer driver has been installed.

○ d. There is not enough hard disk space for spooling.

Question 48

Your organization uses group policies to enforce and restrict computer usage on all Windows 95 computers. You have four groups with the following restrictions:

➤ **Admin** No restrictions

➤ **Sales** Restricted access to Network, Display, and Registry Editor

➤ **Accounting** Restricted access to Network and Registry Editor

➤ **Temporary** Same as Sales, but with the additional restriction of approved applications only.

Some users are members of several groups. If members of Temporary are not also members of Admin and if your organization is concerned about security related to transient workers, what is the best priority ordering of these policies? (Assume that priority *decreases* from left to right.)

○ a. Admin, Temporary, Sales, Accounting

○ b. Temporary, Sales, Accounting, Admin

○ c. Accounting, Temporary, Admin, Sales

○ d. Sales, Accounting, Admin, Temporary

Question 49

You purchase a nonstandard modem to use on your Windows 95 computer. The computer system to which you are attempting to connect is using a similar device. You wish to take advantage of several features of the modem to improve the speed, security, and reliability of your dial-up connections. To do so, you must send a long string of AT commands to the modem before each connection attempt. Where can this be defined?

○ a. Through Dialing Properties

○ b. On the dialog box reached through the Advanced button on the Connection tab of Modem Properties

○ c. The Options tab of Modem Properties

○ d. By editing the MODEMLOG.TXT

Answer Key

1. d
2. c
3. c
4. a
5. a, b, c, d
6. a, c, d
7. a, c
8. a, b, c, d
9. b, c
10. c
11. a, c
12. a, d
13. c
14. a, d
15. c
16. d
17. b, d
18. a, c
19. c
20. b
21. a, b, c, d
22. d
23. c
24. a, c
25. a, b, c, d

26. b
27. c
28. a, b, d
29. b
30. b, c
31. b
32. c
33. b, c, d
34. a, d
35. a, b
36. a, b, c
37. a, b, d
38. a, c
39. c
40. c
41. b, c
42. a, b, c, d
43. c
44. c
45. a, b, c
46. b
47. c
48. a
49. b

Question 1

Inbound faxes must be manually forwarded by an administrator and are not forwarded to user mailboxes automatically by Exchange. Therefore, answer d is correct. MAPI is a communications interface independent of the features and functions of the applications that support it and has no control over how data is received or handled. Therefore, answer a is incorrect. The ability to specify recipients in a fax header or by other means is not a feature in the fax service included with Windows 95 (although this type of feature may be available in other commercial fax products). Therefore, answer b is incorrect. Microsoft Fax has no configurable settings that would enable a fax forwarding feature. Therefore, answer c is incorrect.

Question 2

The attention keystroke (CTRL+ALT+DEL) launches the Task Manager. Therefore, answer c is correct. This keystroke would reboot the system in DOS, but when Windows 95 is active, even in the background, it is intercepted as a call for the Task Manager. If the attention keystroke is pressed a *second* time while the Task Manager is active, the system will reboot. Therefore, answer a is incorrect. The keystroke is not ignored—that is why it is called the attention keystroke. Therefore, answer b is incorrect. The attention keystroke does not automatically terminate any applications, although the Task Manager can be used to terminate an application. Therefore, answer d is incorrect.

Question 3

A single DOS application can be launched with different environment settings by creating a PIF, making a copy of the PIF, then changing the settings of the second PIF. Therefore, answer c is correct. Editing the PIF each time is very tedious and provides two separate launch points. Therefore, answer a is incorrect. Windows 95 does not have a PIF Editor, and a pop-up menu cannot be created with a PIF anyway. Therefore, answer b is incorrect. PIFs are edited through the Properties dialog box of a DOS application. Windows 95 does allow multiple PIFs for the same application. Therefore, answer d is incorrect.

Question 4

The most efficient partition for this data drive is 250 MB because this would offer 4 KB clusters, and all of the files stored are integral multiples of four. Therefore, answer a is correct. 500 MB uses 8 KB clusters, which means both the 4 KB and 12 KB files would waste space. Therefore, answer b is incorrect. 750 MB uses 16 KB clusters, which means the 4, 8, and 12 KB files would waste space. Therefore, answer c is incorrect. 2,000 MB uses 32 KB clusters, which means all of these files would waste space. Therefore, answer d is incorrect.

Question 5

All these actions are useful and valid troubleshooting techniques for profiles. Therefore, answers a, b, c, and d are correct.

Question 6

The files or data components skipped by Safe Mode include AUTOEXEC.BAT, CONFIG.SYS, and the Registry. Therefore, answers a, c, and d are correct. WIN.INI cannot be bypassed because it contains base operational parameters for Windows 95. Therefore, answer b is incorrect.

Question 7

The PING utility's timeout result indicates that the host is offline or that there is too much traffic on the network. Therefore, answers a and c are correct. If your TCP/IP settings are wrong, the PING utility's responses would not inform you or even hint of this. Therefore, answer b is incorrect. If you use the wrong IP address to PING against, you'll get data only on the host you did contact instead of the intended host. PING is not able to inform you that you used the wrong IP address, Therefore, answer d is incorrect.

Question 8

All these methods can return the system to working order. Therefore, answers a, b, c, and d are correct. The first three are the most promising; however, reinstalling Windows 95 is required if backups are unavailable or if corruption has spread to other files.

Question 9

If a user has a defined individual policy, only computer policies can apply. Therefore, answers b and c are correct. However, only one computer policy can apply; if a specific computer policy is defined, it is used rather than the Default Computer. If a user has a defined individual policy, no group polices are used. Therefore, answer a is incorrect. The Default User policy does not apply if a user has a defined individual policy. Therefore, answer d is incorrect.

Question 10

When CTRL+ALT+DEL is pressed while a DOS application that was launched using DEFAULT.PIF is in the foreground, the keystroke is passed to

Windows 95, bringing up the Close Program dialog box. Therefore, answer c
is correct. The computer would reboot if the DOS application were launched
into DOS Mode. Therefore, answer a is incorrect. The application would not
terminate with the CTRL+ALT+DEL keystroke. Selecting the application in
the dialog box and clicking End Task is required to terminate the application.
Therefore, answer b is incorrect. Because the Close Program dialog box appears, answer d is incorrect.

Question 11

Editing the MSDOS.SYS file and using the Startup menu are two methods of
altering how Windows 95 boots. Therefore, answers a and c are correct. It is
not possible to edit the MBR with any tools that are bundled with Windows 95,
nor is this a valid method of altering how Windows 95 boots. Therefore, answer b
is incorrect. BOOT.INI is a file that is present only on systems hosting Windows NT and is not used with Windows 95. Therefore, answer d is incorrect.

Question 12

The File and Printer Sharing for NetWare Networks and Microsoft Client for
NetWare Networks client must be installed to enable Windows 95 to service
NetWare-hosted print queues. Therefore, answers a and d are correct. Microsoft
Print Server for NetWare is a radio button selection on the Print Server tab of
Printer Properties that can be used after File and Printer Sharing for NetWare
Networks has been installed. Therefore, answer b is incorrect. Remember that
IPX/SPX is required only if that is the protocol being used on the NetWare
system. If TCP/IP is being used, installing IPX/SPX is useless, so you must
install whichever protocol is in use. Therefore, answer c is incorrect.

Question 13

USER.DAT is the Registry file used by profiles, so this is the file that must be
renamed to USER.MAN to force mandatory profiles. Therefore, answer c is
correct. SYSTEM.DAT is the Registry file that stores system-related configuration details and is not used by profiles. Therefore, answer a is incorrect.
REGLOG.TXT and PROFILE.DAT are fictional files. Therefore, answers b
and d are incorrect.

Question 14

Windows 95 Dial-Up Server supports PPP and Windows NT clients. In addition, Windows 95 can accept a single inbound connection from Windows 95,
WFW, and LAN Manager. Therefore, answers a and d are correct. IPX and SLIP
are not supported by Dial-Up Server. Therefore, answers b and c are incorrect.

Question 15

Multiple message profiles are created through the Mail and Fax applet. Therefore, answer c is correct. The Passwords applet is used to change passwords and enable user profiles, not to create messaging profiles. Therefore, answer a is incorrect. The Options command in the Inbox cannot be used to create message profiles because any instance of the Exchange client can modify only the settings within the profile it used to launch itself. Therefore, answer b is incorrect. There is no Profiles applet. Therefore, answer d is incorrect.

Question 16

Windows 95 Microsoft Backup does not support SCSI tape devices. Therefore, answer d is correct. The drivers for the SCSI card and the DAT device are not helpful because the device type is not supported. Therefore, answers a and b are incorrect. There is not a configuration command in the Tools menu; there is only a Redetect Tape Backup command that has no options. Therefore, answer c is incorrect.

Question 17

Windows 95 virtual memory combines physical RAM and hard drive storage space to offer applications more memory than would otherwise be available. Therefore, answers b and d are correct. Time slices are associated with CPU execution and not memory. Therefore, answer a is incorrect. EMS is not used by Windows 95. Therefore, answer c is incorrect.

Question 18

Enabling internetwork browsing and mapping NetBIOS names to IP addresses are two of the three functions of WINS. Therefore, answers a and c are correct. The third function is recognizing NetBIOS names on all subnets. Mapping FQDNs to IP addresses is a function of DNS. Therefore, answer b is incorrect. Mapping NetBIOS names to MAC addresses happens in NWLink and NetBEUI. Therefore, answer d is incorrect. Assigning clients IP addresses is a function of a DHCP server. Therefore, answer e is incorrect.

Question 19

The use of PPTP to create a VPN connection is the best way to simplify and decrease costs for the long-distance communication with the home network. Therefore, answer c is correct. Emailing is inefficient and requires someone to perform this task, which is not a cost- or time-effective solution. Therefore, answer a is incorrect. Faxing the information is not only a waste of time, it costs money for long distance and does not get the data to the salesman in a useful form. Therefore, answer b is incorrect. The current method is not the best solution for this situation; PPTP can be used. Therefore, answer d is incorrect.

Question 20

Legacy Printer Port (11), Legacy Video card (7), NIC (9), Modem (3), and Sound card (5) are the only possible settings for these devices. Therefore, answer b is correct. The other three options either assign the same resource to multiple devices or assign an invalid setting to a device. Therefore, answers a, c, and d are incorrect. You should remember that legacy cards are given their requested resources first (if available), then the Resource Arbitrator determines how to assign the remaining resources to all Plug and Play devices.

Question 21

The Exchange client can be configured to use all these (and many more) information services simply by installing the service (such as drivers) through the Mail and Fax applet. Therefore, answers a, b, c, and d are correct.

Question 22

The last segment of the Windows 95 boot process is the Protected Mode boot. Therefore, answer d is correct. BIOS Bootstrap is the first segment, MBR and boot sector are the second segment, and Real Mode boot is the third segment. Therefore, answers a, b, and c are incorrect.

Question 23

GRPCONV is the utility used to convert Windows 3.x .GRP (group) files to Windows 95 Start menu entries. Therefore, answer c is correct. SETUP is the installation utility, CONVERT is an NT utility for file systems, and NETSETUP is used to create network installation scripts. Therefore, answers a, b, and d are incorrect.

Question 24

A Browser election occurs when a Backup Browser is unable to contact the Master Browser and when a computer boots into the network that is set to become a Master Browser. Therefore, answers a and c are correct. If a Master Browser goes offline, an election does not occur until a Backup Browser attempts to contact it and fails (which can be a delay of up to 15 minutes). Therefore, answer b is incorrect. There is no command that an administrator can give to force a Browser election. Therefore, answer d is incorrect.

Question 25

All these answers indicate situations in which the defragmentation utility should be used. Therefore, answers a, b, c, and d are correct.

Question 26

The AutoPlay feature is disabled on the Settings tab of the Properties dialog box of the CD-ROM drive driver list on the Device Manager tab of the System applet. Therefore, answer b is correct. The CD Player's Options menu contains commands for random, continuous, and intro play as well as to open the player's interface display properties. There is no control for AutoPlay. Therefore, answer a is incorrect. The Multimedia applet does not offer a command to disable the AutoPlay feature. Therefore, answer c is incorrect. The Properties of the CD-ROM drive displays the size of the data stored on the disk and offers control over sharing of the disk, not AutoPlay controls. Therefore, answer d is incorrect.

Question 27

The Exchange client is configured to access information services over dial-up connections through the Mail and Fax applet. Therefore, answer c is correct. The Microsoft Mail Postoffice applet is used to create and administer workgroup postoffices, not DUN-accessed messaging services. Therefore, answer a is incorrect. The Tools|Microsoft Mail Tools menu within the Exchange client does not offer access to modify DUN service settings. Therefore, answer b is incorrect. The Internet applet is used to set autodial and proxy settings for Internet access, not to set the DUN parameters. Therefore, answer d is incorrect.

Question 28

Windows 95 supports DOS, Win16, and Win32 applications. Therefore, answers a, b, and d are correct. Of the Microsoft product line, only Windows NT supports OS/2 and POSIX applications. Therefore, answers c and e are incorrect.

Question 29

DOS Mode is the feature of Windows 95 that allows DOS applications to be run even if they cannot function within a DOS VM. Therefore, answer b is correct. Virtual Memory, Ring 0 Protected Mode, and message queues have nothing to do with the ability of a DOS application to execute. Therefore, answers a, c, and d are incorrect.

Question 30

The communication log files stored in the Windows directory are PPPLOG. TXT and MODEMLOG.TXT. Therefore, answers b and c are correct. DUN.LOG is a fictitious file. Therefore, answer a is incorrect. USERS.DAT is the user-specific portion of the Registry stored in the Windows directory that has nothing to do with communication logging. Therefore, answer d is incorrect.

Question 31

The simplest method is using a Direct Cable Connection. Therefore, answer b is correct. Adding NICs or modems may not be easy, and creating or using system accounts and a directory share is not the easiest method. Therefore, answers a and c are incorrect. A tape backup device is the most difficult of all the solutions. Therefore, answer d is incorrect.

Question 32

The key that stores data about the current session's hardware configuration is HKEY_CURRENT_CONFIG. Therefore, answer c is correct. HKEY_LOCAL_MACHINE stores data on all possible and past configurations of hardware. Therefore, answer a is incorrect. HKEY_DYN_DATA stores OLE and file association information. Therefore, answer b is incorrect. HKEY_CURRENT_USER stores information about the currently active user. Therefore, answer d is incorrect.

Question 33

The Device Manager can be used to disable automatic resource assignment, remove conflicting drivers, and identify available resources. Therefore, answers b, c, and d are correct. The Device Manager cannot be used to edit the Registry directly. Therefore, answer a is incorrect.

Question 34

During the Real Mode portion of setup, the file system's integrity is checked and TSRs are managed. Therefore, answers a and d are correct. The Windows 95 startup disk creation, hardware detection, and Help system building all occur in the Protected Mode portion of setup. Therefore, answers b, c, and e are incorrect.

Question 35

Both SYS and DRV are Real Mode driver types. Therefore, answers a and b are correct. VXD and 386 are Protected Mode driver types. Therefore, answers c and d are incorrect.

Question 36

The Exchange components that can have passwords assigned to them are the Personal Address Book, User's mailbox, and Personal Folders. Therefore, answers a, b, and c are correct. Dialing Properties are not password protected. Therefore, answer d is incorrect.

Question 37

A shortcut can be configured with command-line parameters, window launch size, and a quick-launch keystroke. Therefore, answers a, b, and d are correct. Only DOS PIF shortcuts can have their memory usage configured. Therefore, answer c is incorrect.

Question 38

Performance can be improved through adding physical RAM and reducing applications. Therefore, answers a and c are correct. Reducing the swap file size and installing all networking services will most likely degrade system performance. Therefore, answers b and d are incorrect.

Question 39

Windows 95 utilities can reference LFN files and paths with their 8.3 equivalents. Therefore, answer c is correct. Because directory entries are only 11 characters long, 50-character file names will use at least 5 entries per file, so only about 100 such files can be placed in the root directory. Therefore, answer a is incorrect. Not all backup utilities, especially those built for DOS, support or preserve LFNs. Therefore, answer b is incorrect. LFN path and file names have a total length restriction of 260 characters. Therefore, answer d is incorrect.

Question 40

Windows 95 protects 16-bit non-reentrant code from being used by more than one application at a time by setting the Win16Mutex flag. Therefore, answer c is correct. Thunking is the process of translating a system call between 16-bit and 32-bit. Therefore, answer a is incorrect. Memory swapping and Ring 0 protection do not prevent non-reentrant code from being used by more than one application at a time. Therefore, answers b and d are incorrect.

Question 41

NetBEUI and IPX/SPX are installed by default into Windows 95. Therefore, answers b and c are correct. All these protocols can be installed on Windows 95 because they are included in the distribution files.

Question 42

DUN supports all these protocols. Therefore, answers a, b, c, and d are correct. However, you should note that PPP is a WAN protocol and that the others are LAN protocols.

Question 43

The 4 MB through 2 GB range is used by Win32 and Win16 applications. Therefore, answer c is correct. The 0 through 1 MB range is used by DOS and some Win16 applications. If a DOS VM is not in use, this area is not used by the application but is reserved for Real Mode drivers. Therefore, answer a is incorrect. The 1 through 4 MB range is generally not used but can be used by Win16 applications for backward compatibility. Therefore, answer b is incorrect. The 2 through 3 GB range is used by DLLs and other shared components. Therefore, answer d is incorrect. The 3 through 4 GB range is reserved for exclusive use by Ring 0 components, usually virtual device drivers. Therefore, answer e is incorrect.

Question 44

The System Monitor is used to monitor the activity and performance of several system components and resources. Therefore, answer c is correct. The Task Manager can be used to terminate an application or abort the current computing session. Therefore, answer a is incorrect. The Net Watcher is used to manage remote resources and does not measure performance. Therefore, answer b is incorrect. The Control Panel has several applets that control and manage various aspects of Windows 95, but none is used to measure performance. Therefore, answer d is incorrect.

Question 45

The System VM houses the execution of the kernel, Win16, and Win32 applications. Therefore, answers a, b, and c are correct. Each DOS application is executed within its own separate DOS VM. Therefore, answer d is incorrect.

Question 46

The best way to update a printer driver is to update the driver on the print server. Therefore, answer b is correct. There is no need to update the driver manually on each client computer that is running Windows 95. Therefore, answer a is incorrect. When a client computer sends a print job to the print server, the updated driver is automatically copied to the client. Therefore, answers c and d are incorrect.

Question 47

If an incorrect printer driver has been installed, documents may print illegibly. Therefore, answer c is correct. A print job won't print at all if the wrong protocol is used. Therefore, answer a is incorrect. Likewise, nothing will print without the spooler. Therefore, answer b is incorrect. As in answer b, a print job won't print without proper spooling unless the option to print directly to the printer is selected. Therefore, answer d is incorrect.

Question 48

The best priority order is Admin, Temporary, Sales, Accounting. Therefore, answer a is correct. Because no member of Temporary is also a member of Admin, Admin can be given the highest priority. This ensures that Sales and Accounting members who are also Admins will be given the correct level of access. In addition, placing Temporary above Sales and Accounting ensures that they have tighter restrictions than the normal Sales and Accounting members. The other three orders do not provide for optimal access. Therefore, answers b, c, and d are incorrect.

Question 49

An AT command can be defined on the dialog box reached through the Advanced button on the Connection tab of Modem Properties. Therefore, answer b is correct. Dialing Properties does not offer an AT command option but is used to set the location, credit card, and line commands. Therefore, answer a is incorrect. The Options tab of Modem Properties is used to set a terminal window and operator-assisted or manual dial, and it has a checkbox for displaying modem status during connection establishment. Therefore, answer c is incorrect. The MODEMLOG.TXT records modem-related events. AT commands are not defined in this file, although the results of AT commands may be listed. Therefore, answer d is incorrect.

Glossary

AATP (Authorized Academic Training Program)—A program that authorizes accredited academic institutions of higher learning to offer Microsoft Certified Professional testing and training to their students. The institutions also are allowed to use the Microsoft Education course materials and Microsoft Certified Trainers.

Access Control—A "security watchdog" that intercepts requests for certain resources (e.g., printers or network shares) and requires a password before permitting further access.

address book—A utility accessed through the Tools|Address Book command that allows users to edit, add, or delete addresses stored in their Personal Address List or any other address list to which they are allowed access.

ADMIN.ADM—A default template in the System Policy Editor that contains many popular Registry settings that can be used to create system policies.

administrator—The person responsible for the upkeep, management, and security of a network. Also, when capitalized (Administrator), a built-in user in Windows NT that has full control of the system.

ANDing process—The process by which a TCP/IP host, when initialized, compares its own IP address to its given subnet mask and stores the result in memory.

APPS.INF—The file that contains a master list of settings for common DOS applications.

ASCII (American Standard Code for Information Interchange)—A way of coding that translates letters, numbers, and symbols into digital form.

assessment exam—Similar to the certification exam, a type of exam that gives you the opportunity to answer questions at your own pace. This type of exam also utilizes the same tools as the certification exam.

ATEC (Authorized Technical Education Center)—The location where you can take a Microsoft Official Curriculum course taught by Microsoft Certified Trainers.

AUTOEXEC.BAT—A DOS batch file launched when a Windows 95 computer is started or booted.

AUTORUN.INF—An AutoPlay feature that automatically launches application CD-ROMs when they are inserted into the CD-ROM drive.

.AVI—The file extension used to name digital video format files, commonly used in multimedia players.

Backup Browser—The computer on a Windows NT network that maintains a duplicate list of available resources and acts as a backup information provider for the Browser Service, as a BDC does within a Windows NT domain.

BATCH.EXE utility—A utility that appears in the *Windows 95 Resource Kit* that's used to create the MSBATCH.INF files that automate a batch install.

beta exam—A trial exam that is given to participants at a Sylvan Prometric testing center before the development of the Microsoft Certified Professional certification exam is finalized. The final exam questions are selected on the basis of the beta exam's results. For example, if all beta exam participants get a particular answer correct or wrong, that question generally will not appear in the final version.

BIOS bootstrap—The segment of the boot process that is handled by the computer itself and performs four distinct activities: POST (Power On Self Test), Plug and Play (P&P), Bootable partition, and MBR (Master Boot Record) initialization.

boot disk—A hard drive or floppy drive that has bootstrap files on it. The bootstrap files enable an operating system to launch.

Boot Manager—An application that supports the selection and bootup of multiple operating systems on a single system (or even from a single hard drive). Windows NT, OS/2, and Linux all include built-in boot managers, and several third-party boot manager products are also available (e.g., System Commander and Partition Manager both provide this function).

boot menu—The text menu that appears immediately after the hardware test on a Windows NT computer. It lists all the known operating systems present.

The operating system listed first will be booted by default when the timeout period expires unless an alternate operating system is selected manually.

BOOT.INI—The file on the system partition that contains the location of the system files for each operating system installed on the computer. The locations are listed using ARC names.

briefcase—A Windows 95 built-in utility that provides two-way file synchronization.

browse—A command used to view local and network resources within File Open and File Save dialog boxes, Explorer, My Computer, and other windows or utilities with file system access.

browser election—The process whereby a potential or Master Browser forces selection of a designated Master Browser on a Microsoft network organized as a browse domain.

C2 Level security—A U.S. Department of Defense security designation for computer systems that comply with a specific set of military standards (DOD 5200.28-STD-December 1985).

CDFS (Compact Disk File System)—A special read-only file system supported by both Windows 95 and Windows NT 3.51 and later. CDFS permits easy access to CDs in these operating systems.

client—A network user or a computer on a network used to access resources hosted by other network computers or servers.

COM (communication) port—A serial port that connects communication devices to a computer.

command line—A DOS prompt that accepts DOS-based commands.

compression agent—A method or device used to compress data.

CompuServe—One of the world's most well known online dial-up services.

computer name—The name of a computer on a LAN that is specific to an individual workstation or server.

CONFIG.POL—In the NETLOGON share, the file where all policies are stored.

CONFIG.SYS—A utility used to modify various settings and load drivers on DOS bootup.

Control Panel—In Windows, the area where settings such as fonts, screen color, SCSI hardware, and printers are modified.

Control Panel applets—The utilities located in the Control Panel that control various system and configuration settings (including protocols and hardware and software settings).

CPU (Central Processing Unit)—The brains of your computer; the area where all functions are performed.

cut score—On the Microsoft Certified Professional exam, the lowest score a person can receive and still pass.

DA0—The automatic backup file that Windows 95 makes of SYSTEM.DAT and USER.DAT, the two Windows 95 Registry files.

DCC (Direct Cable Connection)—A utility that uses a null-modem cable to establish a network link between two Windows 95 computers.

DDE (Dynamic Data Exchange)—A Windows process by which two or more applications communicate with each other through the interprocess communication system in Windows 95.

DEBUG.EXE—A distribution file that should be copied to the Windows 95 startup disk during the installation process.

default—A setting that is configured by the manufacturer and used until the user specifies otherwise.

default gateway—The IP address of a computer or device that serves as a router, a format translator, or a security filter for a network.

defragment—The reorganization of a hard disk by arranging the files in contiguous order. This groups sections of unused disk space in a single block so new data can be stored more efficiently.

demand paging—The process whereby a request for a virtual memory resource results in the transfer of information from the swap file into RAM (often by clearing space in RAM that's occupied by stale or old data by transferring it from RAM into the swap file).

DETLOG.TXT—A detection log file written during the initial installation of Windows 95 that records information about devices and configuration information encountered.

Device Manager—A tab on the System applet that offers a graphical interface to all the drivers installed under Windows 95.

DHCP (Dynamic Host Configuration Protocol)—A service that enables dynamic assignment of IP addresses on the basis of a specified pool of available addresses.

Dialing Properties—A dialog box (reached through the Modem applet or through the Connect To window) that controls how TAPI places calls (e.g., dialing 9 to reach an outside line and *70 to disable call-waiting services).

disk partition—A portion of a hard disk that acts like a physically separate unit.

disk volumes—A formatted disk partition with an associated drive letter and (an optional) volume name.

Display Properties—A dialog box that allows you to modify certain properties of your desktop, such as the background, screensaver, settings, and so on.

DLC (Data Link Control)—A protocol used to gain access to network-attached printers and IBM mainframe or AS/4000 hosts.

DLLs (Dynamic Link Libraries)—Small executable program routines or device drivers stored in separate files. DLLs are loaded by the operating system when called on by a process or hardware device.

DMP file—A memory dump file with the extension .DMP that captures an image of memory during a crash or system failure for subsequent analysis and debugging purposes.

DNS (Domain Name Service)—A service that resolves hostnames (such as microsoft.com) into IP addresses (such as 207.68.145.42).

domain—A group of computers and peripheral devices that share a common security database.

domain name server—An Internet host that translates Fully Qualified Domain Names (FQDNs) into IP addresses using the DNS service.

DOS (Disk Operating System)—The most popular of all PC operating systems; it provides a primitive command-line-driven, runtime environment for x86-based computers.

DPMI (DOS Protected Mode Interface)—A DOS extension technology defined by Microsoft that lets specially constructed DOS programs run under Windows 3.x and Windows 95.

driver—Software that permits an operating system to communicate with a particular peripheral device.

DUN (Dial-Up Networking)—A utility, found in the RAS Phonebook| Programs|Accessories folder of the Start menu, that controls the dial-out capabilities of Windows 95's Remote Access Service (RAS).

EBD.SYS—A special file that appears on a Windows 95 startup disk that identifies it as a Windows 95 startup disk (EBD is an abbreviation for Emergency Boot Disk).

ECP (Extended Capabilities Port) support—A hardware add-on that improves print speed and transfer efficiency.

encryption—A method of encoding data that requires knowledge of a unique decoding key to decipher such information.

ERD (Emergency Repair Disk)—A floppy disk that contains all the files needed to repair a damaged or corrupt system partition and many boot partition-related problems.

ESDI (Enhanced Small Device Interface)—A pre-IDE storage device that is low-level formatted with various values of sectors per track.

Ethernet—The most widely used type of LAN; originally developed by Xerox and standardized by the IEEE 802.3 specification.

Exam Preparation Guides—Guides that provide information specific to the material covered on Microsoft Certified Professional exams to help students prepare for them.

Exam Study Guide—Short for Microsoft Certified Professional Program Exam Study Guide; this contains information about the topics covered on more than one of the Microsoft Certified Professional exams.

Exchange client—A peer-to-peer communication system that can operate without special server software.

Exchange Client Services—Any of the information services supported by Exchange, including Internet mail, CompuServe mail, MS Mail, Personal Address Book, and personal folders.

Expanded Memory Manager (EMM)—A DOS memory management specification that permits the operating system to address memory above the 1 MB upper bound on conventional 16-bit DOS addresses as a single, linear address space (up to a 16 MB upper bound).

FAT (File Allocation Table)—A file system originally used by DOS to hold information about the properties, location, and size of files being stored on a disk.

fault tolerance—The ability of a computer to work continuously, even when there is system failure.

FDISK command—A DOS command used to partition a hard disk.

FIFO (First-In First-Out) buffers—A set of data storage buffers often used in serial interfaces to speed input or output where data written first into the buffer will be transmitted first (to the CPU for incoming data or to the serial port for outgoing data).

firewall—A barrier (made of software and/or hardware) between two networks that permits only authorized communication to pass.

firmware—A type of software that becomes part of the hardware function after it has been saved into a programmable read-only memory (PROM) chip.

FQDN (Fully Qualified Domain Name)—The complete site name of an Internet computer system (e.g., http://www.microsoft.com).

frames—The segments created by the access method used when packets are being sent across a network.

FTP (File Transfer Protocol)—A protocol that transfers files to and from a local hard drive to an FTP server located on another TCP/IP-based network (e.g., the Internet).

gateway—The service a computer performs that converts the protocols between different types of networks or computers.

GDI (Graphics Device Interface)—A system component that provides net-worked applications a method to present graphical information. The GDI translates between an application's print request and a device driver interface (DDI), ensuring that the job is rendered correctly.

General Protection Faults (GPFs)—An application failure that occurs when a process attempts to violate system integrity, such as accessing Ring 0 system components directly or attempting to access memory outside an assigned address space. A GPF normally results in a system halt or crash.

global address list—The shared address list maintained within the main workgroup postoffice that contains a master address list for MS Mail workgroups under its control.

graphics—Pictures and images created on a computer.

GRPCONV—A utility used to transfer program groups into Windows 95 if Windows 95 was not originally installed in the same directory as an existing Windows 3.x installation.

GUI (Graphical User Interface)—A computer setup that uses graphics, windows, and a trackball or mouse to interact with a computer.

hard drive—The permanent storage area for data. Also called the hard disk.

hardware—The physical components of a computer system.

hardware profile—A profile that corresponds to a specific hardware device attached to a computer.

HCL (Hardware Compatibility List)—A list that indicates which hardware is compatible with the software. The most updated version of the Microsoft HCL can be found on the Microsoft Web site or on the TechNet CD.

HKEY_CLASSES_ROOT—The Registry key that stores the mappings between file extensions and the applications that support them. It also stores other OLE-related data.

HKEY_CURRENT_CONFIG—The Registry key that points to the set of Registry settings stored in the HKEY_LOCAL_MACHINE key that pertains to the current configuration and setup of the hardware.

HKEY_CURRENT_USER—The Registry key that contains a copy of data in the HKEY_USERS key that corresponds to the currently active user.

HKEY_DYN_DATA—The Registry key that contains details about hardware devices that can be altered while active, such as Plug and Play devices, PCMCIA cards, and removable media.

HKEY_LOCAL_MACHINE—The Registry key where all hardware settings for a computer are stored, including IRQs, I/O addresses, driver controls, and any other hardware-specific information.

HKEY_USERS—The Registry key that stores user-specific settings, including desktop settings, drive mappings, Start menu configurations, and so on, for all users with named accounts on the computer.

Host ID—The part of an IP address that identifies a specific host on a particular network, much like a street address identifies a home among all others on the street.

HOSTS—A specially formatted text file that provides mapping information between IP host names and numeric IP network addresses.

HPFS (High Performance File System)—The first PC-compatible file system that supported LFNs. Like FAT, HPFS maintains a directory structure but adds automatic sorting of the directory and includes support for special attributes to better accommodate multiple naming conventions and file-level security.

hung process—A program that has stopped responding to the system.

INFINST.EXE—A tool from the *Windows 95 Resource Kit* that is used to add more details to the MSBATCH.INF file to install other applications (e.g., Microsoft Office).

INI—Files that contain all startup information needed to launch a program or an operating system.

Input/Output System—A system that handles input from input devices (e.g., a keyboard) and directs outputs to output devices (e.g., CRTs and printers).

Internet—The collection of publicly accessible TCP/IP-based networks around the world.

intranet—An internal, private network that uses the same protocols and standards as the Internet.

IP address—Four sets of numbers (called octets), separated by decimal points, that represent a unique numeric address for a computer attached to a TCP/IP network (e.g., the Internet).

IPC (InterProcess Communications)—Within an operating system, the service that facilitates the exchange of data between applications.

IPX/SPX (Internetwork Packet Exchange/Sequenced Packet Exchange)—Novell's NetWare protocol, reinvented by Microsoft and implemented in Windows NT under the name NWLink. It is fully compatible with Novell's version and in many cases runs slightly faster than the original.

IRQ (Interrupt Request)—On a PC, a hardware interrupt address that devices use to signal the CPU of a need for immediate service or handling.

IRQ channels—Any of a named set of IRQ addresses (typically numbered from 0 to 15) used to create a unique communications link (or channel) between a PC's CPU and some external device (e.g., a disk controller, network interface, or keyboard).

ISP (Internet Service Provider)—An organization that charges a fee for providing Internet connections and other related services.

job function expert—A person with extensive knowledge about a particular job function and the software products/technologies related to that job. Typically, a job function expert is currently performing the job, has recently performed the job, or is training people to do this job.

kernel—The essential part of an operating system; provides basic operating system services.

LAN (local area network)—A network confined to a single building or geographic area that connects servers, workstations, peripheral devices, a network operating system, and a communication link.

LFN (Long File Names)—File names up to 256 characters in length supported by the VFAT, NTFS, and FAT32 file systems.

LMHOSTS—The predecessor to WINS, a static list of NetBIOS names mapped to IP addresses.

local profile—A user profile that is present only on the Windows 95 computer where it was created.

logical partitions—The multiple segments of a physical hard drive. Each segment can be used independently of the others, including belonging to separate volumes and hosting different file systems. Most logical partitions have a drive letter assigned to them and can be referred to by an ARC name.

logical printers—The software component used by NT to direct print jobs from applications to a print server. A physical printer can be serviced by numerous logical printers.

logoff—The process by which a user quits a computer system.

logon—The process by which a user gains access or signs on to a computer system.

LPT ports—A series of I/O addresses that let a computer and a parallel printer communicate.

mandatory profile—A user profile with a .MAN extension. By giving a profile this extension, Windows 95 will not save any modifications to the environment; this forces users to work with an organization-approved desktop look and feel, layout, and design.

MAPI (Message Application Programming Interface)—A Microsoft standard that enables communication software and hardware to interface for the purpose of exchanging messages.

Master Browser—A computer on an NT network that maintains the main list of all available resources within a domain (including links to external domains). *See also* Backup Browser.

MCA—IBM's MicroChannel Architecture, another 32-bit PC bus scheme that never completely succeeded in the marketplace, owing to IBM's determined decision to keep strict controls on licensing the technologies involved in its implementation.

MCI (multiple-choice item)—An item (within a series of items) that is the answer to a question (single-response MCI) or one of the answers to a question (multiple-response MCI).

MCP (Microsoft Certified Professional)—An individual who has taken and passed at least one certification exam and has earned one or more of the following certifications: Microsoft Certified Trainer, Microsoft Certified Solution Developer, or Microsoft Certified Systems Engineer.

MCSD (Microsoft Certified Solution Developer)—An individual who is qualified to create and develop solutions for businesses using the Microsoft development tools, technologies, and platforms.

MCSE (Microsoft Certified Systems Engineer)—An individual who is an expert on Windows NT and the Microsoft BackOffice integrated family of server software. This individual also can plan, implement, maintain, and support information systems associated with these products.

MCT (Microsoft Certified Trainer)—An individual who is qualified by Microsoft to teach Microsoft Education courses at sites authorized by Microsoft.

message profile—A utility used by Microsoft Exchange to define how data is handled and transmitted. Message profiles are managed through the Mail and Fax applet.

Microsoft certification exam—An exam created by Microsoft to verify an exam taker's mastery of a software product, technology, or computing topic.

Microsoft Certified Professional Certification Update—A newsletter for Microsoft Certified Professional candidates and Microsoft Certified Professionals.

Microsoft Exchange—Windows 95's universal messaging client that controls email, faxes, online services, and more.

Microsoft official curriculum—Microsoft education courses—created by various Microsoft product groups—that support the certification exam process.

Microsoft Roadmap to Education and Certification—An application, based on Microsoft Windows, that takes users through the process of determining their certification goals and then informs them of the best way to achieve those goals.

Microsoft Sales Fax Service—A service through which you can obtain Exam Preparation Guides, fact sheets, and additional information about the Microsoft Certified Professional Program.

Microsoft Solution Provider—An organization, not directly related to Microsoft, that provides integration, consulting, technical support, and other services related to Microsoft products.

Microsoft Technical Information Network (TechNet)—A service provided by Microsoft that provides helpful information, on a monthly CD-ROM.

TechNet is the primary source of technical information for people who support and/or educate end users, create automated solutions, or administer networks and/or databases.

.MID—The file extension given to a MIDI sound file. *See also* MIDI.

MIDI (Musical Instrument Digital Interface)—An interface definition that allows musical instruments to communicate with computers and computers to store musical data.

minidriver—Device-specific drivers supplied by a manufacturer that add sections of code needed to control the special features of a printer or other external peripheral devices.

MOLI (Microsoft Online Institute)—A division of Microsoft that makes training materials, online forums and user groups, and online classes available through the Internet.

motherboard—The main circuit board in a computer system that includes a socket or daughterboard for the CPU, one or more sockets for main memory (RAM), and slots into which adapter cards of many kinds can be inserted.

MRI (multiple-rating item)—An exam item that defines some task and a proposed solution. Every time a task is set, an alternate solution is given, and the candidate must choose the answer that gives the best results produced by the proposed solution.

MS Exchange—An enterprise-wide messaging and mail system developed by Microsoft.

MSDN (Microsoft Developer Network)—The official source for Software Development Kits (SDKs), Device Driver Kits (DDKs), operating systems, and programming information associated with creating applications for Microsoft Windows and Windows NT.

MSDOS.SYS—In DOS, an executable used to manage part of the operating system; in Windows 95, a text file in which boot details are defined and controlled.

multitasking—Running more than one computer application on a system at a time.

NDA (nondisclosure agreement)—A contract between two parties that enjoins one or both parties from discussing identified confidential information with any third parties.

NDIS (Network Driver Interface Specification)—An industry-standard specification for how protocols and adapters should be bound.

Net Watcher—An application used in Windows 95 to manage shared resources and the users who access those resources.

NetBEUI (NetBIOS Extended User Interface)—A simple Network layer transport protocol developed to support NetBIOS networks.

NetBIOS (Network Basic Input/Output System)—Originally developed by IBM in the 1980s, a protocol that provides the underlying communication mechanism for some basic Microsoft Network functions, such as browsing and interprocess communication between network servers.

NETSTAT—A Windows 95 networking status utility that displays protocol statistics and current TCP/IP network connections.

NetWare—A popular network operating system developed by Novell.

Network Filing System—A popular distributed file system on Unix networks.

Network ID—The part of an IP address that identifies the particular network (or segment) on which a host physically resides, much like the name of a street identifies where a house is located.

Network Neighborhood—Within Explorer or My Computer, the area in which other computers on the network are accessed.

NIC (network interface card)—An adapter card used to connect a computer to a network.

nodebug—A BOOT.INI switch that informs you that debugging information is being used.

non-reentrant—Identifies code segments that are unable to be used by more than a single process or execution thread at any one time.

null-modem cable—An RS-232 cable used to enable two computers in close proximity to communicate across their serial ports without requiring access to a pair of modems.

NWLink—Microsoft's implementation of Novell's Internetwork Packet Exchange/Sequenced Packet Exchange (IPX/SPX) protocols.

objects—Everything in Windows 95 is considered by the operating system to be an object.

ODI (Open Data-Link Interface)—A device driver standard developed by Novell and Apple that allows multiple protocols to run on a single network adapter card.

OEM version—The standard character set of DOS programs; the original IBM PC-8 character set.

OLE (Object Linking and Embedding)—A Windows process by which one application can reference elements from another application.

operating system (OS)—A software program that controls the operations on a computer system.

OSI reference model (OSI model)—Developed by the ISO, a seven-layer reference model that defines a comprehensive networking communication model and information-exchange architecture.

PAB (Personal Address Book/List)—A personal list of email and street addresses, phone and fax numbers, and other contact information maintained locally within a personal file with a .PAB extension.

partition—A portion of memory or a portion of a hard disk.

password—A word used by an individual to gain access to a particular system.

PBX systems (Private Branch Exchange)—A privately owned telephone system that connects telephone extensions and permits them to place or receive calls from some external telephone network.

PCMCIA card—A card used to connect external devices (modems, hard drives, network adapters, and so on) to a laptop or other portable computer. Also called a PC card.

peripheral device—An external hardware device connected to a computer.

physical disk—The hardware component that adds additional storage space. A physical disk must be partitioned and formatted with a file system before data can be stored on it.

PIF (Program Information File)—A program description file for DOS applications that defines and restricts their runtime environments.

PING (Packet InterNet Groper)—A TCP/IP command used to verify the existence and connection to remote hosts over a network.

pixel—The smallest addressable unit on a video display screen.

Plug and Play—A feature of Windows 95 that automatically detects attached devices and configures those that are Plug and Play-compatible. Also called a P&P device.

.POL—The file type used to store system policies, usually in a file named CONFIG.POL.

policy template—The ADM files that define which controls a policy file can contain.

POSIX—An operating system type that complies with the IEEE 1003.1 standard. NT supports only POSIX.1.

postoffice—A designated directory in which MS Exchange files are stored.

Potential Browser—A computer able to maintain a list of resources for a domain. A Potential Browser may be elected to become a Backup Browser or Master Browser by the browser service, as needed. *See also* Backup Browser; Master Browser.

POTS (Plain Old Telephone System)—The conventional phone system that uses analog lines and equipment for voice- or modem-based communications.

PPP (Point-to-Point Protocol)—An industry-standard protocol used to establish network links over a variety of communication links, from analog telephone lines to a variety of digital technologies.

PPTP (Point-to-Point Tunneling Protocol)—A communications protocol based on PPP that establishes a secure communication channel between a client and a network (or a single server) over an existing Internet connection.

preemptive multitasking—When multiple processes or threads are running concurrently, processing is allocated to the process with the highest priority at any given time (should a lower-priority process be executing and a higher-priority process appear, the higher-priority process would take over the CPU, thereby preempting the lower-priority process).

Primary Network Logon—Appears on the Configuration tab of the Network Applet; defines which network Windows 95 attempts to log on to when booted.

print client—A computer on a network (called a client computer) that transmits the print jobs to be produced by a physical print device.

print device—The physical hardware device that produces printed output (what most people call a printer).

print driver—The software component that enables communication between the operating system and the physical printing device.

print job—A document or image sent from a client to a printer; a print job is typically coded in Windows EMF or the RAW language of the printer.

print server—The computer that hosts the spool file for a printer and/or that is physically attached to the printer.

print spooler—A collection of Dynamic Link Libraries (DLLs) that acquire, process, catalog, and disburse print jobs.

printer—Typically, a logical printer (software component) within the NT environment, as opposed to a physical printing device.

printer pool—A collection of identical printers served by a single logical printer.

process priority—A priority setting, established by the Windows 95 kernel when cooperative multitasking occurs, that sets the level of system access for processes running in the background and in the foreground.

Protected Mode—A mode of operation in the Intel x86 processor family wherein it's possible to address memory above the 1 MB upper bound on DOS memory.

protocol—In networking, a set of rules that defines how information may be transmitted and received across a network.

PS (PostScript) format—An Adobe page description language used to create print images for output on suitably equipped print engines.

.PST—The file extension used to designate a personal folder file.

PSTN (Public Switched Telephone Network)—Another term for the world-wide telephone network or a local telephone company.

queue—A storage area for tasks that are waiting to be serviced or run.

RAM (Random Access Memory)—Short-term storage contained in a computer's memory chips. Computers use RAM to process computer applications; therefore, the more RAM a computer has, the more efficiently its applications will run.

Real Mode—A mode of operation for the Intel x86 processor family where memory is broken into 16 64-KB segments, addressed by segment number, and offset within a segment. For DOS, the lower 10 segments (640 KB) define the memory space in which applications run; the 384 KB of the so-called High Memory Area (HMA) from 640 KB to 1,024 KB is reserved for operating system and device use.

Recycle Bin—A temporary storage space for deleted files.

redirector—A networking software component that acts as a traffic director for resource requests and separates requests for local resources (passed on to the local operating system) from requests for network resources (passed across the network to whatever resource is addressed).

REGEDIT—The Windows 95 Registry editor program; Windows NT also supports a Registry editor of the same name with an identical interface.

Registry—The hierarchical database that serves as a repository for hardware, software, and operating system configuration information in Windows 95 and Windows NT.

Resource Kit—Additional documentation and software utilities distributed by Microsoft to provide information and instruction on the proper operation and modification of its software products.

roaming profile—A user profile that can be loaded from a shared network drive so it can be used no matter which Windows 95 computer users log on to.

Safe Mode—The mode Windows 95 loads in VGA mode (minus network support and 32-bit drivers).

SAP (Service Advertisement Protocol)—An IPX service that broadcasts a list of services and their corresponding network addresses.

ScanDisk—A DOS and Windows 95 disk repair tool that checks and corrects disk errors.

SCSI (Small Computer System Interface)—A standard interface, defined by ANSI, that provides high-speed connections to devices such as hard drives, scanners, and printers.

security—A manner of protecting data by restricting access to authorized users.

SETUP.EXE—The program that begins the installation of Windows 95.

shortcuts—A small pointer that can be placed in a folder, on the desktop, or in the Start menu to reference an application or file.

SLIP (Serial Line Internet Protocol)—An older industry standard for remote communication links. It is included with NT only to establish connections with Unix systems that do not support the PPP standard; it is not available for DUN use.

SMTP (Simple Mail Transfer Protocol)—An Internet protocol used to distribute email from one mail server to another over a TCP/IP network.

SPE (System Policy Editor)—The administrative tool used by Windows 95 to create and modify system polices for computers, groups, or users. The SPE must be manually installed because it is not installed by default.

spooler—A software component of the print system that stores print jobs on a hard drive while the jobs wait in the print queue.

Start menu—Found in the lower left-hand corner of the Windows 95 desktop, the Start menu lets users start a variety of programs and applications from a centralized area.

static address—A preassigned IP address set in the TCP/IP properties windows in the Network applet.

subnet—A portion or segment of a network.

subnet mask—A 32-bit address that indicates how many bits in an address are being used for the network ID.

swap file—The hard drive storage file used to support virtual memory in Windows 95.

sysedit (System Configuration Editor)—The utility that allows you to quickly gain access to six of the most common INI files. It is simply a multiple-window notepad.

system policies—Tools used to restrict or limit the operational environments for users, groups, or computers. A system policy selectively edits the Registry each time a user logs in.

SYSTEM.DAT—One of the files that stores the Windows 95 Registry. USER.DAT is the other file.

tape drives—Devices, used for backing up data, that employ various recording tape formats for storage and backup.

TAPI (Telephony Application Programming Interface)—An interface and API that defines how applications can interact with data, fax, and voice devices and with calls.

Task Manager—A utility used to view applications and processes where such processes may be stopped or started. The Task Manager in Windows NT also offers CPU and memory status information, but is not available for Windows 95.

taskbar—The area on the desktop of Windows 95 that lets users toggle between applications.

TCP/IP (Transmission Control Protocol/Internet Protocol)—The most widely used protocol in networking today because it is the most flexible of the transport protocols and is able to span wide areas.

telecommunication lines—Lines used to transmit messages as either data communication or voice information.

TELNET—A TCP/IP-based terminal emulation utility used to interact with remote computers.

Terminate and Stay Resident (TSR)—A program that stays in memory, even while not in active use, that is always available at the touch of a "hotkey."

thunking—The process Windows uses to translate 16-bit system calls into 32-bit calls, and vice versa.

topology—The way a computer system is attached to a network. Star and Bus are two common network topologies.

TRACERT utility—The service that displays the route taken by IP packets to a remote system.

TrueType—A special Microsoft font technology that permits fonts to be adjusted to any height or angle and to appear the same in print as they do on screen.

TSR (Terminate and Stay Resident) program—A program that runs under MS-DOS that remains loaded in memory even when it is not running, so it can be invoked quickly for a specific task performed while any other application is operating.

UNC (Universal Naming Convention)—A standardized naming method for networks that takes the form \\servername\sharename.

UNINSTAL.EXE—A utility that gives you the option of uninstalling a program; can be used only if a new program has not been installed over a previous version of itself.

Unix—An interactive, time-sharing operating system developed in 1969 by a hacker to play games. This system developed into the most widely used industrial-strength computer operating system in the world and ultimately supported the birth of the Internet.

user profile—A stored collection of details and configuration settings for a user.

USER.DAT—One of the files that stores the Windows 95 Registry. SYSTEM.DAT is the other file.

VFAT (Virtual File Allocation Table)—This file system is currently supported by Windows 95, OSR1, Windows NT 3.51, and Windows NT 4; VFAT provides 32-bit Protected Mode access for file manipulation.

VGA (Video Graphics Array)—A PC display standard of 640 by 480 pixels, 16 colors, and a 4:3 aspect ratio.

virtual memory—The feature of Windows 95 that enables a greater amount of memory to be available to programs than is physically present in RAM by treating a swap file on disk as an extension of physical RAM.

VM (Virtual Machine)—A software construct within which applications are executed.

VXD (Virtual Device Driver)—A driver, unique to Windows, that manages software or devices to allow multiuser access.

WAN (wide area network)—A network that spans geographically distant segments. Often, a distance of two or more miles is used to define a WAN; however, Microsoft considers that any RAS connection establishes a WAN.

.WAV—The file extension used to designate a waveform audio file; typically associated with sound playback.

Win16Mutex flag—A flag that is set when a thread uses a non-reentrant segment of code. The flag indicates to the system that no other thread can make a call to this code segment until the flag has been unset.

WINIPCFG utility—A service that allows a client to display its IP configuration and lease information.

WINS (Windows Internet Name Service)—A Windows network service used to resolve NetBIOS names to IP addresses.

workgroup—A collection of networked computers that participate in a peer-to-peer relationship.

Workgroup Postoffice—The MS Mail service that ships with Windows 95 (a peer-to-peer service only). In this environment, a single-user computer acts as a workgroup postoffice to store email messages until recipient users log in, at which point such messages are delivered to their machines.

World Wide Web (WWW or Web)—An information distribution system hosted on TCP/IP networks. The Web supports text, graphics, and multimedia. The IIS component of NT is a Web server that can distribute Web documents.

x86 platform—Intel's family of processors that are the most common CPUs employed in PCs.

XMS (Extended Memory Specification)—A programming interface through which DOS programs (286 and later) can use extended memory.

Index

Numbers And Symbols